D0148715

(Mis)recognition, Social Inequality and Social Justice

Nancy Fraser's work provides a theory of justice from multiple perspectives, which has created a powerful frame for the analysis of political, moral and pragmatic dilemmas in an era of global capitalism and cultural pluralism. It has been developed through dialogue with key contemporary thinkers, including an extended critical exchange with Axel Honneth that touches importantly upon the work of the late Pierre Bourdieu on social suffering.

This collection of essays considers some of the conceptual and philosophical contentions that Fraser's model has provoked and presents some compelling examples of its analytical power in a range of contexts in which the politics of social justice are at issue, including the politics of justice in South Africa, and social policy. It includes essays on queer theory and the paradoxical effects of gay marriage and civil partnerships, on the imbalance in the social composition of UK parliamentary representation and on the significance of class.

Terry Lovell is a Professor in the Department of Sociology at Warwick University and has published on feminist social and cultural theory.

Critical realism: interventions
Edited by Margaret Archer, Roy Bhaskar, Andrew Collier, Kathryn Dean, Nick Hostettler, Jonathan Joseph, Tony Lawson, Alan Norrie and Sean Vertigan

Critical realism is one of the most influential new developments in the philosophy of science and in the social sciences, providing a powerful alternative to positivism and post modernism. This series will explore the critical realist position in philosophy and across the social sciences.

Critical Realism
Essential readings
Edited by Margaret Archer,
Roy Bhaskar, Andrew Collier,
Tony Lawson and Alan Norrie

The Possibility of Naturalism, 3rd edition
A philosophical critique of the contemporary human sciences
Roy Bhaskar

Being and Worth
Andrew Collier

Quantum Theory and the Flight from Realism
Philosophical responses to quantum mechanics
Christopher Norris

From East to West
Odyssey of a soul
Roy Bhaskar

Realism and Racism
Concepts of race in sociological research
Bob Carter

Rational Choice Theory
Resisting colonisation
Edited by Margaret Archer and
Jonathan Q. Tritter

Explaining Society
Critical realism in the social sciences
Berth Danermark, Mats Ekström,
Jan Ch Karlsson and
Liselotte Jakobsen

Critical Realism and Marxism
Edited by Andrew Brown,
Steve Fleetwood and
John Michael Roberts

Critical Realism in Economics
Edited by Steve Fleetwood

Realist Perspectives on Management and Organisations
Edited by Stephen Ackroyd and
Steve Fleetwood

After International Relations
Critical realism and the
(re)construction of world politics
Heikki Patomaki

Capitalism and Citizenship
The impossible partnership
Kathryn Dean

**Philosophy of Language and the
Challenge to Scientific Realism**
Christopher Norris

Transcendence
Critical realism and God
*Margaret S. Archer, Andrew Collier
and Douglas V. Porpora*

**Critical Realist Applications in
Organisation and Management
Studies**
*Edited by Steve Fleetwood and
Stephen Ackroyd*

Making Realism Work
Realist social theory and empirical
research
*Edited by Bob Carter and
Caroline New*

Rethinking Marxism
From Kant and Hegel to Marx and
Engels
Jolyon Agar

**(Mis)recognition, Social Inequality
and Social Justice**
Nancy Fraser and Pierre Bourdieu
Edited by Terry Lovell

Also published by Routledge
Routledge studies in critical realism
Edited by Margaret Archer, Roy Bhaskar, Andrew Collier, Kathryn Dean, Nick
Hostettler, Jonathan Joseph, Tony Lawson, Alan Norrie and Sean Vertigan

1 **Marxism and Realism**
   A materialistic application of
   realism in the social sciences
   Sean Creaven

2 **Beyond Relativism**
   Raymond Boudon, cognitive
   rationality and critical realism
   Cynthia Lins Hamlin

3 **Education Policy and Realist
   Social Theory**
   Primary teachers, child-centred
   philosophy and the new
   managerialism
   Robert Wilmott

4 **Hegemony**
   A realist analysis
   Jonathan Joseph

5 **Realism and Sociology**
   Anti-foundationalism, ontology
   and social research
   Justin Cruickshank

6 **Critical Realism**
   The difference it makes
   Edited by Justin Cruickshank

7 **Critical Realism and
   Composition Theory**
   Donald Judd

(Mis)recognition, Social Inequality and Social Justice

Nancy Fraser and Pierre Bourdieu

Edited by Terry Lovell

Routledge
Taylor & Francis Group

LONDON AND NEW YORK

First published 2007
by Routledge
2 Park Square, Milton Park, Abingdon, Oxon, OX14 4RN

Simultaneously published in the USA and Canada
by Routledge
270 Madison Ave, New York NY 10016

Routledge is an imprint of the Taylor & Francis Group, an informa business

Transferred to Digital Printing 2008

© 2007 Terry Lovell

Typeset in Times by Wearset Ltd, Boldon, Tyne and Wear

British Library Cataloguing in Publication Data
A catalogue record for this book is available from the British Library

Library of Congress Cataloging in Publication Data
A catalog record for this book has been requested

ISBN10: 0-415-40466-5 (hbk)
ISBN10: 0-415-46494-3 (pbk)

ISBN13: 978-0-415-40466-2 (hbk)
ISBN13: 978-0-415-46494-9 (pbk)

Contents

Contributors

Loraine Blaxter is an Associate of the Institute of Health in the School of Health and Social Studies at the University of Warwick. She originally trained as an anthropologist, undertaking fieldwork in rural France. Throughout her career she has attempted to combine teaching and research with community engagement.

Robert Fine is Professor of Sociology at the University of Warwick. He has made extensive contributions to the sociology of law and to social and political theory. His current research interests are on the sociology of the holocaust. His publications include: *Political Investigations: Hegel, Marx, Arendt*, Routledge, 2001; *Social Theory after the Holocaust* (with Charles Turner), Liverpool University Press, 2000; *People, Nation, State* (with Edward Mortimer), IB Tauris, 1999.

Nancy Fraser is Henry A. and Louise Loeb Professor of Philosophy and Politics in the graduate faculty of New School University, New York. Her research focuses on issues of social justice, feminism and the politics of identity. Her work has investigated the normative basis of social rights in a transnational frame. Her publications include: *Redistribution or Recognition? A Political–Philosophical Exchange* (co-authored with Axel Honneth), Verso, 2003; *Justice Interruptus: Critical Reflections on the "Postsocialist" Condition*, Routledge, 1997; *Unruly Practices: Power, Discourse and Gender in Contemporary Social Theory*, Polity Press, 1989.

Christina Hughes is a Reader in Sociology at the University of Warwick. Her research interests include the interrogation of feminist theory and its application in the domains of education and employment with particular attention to the role of conceptual development. She was the founding co-chair of the Gender and Education Association, and currently serves on the boards of *Gender, Work and Organisation* and *Sociological Research On-Line*. Her publications include: *Contemporary Women's Lives*, Routledge, 2002; *Key Concepts in Feminist Theory and Research*, Sage, 2002; *Disseminating Qualitative Research*, Open University Press, 2003; *How to Research* (with Loraine Blaxter and Malcolm Tight), Open University Press, Third Edition, 2006.

María Pía Lara is Professor of Philosophy at the Universidad Autónoma Metropolitana de Barcelona. She has made extensive contributions to feminist political philosophy and social theory. She is preparing a collection of essays on globalization, many of which have already appeared in several journals in English, Spanish and Italian, and is currently engaged in research on political authority. Her publications include: *La Democracia como proyecto de Identidad Etica*, Anthropos, 1992; *Moral Textures: Feminist Narratives in the Public Sphere*, University of California Press, 1999, and Polity Press, 1998; (Editor) *Rethinking Evil: Contemporary Perspectives*, University of California Press, 2001; *Narrating Evil: a Postmetaphysical Theory of Reflective Judgement*, Columbia University Press, forthcoming.

Joanna Liddle is Senior Lecturer at the Centre for the Study of Women and Gender in the Department of Sociology, University of Warwick. She teaches in the areas of Women and Gender Studies, and Gender and International Development. She has carried out international collaborative research on gender, class and public power in several countries. Her publications include: *Daughters of Independence: Gender, Caste and Class in India* (with Rama Joshi), 1986, Zed Books *Rising Sons, Rising Daughters: Gender, Class and Power in Japan* (with Sachiko Nakajima), Zed Books, 2000.

Sandra Liebenberg currently holds the H.F. Oppenheimer Chair in Human Rights Law in the Law Faculty of the University of Stellenbosch. She previously served as a member of the Technical Committee advising the Constitutional Assembly on the Bill of Rights in the 1996 Constitution of South Africa. She founded and directed the Socio-Economic Rights Project based at the Community Law Centre (University of the Western Cape) where she was involved in research, advocacy and supporting litigation in the area of socio-economic rights. She has published widely in the field of socio-economic rights and serves on the editorial board of the *South African Journal on Human Rights*, the *African Human Rights Law Journal* as well as the board of trustees of a number of human rights non-governmental organisations. Her publications include: 'Social and economic rights: a critical challenge', in S. Liebenberg (ed.) *The Constitution of South Africa from a Gendered Perspective*, Cape Town: The Community Law Centre, University of the Western Cape, in association with David Phillip, 79–96, 1995; 'South Africa's evolving jurisprudence on socio-economic rights: an effective tool in challenging poverty?' *Law, Democracy and Development*, 6, 159–191, 2002; 'The value of human dignity in interpreting socio-economic rights', *SA Journal on Human Rights*, 21, 1–31, 2005; 'South Africa', in M. Langford (ed.) *Socio-economic Rights Jurisprudence: Emerging Trends in Comparative and International Law*, Cambridge University Press, forthcoming.

Ruth Lister is Professor of Social Policy at Loughborough University and a former director of the Child Poverty Action Group. She works in three broad areas: poverty, welfare reform and citizenship. Her work on citizenship addresses questions of difference and exclusion at national and international level, with a particular focus on gender, and, more recently, children. She has also researched how young people negotiate the transition to citizenship. Her publications include: *Citizenship: Feminist Perspectives*, Palgrave, 1997/2003; *Poverty*, Polity, 2004; 'Young people talk about citizenship: empirical perspectives on theoretical and political debates', *Citizenship Studies*, 7(2), 2003 (with N. Smith, S. Middleton and L. Cox); 'Investing in the citizen-workers of the future: transformations in citizenship and the state under New Labour', *Social Policy and Administration*, 37(5), 2003; 'Being Feminist', *Government and Opposition*, 40 (3), 2005.

Terry Lovell is Emeritus Professor in the Department of Sociology and the Centre for the Study of Women and Gender, University of Warwick. She has worked in the area of feminist social and cultural theory, and the sociology of film and literature. She is currently working on a study of feminism in contemporary sociology. Relevant publications include: *Pictures of Reality*, BFI Publishing, 1983; 'Thinking feminism with and against Bourdieu', *Feminist Theory*, 1(1), April 2000; 'Resisting with authority: historical specificity, agency and the performative self', *Theory, Culture and Society*, 20(1), 2003; 'Bourdieu, class and gender: the return of the living dead?', in L. Adkins and B. Skeggs (eds) *Feminism After Bourdieu*, Blackwell, 2004.

Mandy Merck: is Professor of Media Arts at Royal Holloway, University of London. She is the author of *Hollywood's American Tragedies*, Berg, 2007; *In Your Face: Nine Sexual Studies*, New York University Press, 2000; and *Perversions: Deviant Readings*, Virago and Routledge, 2000. She has edited *America First: Naming the Nation in US Film*, Routledge, 2007 and *After Diana*, Verso, 1998, and co-edited *The Art of Tracey Emin*, Thames and Hudson, 2002 and *Coming Out of Feminism?* Blackwell, 1998.

Elisabeth Michielsens is Senior Lecturer in Business Studies at the University of Westminster, London. She teaches international business and equality and diversity at undergraduate and postgraduate level. She worked with Joanna Liddle as a researcher on the comparative Leadership Study (on which the paper in this volume is based) under the EU's Human Capital and Mobility Programme.

Andrew Sayer is Professor of Social Theory and Political Economy in the Department of Sociology, Lancaster University, Lancaster. He currently holds an ESRC fellowship to work on the moral dimension of social life, particularly with regard to economic relationships or 'moral economy', and on lay normativity generally. His books include: *Realism and Social Science*, Sage, 2000; *The Moral Significance of Class*, Cambridge University Press, 2005.

Acknowledgements

Nancy Fraser, 'Reframing justice in a globalizing world', *New Left Review*, 36, November–December 2005. Reprinted by kind permission of *New Left Review*.

Mandy Merck, 'Sexuality, subjectivity and … economics?', *New Formations*, 52, Spring 2004. Reprinted with an 'Afterword' by kind permission of *New Formations*.

Andrew Sayer, 'Class, moral worth and recognition', *Sociology*, 39, 2005, copyright BSA Publications Ltd. Reprinted here by kind permission of Sage Publications Ltd.

Joanna Liddle and Elisabeth Michielsens, 'NQOC: social identity and representation in British politics', *British Journal of Politics and International Relations*, 2007 (forthcoming). A longer version of this paper is printed here with the kind permission of Blackwell Publishing.

Sandra Liebenberg, 'Needs, rights and transformations: adjudicating social rights' *Stellenbosch Law Review*, 1, 1–36, 2006. A shorter version of this paper is reprinted here by kind permission of the editorial board and management of the Stellenbosch Law Review.

The cartoon by David Austin (p. 60) appeared in the *Guardian* on November 27, 2003, and is reproduced here by kind permission of his widow, Janet Slee.

My thanks are due to Kathryn Dean from the editorial board in her role as editor for this collection for the Routledge critical realism series.

1 Introduction

Terry Lovell

Nancy Fraser's 'integrated theory of justice' was the starting point of this collection and remains at its core. Pierre Bourdieu's sociology of domination finds prominence for its deep relevance to a project that has been described as 'sociologically rich' (Honneth, in Fraser and Honneth 2003: 110). All the papers locate themselves in engagement with one or another or both of these two key thinkers. I shall begin with a brief account of its concerns, and then say a word about the location of this volume in a series dedicated to critical realism.

Fraser's theory was developed and refined through a series of dialogues with colleagues engaged in projects close to her own in relation to critical theory and feminism in Europe and the US. She engaged in exchanges with Iris Marion Young, whose *Justice and the Politics of Difference* had argued for a non-distributive theory of justice (Young 1990). While recognizing with Young the critical importance 'difference' that had been central to poststructuralism and 'the cultural turn', Fraser was troubled that issues of inequality and maldistribution, in Young's work and more generally with the rise to dominance of 'the politics of recognition' from the late 1980s, had fallen into the margins. Her theory of justice emerged initially as a double-headed one that held together recognition with redistribution. The possibility of a third, specifically political dimension had been signalled up, and in her recent work, represented in Chapter 2 in this collection, (political) representation has been more fully integrated into the model.

Fraser's critique of recognition theories, including that of Axel Honneth and Charles Taylor as well as of Young's work, led to the first articulation of her theory of justice (Fraser 1995). She regrouped Young's five forms of oppression into two broad kinds, one in which injustice was rooted in the inequities of the economic order, the second in (cultural) misrecognition institutionalized in the status order. Young's rejoinder charged Fraser with a form of 'dual systems' thinking founded on a problematic separation of 'the cultural' from 'the material' that had long since been discredited in feminist as well as socialist theory (Young 1997).

Judith Butler entered the lists with a similar charge in her 'Merely cultural' (Butler 1998). Fraser's robust defence (Fraser 1998) argued the need to maintain an analytical distinction between the cultural and the economic. She further refined her concept of a complex integrated 'dual perspectival' theory and politics of justice in this exchange.[1] The fullest articulation of this 'perspectival dualism' to date is to be found in her dialogue with Honneth in 2003. Honneth rightly identifies their common commitment to 'a sociologically rich interpretation of the normative claims implicit in the social conflicts of the present' (Honneth, in Fraser and Honneth 2003: 110). They are engaged in normative theory therefore, but one that draws on a sociological frame and socio-historical analysis. Both Fraser and Honneth include Bourdieu among the sociological resources upon which they draw.

Bourdieu's influence upon Fraser may be detected in the not infrequent references she makes to his work over the years, and in her analytical distinction between 'the economic' and 'the cultural' which Bourdieu uses as axes of power in his mapping of social space (Bourdieu 1984). In her rejoinder to Butler, Fraser emphasized her debt to Max Weber – a key source, too, for Bourdieu – where Butler had seen only a return to a neo-Marxist reductionism of the cultural to the material. Honneth enlists Bourdieu, specifically the collaborative study *The Weight of the World* (Bourdieu *et al.* 1999) based on a research project dating from the early 1990s, in support of his own contentions over Fraser's theory of justice. Their differences hinge, critically, on issues that are raised by the research, making Bourdieu, in effect, a tacit third party to the exchange.

The famous cultural or linguistic turn had a profound impact across many disciplines, and not least upon feminism. It placed the very concept of 'the material' on the defensive, and with it, realism in social and textual studies. It took feminist *theory* towards poststructuralist, deconstructionist and postmodernist philosophy and away from sociological and Marxist realisms. It was, famously, a shift from 'things' to 'words'. While 'words' were made to extend to social relations and institutions in this shift, these sometimes appeared to dissolve into nothing *but* words. Those feminists who refused this turn sometimes did so at the cost of discounting or sidelining the specifically textual/cultural. Feminist 'high theory' meanwhile shifted its disciplinary base from sociology to literary and other textual studies and, above all, to philosophy.

Across the differences that are explored in depth in their lengthy exchange, a good deal is shared by Fraser and Honneth; both eschew the more abstract forms of normative theory, arguing the need to draw upon sociological concepts, research and analysis. Neither separates normative claims and their assessment, whether these are mounted from within lay discourse or in philosophical theory, from well-founded analysis of the socio-historical contexts in which these claims have arisen. This in turn suggests a strong affinity with the critical realist project. A critical realist social science has normative and emancipatory aspects (Bhaskar 1979, 1986). It identifies unnecessary social suffering, injustice and misconceptions, uncovers and explains their causes and implies an injunction to eliminate them (Sayer 2000: 156). These implications supply the second strong link with critical theory. Finally, emancipatory projects presuppose and require human agency: the ability to intervene effectively to achieve positive social transformation. At the centre of Fraser's politics is the commitment to both defining emancipatory goals – 'the good life' – and to intervention to achieve it, only through the mediation of public dialogics: democratic debate, with full parity of participation. At the centre of Bourdieu's sociology is a sober analysis of the strength and depth of the impediments to participatory parity which may reside deep in the habitus as well as in the institutions of power in the social world.

If normative critical theory has a stake in sociological analysis, then, critical realist sociology has an equal stake in normative theory. So, while neither Fraser nor Honneth nor Bourdieu has been directly associated with the critical realist movement, their work has close affinities with that movement's project. However, Bourdieu's sociology has had a mixed reception within that movement as we shall see. And while a number of feminists have drawn on Bourdieu's work, they have done so cautiously and critically.[2] Equally there has been limited engagement between the dominant forms of feminist theory and sociological critical realism.

Critical realists, following Roy Bhaskar (1979), distinguish between the 'real' – whatever exists in the world regardless of if, and how, we experience or know it – the 'actual' and the 'empirical'. Real objects have more or less enduring structures, causal powers and potentials, and realists are concerned with them because they 'seek to identify both necessity and possibility or potential in the world' (Sayer 2000: 11). The 'actual' refers to 'what happens if and when these powers are activated' (ibid.: 12). The empirical belongs to the domain of experience.

Critical realism furnishes the world, therefore, with intransitive objects that exist independently of our knowledge of them. This does not mean that they are immutable, that they all exist outside of culture, or that knowledge of them cannot be used to effect changes in them. Our understanding of these objects is however transitive, relative and fallible. It is at this point that critical realism is open to engagement with aspects of postmodernism, and with feminism after the cultural turn, including feminist standpoint epistemology. The first part of Sayer's work on realism and social science is entitled 'postmodern-realist encounters', and is by no means dismissive. He confesses to no more than 'mixed feelings' (ibid.: 7) and distinguishes between the relativism of 'defeatist postmodernists' and others that 'point to a renewed social science' (ibid.: 6) and to the possibilities for a more fruitful interchange. 'Strategically', he argues, 'the main mistake made by critical realists in academic debate is to have ignored rather than engaged with poststructuralist and postmodernist thought' (ibid.: 30). Again the convergence with Fraser is striking (Fraser and Nicholson 1990). However, most critical realists retain a distinction between the cautious relativism of critical realist epistemologies and the heady lightness of being of the epistemology that emerged in the post-Kuhnian era (Feyerabend 1978) that sometimes gave the impression of throwing all caution to the wind. Bhaskar identifies this distinction in terms of epistemic judgement:

> Critical realism *accepts* 'epistemic relativism', that is the view that the world can only be known in terms of available descriptions or discourses, but it rejects 'judgemental relativism' – the view that one cannot judge between different discourses and decide that some accounts are better than others.
>
> (Bhaskar 1986: 72, cited in Sayer 2000: 47)

However it must be said that this settles little, since judgement is hardly less fallible than claims to knowledge.

The distinction between intransitive 'objects' and transitive knowledge of them is not the same as the Foucauldian distinction between 'things' and 'words'. Words may have the power of objects. Social and cultural 'objects' are meaningful, and discursive 'objects' have powers in the social world, including powers that may be directed towards changing it. But critical realism avoids reductionism upwards: the paradoxical position arrived at when (social) objects are reduced to their meanings – to 'texts'. Social theory offers causal explanations but does not and cannot dispense with a (double) hermeneutic.

The opposition between 'the cultural' and 'the economic', utilized by both Fraser and Bourdieu, was, as we have seen, at issue in Fraser's dialogues with Young, Butler and Honneth, all three contesting this dualism. Fraser defended it as a necessary analytical distinction, a defence that would readily find acceptance on a critical realist but not a postmodernist reading. 'The economic' and 'the cultural', on a realist reading, are 'good' abstractions (Sayer 1992: 127) because they are used in relation to real structural conglomerations in socio-cultural orders that are *relatively* enduring (though variably so: 'open' systems open to change), intransitive and real: the orders of class, founded in economic structures and relations, and the cultural distinctions institutionalized in the status order. With the development of modern capitalist society, these orders are no longer tightly bound together as they were in many earlier social formations. Links and ties are longer and looser; the more so, argues Fraser, under the contemporary conditions of global capitalism. They have their own causal powers, and they form distinctive 'clusters'. This does not mean, *pace* Honneth, that the economic order is without cultural meanings and processes, nor that status orders are untouched by economics. Bourdieu, it must be said, holds them more closely together than does Fraser. In his sociology of domination they are double aspects of social class.

Accounts, explanations and assessments of actual injustice claims in specific historical and socio-cultural context may need to draw on the mechanisms/processes of both economic and status orders, and indeed other levels of 'the real'. For another key component of critical realism is its stratified ontology, in which there are emergent levels of existence that are not reducible to 'deeper' levels whose structures and processes, nevertheless, circumscribe them in ways that are both enabling and restricting: their conditions of existence.

This concept of depth marks another point of difference between critical realism and a postmodernism that operates with a plane surface. At every emergent level, for critical realists, there will be others that may be seen as 'more basic' – human physiology and biology, for example, with respect to emergent socio-cultural levels. Their status as 'basic' rests on the fact that they condition what is possible at 'emergent' levels, and also in part upon the *relative* durability of the 'things' that furnish them. However, it is more difficult to maintain such a hierarchical model between emergent psychic, social and cultural levels (New 2005: 61). Higher-level systems are open systems. Indeed, it is in part this openness of social worlds that fuels postmodernist and poststructuralist preference for the language of flux over that of structure and system.

Feminism after the cultural turn likewise eschews theories of depth, as may be seen in relation to that old chestnut among contentious feminist distinctions, the sex/gender couplet. Those feminists who, like Butler, wish to dismantle the opposition between the cultural and the material have applied their tools of deconstruction additionally to the distinction between sex and gender. Yet this distinction remains prominent in – indeed it is the starting point for – feminist critical realism (ibid.; Hull forthcoming). Biological sex belongs to a relatively deep ontological level within the critical realist model, while gender is placed firmly within the emergent, more open domain of culture. Some settling of accounts on this matter will be a condition for fruitful engagement.

This is not the place, however, for such a settling of accounts, since the sex/gender distinction is not at issue in the concerns of this collection.[3] But the account might be opened by noting the absence of a term that has become ubiquitous in other contexts – that of 'the (lived) body'. The body has an ambivalent status in relationship to sex and gender. It is this ambivalence that ensures that they cannot be assimilated to the philosophical distinction between body and mind.

Phenomenological philosophy and social theory has been used as a potent resource for feminist theories of sexed subjectivity, alongside and often in conjunction with feminist psychoanalysis. Moira Gatens, in her justly praised 'A critique of the sex/gender distinction' (Gatens 1989), took as her point of departure the sexually differentiated 'lived body', an active participant in the formation of sexed subjectivities, reducible neither to its biology nor to socio-cultural imprinting. The feminist literary theorist Toril Moi (1999) takes a similar position. She, too, makes sexual difference her starting point and has no problems in acknowledging the claims of biology. Rather it is gender that troubles her: the ways in which, as Gatens puts it: 'we are historically and culturally situated in a society that is divided and organized in terms of sex' (Gatens 1989: 148).

Caroline New does not discuss specifically the feminisms of 'the lived body' (New 2005). She incorporates them, rather, within the general category of 'difference feminism'. Conversely, Gatens bases her critique of realist usage of the sex/gender distinction on *naïve* rather than critical realism. So feminist critical realists and feminists of the lived body tend to talk past one another. They attack the weakest versions of the positions they oppose. Yet critical realism, with its stress on human *agency*, might engage profitably with feminism of 'the lived body'. As New remarks: 'the fact that we are embodied is always crucial to our agency' (ibid.: 60)

Like these feminists, Bourdieu has been deeply influenced by phenomenology. Unlike them, he fully socializes the *dispositional* structure of his social agents: their habitus. He has virtually no recourse to psychoanalysis. Habitus and field provide the main conceptual tools through which he endeavours to negotiate the structure/agency opposition. All such attempts must walk the line that separates the Scylla of reducing agents to mere 'bearers' of incorporated social structures and the Charybdis of dismantling social structure so that it is nothing more than the sum of the current activities of human agents alongside the unintended consequences of their actions and interactions.

Margaret Archer is foremost among Bourdieu's critics from a critical realist perspective. She focuses particularly on his concept of 'habitus', and her concern is that this Pascalian concept leaves too little space for reflexivity and therefore for human agency. She argues that field and habitus collapse into one another, and as a result, Bourdieu fails to maintain the necessary distinction between social systems and human agents whose social relations, interactions and decisions are constrained but not determined either by the causes and mechanisms of such structures, or by social practices whose residue lies at a level below that of conscious reflexivity in (embodied) habitus (Archer 2007). It is interesting that Judith Butler, too, from a very different perspective, one far distant from that of Archer, makes the same charge that habitus collapses too readily and without remainder into the social field of its production to provide an adequate approach to agency (Butler 1997).

Sayer shares Archer's concerns. But in mounting his critique of Bourdieu, he draws also on the school of feminists who have engaged with Bourdieu with a view to *using* his concepts. Sayer, Skeggs and others interrogate and critique both habitus and Bourdieu's capitals, whilst acknowledging that they are, potentially, powerful analytical tools. The economic metaphor has been telling in many respects. But Sayer and Skeggs wish to make room for related concepts that Bourdieu's metaphorical repertoire tends to squeeze out.

Habitus is related to possession of cultural and social capital. Skeggs distinguishes between the secure possession of cultural capital and a representational display that may have no solid dispositional foundation and that may be seen, as in many forms of reality TV, and more painfully, in social situations in which pretensions to distinction in matters of taste may be exposed and found wanting (Skeggs 1997: 86). Her work, and that of the group of sociologists with which she has been associated and that includes Sayer, makes a further related distinction between social relations and attributes that are developed and treated as *mere* capital investments, to be traded in for profits that carry themselves or their children along valued life trajectories, and those that are developed and valued for their own sake. Sayer develops these distinctions in relation to the Marxist opposition between exchange value and use value, and Alasdair McIntyre's distinction between 'internal' and 'external' goods: the former intrinsic to specialized practices and social activities, the latter their result in terms of status, power and prestige (MacIntyre 1981). Here, the language of 'depth' is apposite and has a force that is lost when commitments are reduced to matters of taste or choice (Sayer, in this collection, Chapter 6).

In order to push back the frontiers of 'unwanted determination', real constraints have to be recognized in the variety of different structures that human agents confront, differentially, depending on their position in social space. Structures are necessary and may be enabling – in this sense, they are wrongly opposed to agency. If there were no relatively enduring intransitive objects in the psyche, social worlds or cultures, only absolute flux and free choice, it would be extremely difficult for human beings to act effectively on their own behalf as individuals, or to come together with others to make effective interventions in the world. It is less a question of 'structure versus agency', than of how to understand existing structures, to identify and critique the injustices they carry, and of how to transform them; a matter, too, of the structures and processes we might legitimately want to put in their place. This is very much Fraser's concern, but she works at more than one level. Fraser moves between 'thought experiments' in which she uses ideal types to explore what would be needed in order to achieve parity between men and women without any 'trade-offs' of one 'good' for another – see, for example, 'After the family wage: a postindustrial thought experiment' (Fraser 1997) – and political pragmatism in which trade-offs are unavoidable, but in which she seeks those that have the potential to trigger a more transformative trajectory.[4]

Critical realists argue, following Bhaskar, for 'ethical naturalism' – for the ability to determine 'what is good' for human beings – and this seems to resonate more with Honneth than with Fraser. Fraser's approach is motivated by principle – her passionate commitment to needs-determination and social change through public dialogics – but also by pragmatics in the face of value relativism and the need to make practical, political judgements. Above all, for Fraser, it would not be enough to be able to develop sound knowledge of, or to make judgements on, what is 'good' for human beings. This question must remain open in principle, for determination within the exchanges of the democratic public sphere.

So, 'no structures, no agency and no structures without agency': the emancipatory aspect of critical theory does not aim to demolish all structures but to reach agreement through processes of deliberation undistorted by social injustice, on the structures of our choice in given circumstances. This is entirely commensurable with the critical realist project.

Fraser holds the place, therefore, for participatory parity, dialogics and agency in normative social transformation. Bourdieu, on the other hand, holds the place for the powers that thwart these processes and that condition and shape agency. His 'central conflationism', if such it be, has a certain heuristic value in 'bending the stick' towards structure and power, and the ways in which injustice may be embedded not only in power structures but also in dispositions. He is a pessimist rather than a determinist, and his pessimism is sometimes salutary. Fraser's integrated theory of justice, in the stage it had reached in her exchanges with Honneth, allowed these differences to be addressed very sharply over Bourdieu and his collaborators' research in *The Weight of the World*.

In the remainder of this introduction I shall say something about each of the contributions.

Fraser's integrated theory of justice signalled in its earliest forms her concern with the global context, but she has taken a full 'post-Westphalian' turn only recently, after her series of exchanges with Honneth. 'Globalization' she argues, 'is changing the way we argue about justice' (p. 17). Justice claims can no longer be assessed in terms of what is owed to members of a given community, since the injustices suffered by groups and individuals increasingly have their sources outside the boundaries and the reach of national states. '[T]he grammar of argument has altered'. Whether it is distribution or recognition that is contested, it is no longer a matter of '*what* is owed ... [but] *who* should count as a member and *which* is the relevant community' (p. 19). She argues that these issues may be addressed through the incorporation of a third, specifically political, dimension to her model, alongside the economic dimension of distribution and the cultural dimension of recognition. The injustices specific to this level she names as injustices of *representation*. The political is distinct from the other two aspects of participatory parity, her general criterion of justice, insofar as it *specifies the reach* of the other two, to tell us 'who is included and who excluded from the circle of those entitled to a just distribution and reciprocal recognition' (p. 21).

Fraser distinguishes two levels of (mis)representation: 'ordinary-political misrepresentation' that is the object of much of the literature on political systems of representation, and the higher order concern with frame-setting, for 'the Keynesian-Westphalian frame is a powerful instrument of injustice, which gerrymanders political space at the expense of the poor and despised'. Her paper identifies a task that is at once urgent and formidable: 'How can we integrate struggles against maldistribution, misrecognition, and misrepresentation within a *post-Westphalian* frame?' (p. 24). The Introduction to her earlier exchanges with Honneth (Fraser and Honneth 2003: 5) closes with a brief comment on their differences over the nature of contemporary capitalism. Honneth claims that the capitalist economic order is subject to an overarching normative recognition order, while Fraser argues that modern global capitalism is relatively autonomous, with its own mechanisms and processes that are not directly so regulated. However, in her contribution to this collection, Fraser moves away from 'systems talk' as she draws on Castells' model of 'the network society': '[M]atters, so fundamental to human well-being ... belong not to "the space of places"' – the space in which nation-states reside – but to '"the space of flows"' (p. 25).

Within a post-Westphalian model of justice, the 'all affected' principle of representation can no longer depend on state-territoriality (p. 25). Fraser shifts attention to the struggle for 'meta political democracy' as she turns her attention and ours to the *how* of post-Westphalian justice and the demands of a transformative politics of framing that remains dialogic, reflexive and participatory: to processes of collective democratic deliberation.

María Pía Lara and Robert Fine in their response locate Fraser's theory in relation to Rawls' concept of justice as fairness, but particularly to Habermas' shift of focus to the social institutions and practices where deliberation takes place, in a decentred idea of justice. They identify Fraser's key intervention through her feminist-inspired critique of Habermas in relation to power and its effects upon the structural exclusions from the public sphere. At the same time, she drew attention to power struggles within that sphere; it is contested internally thanks to the deliberations of a plurality of competing publics drawn from among the dominated. The force of Fraser's critique was acknowledged by Habermas.

Lara and Fine then go on to trace the development of Fraser's theory of justice through the various stages of her familiar double-headed account in terms of recognition and redistribution, to its current form in which, in the post-Westphalian context, the third dimension of 'the political' site of the injustice of misrepresentation has been integrated. They argue that this new prominence given to 'the political' is in part the result of the exchange with Honneth, although Fraser had previously signalled the need for this addition, which would of course bring it into alignment with Max Weber's triple distinction between class, status and party (Fraser 1998). She delivered on this promissory note with the 'post-Westphalian turn' in her thinking:

> If we now face the challenge of thinking about justice in a global frame, we need to address normative standards of representation and misrepresentation to deal with people's right to participate in political arenas on a par with others. With predatory states, transnational private powers, transnational corporations, international speculators and the way the global economy dictates systems of social interaction, the participatory imparity of more than half the world population has now become a stark and devastating reality.
>
> (Lara and Fine, this collection, p. 43)

Lara and Fine are not entirely persuaded by Fraser's 'all-affected' principle of representation, and turn instead to the concept of a nascent 'world public sphere', using the example of the challenges to the legitimacy of the US and UK decision to declare war against Iraq. They argue that:

> the most important question about the space of a world public sphere is whether actors can acquire the capacity to act politically within it and how in turn these performances can lead to new processes of lending authority to the world community.
>
> (Lara and Fine [p. 46])

They develop this idea along the lines of Habermas' decentred notion of authority, and suggest that this signals one way which Fraser's thinking might take to solve the problems she raises with regard to post-Westphalian democratic justice.

Mandy Merck's contribution looks at the politics of sexuality and subjectivity – specifically, queer subjectivity – in relation to the exigencies of global capitalism and the marketplace. She takes as her point of departure Fraser's exchange with Butler over the status of normative and transgressive sexualities in this context. Fraser's argument was that the capitalist economic system in the era of globalization is unfazed by queer subjectivity and identity. Some of the contemporary writings on this topic, such as that of Rosemary Hennessey, go further, to relate this insouciant tolerance to the charge that such 'postmodern' subjectivities are actually the product of the global capitalist marketplace in which they flourish (p. 56). While critical of what she sees as Fraser's 'tendency to reify identity categories' by separating groups suffering injustices along her continuum from those that she locates at the 'economic' end of her continuum, to those that are produced by cultural status distinctions, she makes an unequivocal judgement: 'Butler does not win this debate' (p. 52).

Merck traces an unexpected 'economic turn' that has been taken in the field of a queer theory that had emerged as an area of study with the earlier 'cultural turn' to institute itself within literary critical theory, visual culture, media studies and rhetoric, turning its back upon the earlier allegiance of lesbian and gay studies to political economy. Merck echoes Fraser's critique of Butler's functionalist tie-in of the family, instituted on the base of normative or compulsory heterosexuality, to the economic imperatives of capitalism. The literature that she reviews here is at its best when it analyses the relationship between sexuality, subjectivity and socio-economic system as contingent and historically specific. We cannot assume any automatic interdependency between capitalist imperatives and normative heterosexuality, nor on the other hand any automatic transformative or disruptive effects for transgressive sexualities, but we can uncover these relationships at a given point in time and place through conjunctural analysis.

Merck's paper takes us through a range of contributions to the revamped 'political economy' of transgressive subjectivities and identities that are, according to Hennessy, no more than expressions and instruments of globalization (p. 56). In other words, Hennessy paradoxically ties a knot between sexual transgression and modern global capitalism that is as tight as that drawn in the 1970s by Marxist feminists to whom Butler returns; between normative heterosexuality and capitalism. Merck accuses her of a 'head-banging reduction of all contests over meaning to those of resources' (p. 58) and finds more promise in the work of Miranda Joseph and Bill Maurer: 'their increasingly shared opposition to the economic order from which queer theory has arguably both emerged and departed signals a significant turn in sexual scholarship' (p. 60).

In an afterword, Merck gives extended consideration to the topical issue of same-sex marriage and civil unions.

The next contribution, my own, is the first paper in the collection to discuss Bourdieu's sociology of domination alongside Fraser's critical theory of justice, and the only one that engages extensively with both thinkers. Although Fraser's theory is a sociologically informed one, and although she has developed her model, as her theory indeed dictates, through dialogics, her exchanges have not taken place across this disciplinary boundary. My sense that it might be fruitful to bring them together was confirmed by the pivotal role that Bourdieu's research in *The Weight of the World* had in Fraser's exchange with Honneth, and then by Andrew Sayer's most recent work on *The Moral Significance of Class*, as discussed in the first part of this introduction. My paper brings out some of the issues that remain unresolved in the Fraser–Honneth exchange as they touch on Bourdieu's work. These include the analytical distinction between 'the economic' and 'the cultural' that is also at issue in Merck's contribution. My paper rehearses the case for a *dual* perspectival approach to injustice under her general criterion of justice, participatory parity, as against Honneth's inclusion of distributive justice within a broader, encompassing but layered category of recognition. At the core of the dispute between them is Honneth's attempt to found injustice in 'social suffering', that expresses a deep sense of violation, lodged in the psyche. Honneth makes repeated use of the language of 'core' and 'depth': 'an institutional rule that, in the light of generally accepted grounds, violates deep-seated claims on the social order, is experienced as social injustice' (Honneth in Fraser and Honneth 2003: 130); 'If the adjective "social" is to mean anything more than "typically found in society", social suffering and discontent possess a *normative* core' (ibid.: 129); 'Only if the idea of a human psyche structurally directed against the unreasonable demands of society is added to the ... connection between social order and subversion can one speak of the necessity of a practice of transgression' (ibid.: 243). Fraser resists because she wishes to found her theory of justice dialogically, and to keep the democratic public sphere open with regard to definitions of what constitutes 'human flourishing' and 'the good life'. Fraser's theory has taken 'the cultural turn' insofar as she retains the postmodern understanding that values concerning 'the good' are culturally relative. This is a matter of principle, but also of pragmatics. For whether or not we might develop a sound understanding of 'what is good for human beings', as the naturalist ethics of critical realism suggests, it is strategically important that any such understanding should emerge through the transactions of a truly democratic discursive process.

The significance of Bourdieu in the work of our next contributor, Andrew Sayer, but also his reservations concerning some aspects of his theory, may be seen in *The Moral Significance of Class* (Sayer 2005). A critical realist, Sayer is concerned above all to make good the normative commitments on which he judges realist social science to have fallen short, 'hampered by the absence of normative reasoning' (Sayer 2000: 156). Sayer's interest begins, however, not with philosophical analysis, but with the discourses of 'lay normativity'; it is underestimated, he charges, in much sociology, including that of Bourdieu, which thereby runs the risk of reducing lay discourse to social locations and structural determinations. While Bourdieu highlights such discourse, he does so in relation to practical activity rather than its normative force.

Sayer's starting point reveals his close affinity with Fraser, who, in her exchanges with Honneth, begins the elaboration of her model with what she terms 'folk paradigms' of justice that inform 'present-day struggles in civil society' (before moving on to the plane of moral philosophy and finally, to the socio-theoretical level: to class and status Fraser, in Fraser and Honneth). Sayer argues that lay normativity constitutes emotional *reasoning*. It has cognitive as well as affective weight: 'emotional' because it concerns things that matter to people. Like all reasoning, it is fallible, but it is not reducible to alienated dispositions that are the product of particular social positionings. Lay normativity has generalizing tendencies: it may arise from particular identities, experiences or dispositions, garnered within specific socio-cultural contexts, but it makes judgements that are cast in universal terms.

What is at stake in the Fraser–Honneth debate, then, is also at the centre of Sayer's concerns here, in particular, the relationship between distributive injustice and (class) contempt. He comes close to Honneth in his concern with the subjective, psychological levels at which these injustices are so damaging, and in his reference of justice to well-being and the capacity to pursue 'the good life'. But with Fraser, he recognizes cultural and moral pluralism: there may be many definitions of what constitutes the good life in any given 'social field'.

While, with Honneth, Sayer notes the dependency of a moral stance regarding economic inequality upon recognition – specifically, the recognition of the equal moral worth of persons – he insists, with Fraser, and more strongly than is the case with Honneth, on the opposite pull of recognition towards redistribution. Class contempt is an injustice of misrecognition, but its remedy demands more than a politics of recognition, for it is rooted in 'identity-indifferent mechanisms of capitalism' (p. 99). At this point he cites Fraser's slogan, 'no recognition without redistribution'.

For Sayer, the critical realist sociologist, and for Fraser, the critical theorist philosopher, cognitive and normative claims are fallible, and judgements of these claims must be provisional. But for neither are these provisional judgements arbitrary: they have no absolute guarantees, but may find support in the outcome of open and public deliberations, and in the findings of a scrupulous *critical* realist social theory.

Christina Hughes and Loraine Blaxter's paper addresses Bourdieu's concept of 'social capital', one that is in widespread circulation in contemporary discourses of public policy, but within them Bourdieu's distinctive approach is marginalized. This paper surveys the shifting meaning of the concept in the work of those most closely associated with it in policy studies and public discourses – Coleman, Putnam and Fukuyama – claiming that all have taken a methodological individualist approach that favours rational choice analysis, although in Putnam and Fukuyama we find a move towards a less individualistic, moral social concept.

Bourdieu by contrast defines social capital as 'a network of bonds and connections or social obligations' (p. 108), but because his map of social space, across which his various capitals are very unequally distributed, is defined in *relational* terms, and because 'capitals' are not homogenous – we all possess cultural or symbolic goods and have social connections, but not all of these resources are of equal value as we make our way across social space and time. Access to social goods is very unequally distributed, sustained by a variety of exclusionary practices.

The fact that Bourdieu's capitals are interrelated, argue Hughes and Blaxter, facilitates the making of connections between 'the material' and 'the cultural', and here they invoke Fraser's recognition/redistribution model as one that allows us to consider 'the ways in which inequalities circulate culturally as well as materially': an absence in the dominant public policy discourses of 'social capital'.

The paper ends with some of the critical concerns of feminists who have engaged with and used Bourdieu's sociology, and which have come to rest on his economic metaphor, so prominent in his array of 'capitals'. Like Sayer, as discussed above, they are concerned that the metaphor suggests that 'some activities are not undertaken in the spirit of "investment", rather they are expressive of values' (p. 118) (or, in Sayer's terms, of commitments). Yet they conclude that while the formulations of 'social capital' in Coleman, Putnam and Fukuyama, unlike that of Bourdieu, hides the operation of power in social relations, Bourdieu's exposes it to scrutiny.

The remaining three papers in the collection engage with Fraser's and Bourdieu's conceptual frames in specific socio-historical contexts of political institutions and social policy.

Joanna Liddle and Elisabeth Michielsens' contribution is the last to engage directly with Bourdieu's conceptual frame, but the first to use it in substantive analysis. Its focus is on the processes of injustice in the local frame of one particular political system: a study of 'social bias' in political representation in the British parliament along lines of class and gender. Injustices of representation are difficult to remedy. Bourdieu is valuable because he holds together social identity, subjectivity and self with social structure in his twin concepts of habitus and field. The paper argues that it is possible to do this notwithstanding the danger of conflating the two that has been identified by Archer. Focusing on gendered working-class identity, it offers an in-depth analysis of the narratives of a male MP of working-class origin, and suggests that the concept of entitlement to political power is crucial for understanding why marginalized social categories such as women, working-class people and ethnic minorities do not put themselves forward, proportionally, as parliamentary candidates.

Fraser's inclusion of 'the political' as a distinct dimension, alongside 'the cultural' and 'the economic', in her theory of social justice, with their characteristic injustices of misrepresentation, misrecognition and maldistribution, underscores the relevance of this paper to her concerns. National parliaments remain very significant arenas of power within the democratic deliberative public sphere, even in the age of globalization. This paper uncovers the processes of exclusion that have their roots in the cultural and economic injustices that structure political and other social fields. The research narratives reveal both how it is possible for people to enter, and even flourish in, a field against the grain of habitus and the nomos of the field, but in so doing it simultaneously reveals the obstacles that ensure that this is exceptional. These processes of social injustice remain significant within emerging transnational forums, both hegemonic and counter-hegemonic.

Fraser has been an important influence upon critical social policy, and Ruth Lister's contribution probes the issues that Fraser's political theory addresses, but also some that she does not, primarily but not exclusively in the British context. The first half of the paper looks at feminist welfare politics, focusing on lone mothers and the relationship between paid employment and the care of young children. This is an issue that Fraser has addressed extensively, but Lister's second focus is on a surprising omission in her work: disability.

In spite of this silence, Lister argues that Fraser's model lends itself very well to the analysis of the 'difference' of disability and the politics of disability rights. She invokes Fraser's argument of the need to shift from 'needs talk' (Fraser 1989) to rights: 'the translation of justified needs claims into social rights' (p. 161). What is lost through this omission of explicit consideration of disability is 'the perspective of the care-receiver'.

The second half of the paper looks at Fraser's most recent elaborations of recognition/redistribution. In this, Lister takes up something that is at the heart of the debate between Fraser and Honneth: that of the psychological dimensions of injustice, both the injustice that is rooted in economic inequality and that of misrecognition. She, too, ends with a brief discussion of the global context.

The final contribution to this collection by Sandra Liebenberg gives it a fitting conclusion. Even socio-historically informed normative theory that, like Fraser's, includes substantive considerations in models of justice, and is concerned with pragmatic issues of social policy and political strategy aimed at transformation in the direction of social justice, come fully into their own only in the analysis of specific instances. Liebenberg's paper reveals the benefits of her in-depth engagement not only with Fraser's dual perspectival model of justice, but also with her earlier work on the discourse of social need (Fraser 1989), and she puts Fraser's concepts and arguments *to work* in a testing context: that of a South African state whose constitution affirms social, alongside civil and political rights. The paper takes us through the controversies that this has occasioned over the relationship between the explicitly transformative goals of the South African state that are enshrined in this constitution, and a jurisprudence of basic needs. In Fraser's terms, the difficulty is, on the one hand, in a historical context of long-standing deep social inequality, of securing access to the basic resources needed to redress this inequity through adjudication, and on the other hand, retaining the norm of 'participatory parity'. She cites Fraser's observation that participatory parity 'cannot be applied monologically, in the manner of a decision procedure' but 'must be applied dialogically and discursively, through democratic processes of public debate' (p. 183). But adjudication is precisely a decision-procedure, and the dilemma that this generates is as tough as any that Fraser has 'finessed' in the course of developing her model of justice: 'If the adjudication of basic needs claims operates to obstruct radical participatory democracy and depoliticizes questions concerning the definition and meeting of needs, it will ultimately undermine the project of advancing fundamental transformation in South Africa' (p. 184). Liebenberg's paper picks a careful path through this dilemma. She argues that the courts have the potential to play an important role in the drive towards social transformation. They may do so first, through giving substantive interpretations to the state's constitutional duty to 'act reasonably' in relation to rights claims – groups in urgent need must be catered for, and the process of claims definition, assessment, and implementation must be 'transparent and participatory' (p. 189); second, through the use of their remedial powers to grant more effective remedies and to supervise them; and finally, through their rhetorical role: 'the court's discourse can serve as a constant reminder that the redress of poverty and inequality are questions of political morality and a collective social responsibility' (p. 192). But Liebenberg, in her conclusion, anticipates 'an enduring tension between the depoliticizing tendencies of social rights adjudication and its transformative potential'.

Notes

1 This exchange is discussed in Mandy Merck's paper in this collection (Chapter 4).
2 See the paper by Christina Hughes and Loraine Blaxter in this collection (Chapter 7).
3 Biological sex difference presents a problem for feminism, in large part because it has long been, and still is, the trump card of anti-feminist essentialism. It was bracketed, courtesy of the sex/gender distinction, and placed outside of social space within biology, in order to secure a place for *women* within it under the sign of 'gender'. Because of the history of anti-feminist biological reductionism, some feminists minimize biological sex difference, and maximize the significance of gender in explanations of differences between the sexes. Some make a sharp cut between the two, and make the relationship between them arbitrary and not merely contingent. Butler comes close to this, but she also brings 'sex' into the (cultural/social) domain of gender. Feminist critical realists such as New argue that the relationship is contingent but not arbitrary. All social formations have gender regimes of some kind because of the social significance of human reproduction. All gender regimes *refer*, directly or indirectly, to biological sexual difference, but that difference does not determine the form and content of gender regimes. Such an understanding of the relationship between sex and gender is compatible with much of the most interesting feminist work on sexed subjectivity after the cultural (and psychoanalytical) turn, although the level at which sexed subjectivity is formed is one at which the distinction between what belongs to 'sex' and what to 'gender' is particularly difficult to cut.
4 Sandra Liebenberg's paper analysing the role of the judiciary in furthering or setting back the transformative commitments of the South African constitution provides an excellent example.

References

Archer, M. (2007) *Making our Way Through the World: Human Reflexivity and Social Mobility*, Cambridge: Cambridge University Press.
Bhaskar, R. (1979) *The Possibility of Naturalism*, Brighton: Harvester.
—— (1986) *Scientific Realism and Human Emancipation*, London: Verso.
Bourdieu, P. (1984) *Distinction*, London: Routledge and Kegan Paul.
Bourdieu, P. *et al.* (1999) *The Weight of the World*, Cambridge: Polity.
Butler, J. (1997) *Excitable Speech*, London and New York: Routledge.
—— (1998) 'Merely cultural', *New Left Review*, 227: 33–44.
Feyerabend, P.K. (1978) *Against Method: Outline of an Anarchistic Theory of Knowledge*, London: Verso.

Fraser, N. (1989) *Unruly Practices*, Minneapolis: University of Minnesota Press.

—— (1995) 'From redistribution to recognition? Critical reflections on the "postsocialist condition"', *New Left Review*, 212: 68–93.

—— (1997) 'After the family wage: a postindustrial thought experiment', in Fraser, N. *Justice Interruptus: Critical Reflections on the "Postsocialist" Condition*, London and New York: Routledge.

—— (1998) 'Heterosexism, misrecognition and capitalism', *New Left Review*, 228: 140–149.

Fraser, N. and Honneth, A. (2003) *Redistribution or Recognition? A Political-Philosophical Exchange*, London and New York: Verso.

Fraser, N. and Nicholson, L. (1990) 'Social criticism without philosophy: an encounter between feminism and postmodernism', in Nicholson, L. (ed.) *Feminism/Postmodernism*, New York and London: Routledge.

Gatens, M. (1989) 'A critique of the sex/gender distinction', in Gunew, S. (ed.) *A Reader in Feminist Knowledge*, London and New York: Routledge.

Hennessy, R. (2000) *Profits and Pleasure: Sexual Identities in Late Capitalism*, New York and London: Routledge.

Hull, C. (forthcoming) *The Ontology of Sex*, London: Routledge.

MacIntyre, A. (1981) *After Virtue*, London: Duckworth.

Moi, T. (1999) *What is a Woman?* Oxford: Oxford University Press.

New, C. (2005) 'Sex and gender: a critical realist approach', *New Formations*, 56 (Spring): 54–70.

Sayer, A. (1992) *Method in Social Science: a Realist Approach*, London and New York: Routledge.

—— (2000) *Realism and Social Science*, London: Sage.

—— (2005) *The Moral Significance of Class*, Cambridge: Cambridge University Press.

Skeggs, B. (1997) *Formations of Class and Gender*, London: Sage.

Young, I.M. (1990) *Justice and the Politics of Difference*, Princeton, NJ: Princeton University Press.

—— (1997) 'Unruly categories: a critique of Nancy Fraser's dual systems theory', *New Left Review*, 222: 147–160.

2   Re-framing justice in a globalizing world

Nancy Fraser

Globalization is changing the way we argue about justice.[1] Not so long ago, disputes about justice presumed what I shall call a 'Keynesian-Westphalian frame'. Typically played out within modern territorial states, arguments about justice were assumed to concern relations among fellow citizens, to be subject to debate within national publics, and to contemplate redress by national states. This was true for each of the two major families of justice claims, claims for socioeconomic redistribution and claims for legal or cultural recognition. At a time when the Bretton Woods system of international capital controls facilitated Keynesian economic steering at the national level, claims for redistribution usually focused on economic inequities within territorial states. Appealing to national public opinion for a fair share of the national pie, claimants sought intervention by national states in national economies. Likewise, in an era still gripped by a Westphalian political imaginary, which sharply distinguished 'domestic' from 'international' space, claims for recognition generally concerned internal status hierarchies. Appealing to the national conscience for an end to nationally institutionalized disrespect, claimants pressed national governments to outlaw discrimination and accommodate differences among citizens. In both cases, the Keynesian-Westphalian frame was assumed. Whether the matter concerned redistribution or recognition, class differentials or status hierarchies, it went without saying that the unit within which justice applied was the modern territorial state.[2]

To be sure, there were always exceptions. Occasionally, famines and genocides galvanized public opinion across borders. And some cosmopolitans and anti-imperialists sought to promulgate globalist views.[3] But these were exceptions that proved the rule. Relegated to the sphere of 'the international', they were subsumed within a problematic that was focused primarily on matters of security, as opposed to justice. The effect was to reinforce, rather than to challenge, the Keynesian-Westphalian frame. That framing of disputes about justice generally prevailed by default from the end of World War II through the 1970s.

Although it went unnoticed at the time, the Keynesian-Westphalian frame gave a distinctive shape to arguments about social justice. Taking for granted the modern territorial state as the appropriate unit, and its citizens as the pertinent subjects, such arguments turned on *what* precisely those citizens owed one another. In the eyes of some, it sufficed that citizens be formally equal before the law; for others, equality of opportunity was also required; for still others, justice demanded that all citizens gain access to the resources and respect they needed in order to be able to participate on a par with others, as full members of the political community. The argument focused, in other words, on *what* should count as a just ordering of social relations within a society. Engrossed in disputing the 'what' of justice, the contestants apparently felt no necessity to dispute the 'who'. With the Keynesian-Westphalian frame securely in place, it went without saying that the 'who' was the national citizenry.

Today, however, the Keynesian-Westphalian frame is losing its aura of self-evidence. Thanks to heightened awareness of globalization, many observe that the social processes shaping their lives routinely overflow territorial borders. They note, for example, that decisions taken in one territorial state often impact the lives of those outside it, as do the actions of transnational corporations, international currency speculators, and large institutional investors. Many also note the growing salience of supranational and international organizations, both governmental and nongovernmental, and of transnational public opinion, which flows with supreme disregard for borders through global mass media and cybertechnology. The result is a new sense of vulnerability to transnational forces. Faced with global warming, the spread of AIDS, international terrorism, and superpower unilateralism, many believe that their chances for living good lives depend at least as much on processes that trespass the borders of territorial states as on those contained within them.

Under these conditions, the Keynesian-Westphalian frame no longer goes without saying. For many, it is no longer axiomatic that the modern territorial state is the appropriate unit for thinking about issues of justice. Nor that the citizens of such states are the pertinent subjects. The effect is to destabilize the previous structure of political claims making – and therefore to change the way we argue about social justice.

This is true for both major families of justice claims. In today's world, claims for redistribution increasingly eschew the assumption of national economies. Faced with transnationalized production, the outsourcing of jobs, and the associated pressures of the 'race to the bottom', once nationally focused labor unions look increasingly for allies abroad. Inspired by the Zapatistas, meanwhile, impoverished peasants and indigenous peoples link their struggles against despotic local and national authorities to critiques of transnational corporate predation and global neoliberalism. Finally, WTO protestors directly target the new governance structures of the global economy, which have vastly strengthened the ability of large corporations and investors to escape the regulatory and taxation powers of territorial states.

In the same way, movements struggling for recognition increasingly look beyond the territorial state. Under the umbrella slogan 'women's rights are human rights', for example, feminists throughout the world are linking struggles against local patriarchal practices to campaigns to reform international law. Meanwhile, religious and ethnic minorities, who face discrimination within territorial states, are reconstituting themselves as diasporas and building trans-national publics from which to mobilize international opinion. Finally, trans-national coalitions of human-rights activists are seeking to build new cosmopolitan institutions, such as the International Criminal Court, which can punish state violations of human dignity.

In such cases, disputes about justice are exploding the Keynesian-Westphalian frame. No longer addressed exclusively to national states or debated exclusively by national publics, claimants no longer focus solely on relations among fellow citizens. Thus, the grammar of argument has altered. Whether the issue is distribution or recognition, disputes that used to focus exclusively on the question of *what* is owed as a matter of justice to community members now turn quickly into disputes about *who* should count as a member and *which* is the relevant community. Not just 'the what' but also 'the who' is up for grabs.

Today, in other words, arguments about justice assume a double guise. On the one hand, they concern first-order questions of substance, just as before: How much economic inequality does justice permit, how much redistribution is required, and according to which principle of distributive justice? What constitute equal respect, which kinds of differences merit public recognition, and by which means? But above and beyond such first-order questions, arguments about justice today also concern second-order, meta-level questions: What is the proper frame within which to consider first-order questions of justice? Who are the relevant subjects entitled to a just distribution or reciprocal recognition in the given case? Thus, it is not only the substance of justice, but also the frame, which is in dispute.[4]

The result is a major challenge to our theories of social justice. Preoccupied largely with first-order issues of distribution and/or recognition, these theories have so far failed to develop conceptual resources for reflecting on the meta-issue of the frame. As things stand, therefore, it is by no means clear that they are capable of addressing the double character of problems of justice in a global-izing age.[5]

In this essay, I shall propose a strategy for thinking about the problem of the frame. I shall argue, first, that in order to deal satisfactorily with this problem, the theory of justice must become three-dimensional, incorporating the political dimension of *representation*, alongside the economic dimension of distribution and the cultural dimension of recognition. I shall also argue, second, that the political dimension of representation should itself be understood as encompass-ing three levels. The combined effect of these two arguments will be to make visible a third question, beyond those of the 'what' and the 'who', which I shall call the question of the 'how'. That question in turn inaugurates a paradigm shift: what the Keynesian-Westphalian frame cast as the theory of social justice must now become a theory of *post-Westphalian democratic justice*.

For a three-dimensional theory of justice: on the specificity of the political

Let me begin by explaining what I mean by justice in general and by its political dimension in particular. In my view, the most general meaning of justice is parity of participation. According to this radical-democratic interpretation of the principle of equal moral worth, justice requires social arrangements that permit all to participate as peers in social life. Overcoming injustice means dismantling institutionalized obstacles that prevent some people from participating on a par with others, as full partners in social interaction. Previously, I have analyzed two distinct kinds of obstacles to participatory parity, which correspond to two distinct species of injustice (Fraser 2003). On the one hand, people can be impeded from full participation by economic structures that deny them the resources they need in order to interact with others as peers; in that case they suffer from distributive injustice or maldistribution. On the other hand, people can also be prevented from interacting on terms of parity by institutionalized hierarchies of cultural value that deny them the requisite standing; in that case they suffer from status inequality or misrecognition.[6] In the first case, the problem is the class structure of society, which corresponds to the economic dimension of justice. In the second case, the problem is the status order, which corresponds to the cultural dimension.[7] In modern capitalist societies, the class structure and the status order do not neatly mirror each other, although they interact causally. Rather, each has some autonomy vis-à-vis the other. As a result, misrecognition cannot be reduced to a secondary effect of maldistribution, as some economistic theories of distributive justice appear to suppose. Nor, conversely, can maldistribution be reduced to an epiphenomenal expression of misrecognition, as some culturalist theories of recognition tend to assume. Thus, neither recognition theory alone nor distribution theory alone can provide an adequate understanding of justice for capitalist society. Only a two-dimensional theory, encompassing both distribution and recognition, can supply the necessary levels of social-theoretical complexity and moral-philosophical insight.[8]

That, at least, is the view of justice I have defended in the past. And this two-dimensional understanding of justice still seems right to me as far as it goes. But I now believe that it does not go far enough. Distribution and recognition could appear to constitute the sole dimensions of justice only insofar as the Keynesian-Westphalian frame was taken for granted. Once the question of the frame becomes subject to contestation, however, the effect is to make visible a third dimension of justice, which was neglected in my previous work – as well as in the work of many other philosophers.[9]

The third dimension of justice is *the political*. Of course, distribution and recognition are themselves political in the sense of being contested and power-laden; and they have usually been seen as requiring adjudication by the state. But I mean political in a more specific, constitutive sense, which concerns the constitution of the state's jurisdiction and the decision rules by which it structures contestation. The political in this sense furnishes the stage on which struggles over distribution and recognition are played out. Establishing criteria of social belonging, and thus determining who counts as a member, the political dimension of justice specifies the reach of those other dimensions: it tells us who is included, and who excluded, from the circle of those entitled to a just distribution and reciprocal recognition. Establishing decision rules, likewise, the political dimension sets the procedures for staging and resolving contests in both the economic and the cultural dimensions: it tells us not only who can make claims for redistribution and recognition, but also how such claims are to be mooted and adjudicated.

Centered on issues of membership and procedure, the political dimension of justice is concerned chiefly with *representation*. At one level, which pertains to the boundary-setting aspect of the political, representation is a matter of social belonging; what is at issue here is inclusion in, or exclusion from, the community of those entitled to make justice claims on one another. At another level, which pertains to the decision-rule aspect, representation concerns the procedures that structure public processes of contestation; what is at issue here are the terms on which those included in the political community air their claims and adjudicate their disputes.[10] At both levels, the question can arise as to whether the relations of representation are just. One can ask: Do the boundaries of the political community wrongly exclude some who are actually entitled to representation? Do the community's decision rules accord equal voice in public deliberations and fair representation in public decision-making to all members? Such issues of representation are specifically political. Conceptually distinct from both economic and cultural questions, they cannot be reduced to the latter, although, as we shall see, they are inextricably interwoven with them.

To say that the political is a conceptually distinct dimension of justice, not reducible to the economic or the cultural, is also to say that it can give rise to a conceptually distinct species of injustice. Given the view of justice as participatory parity, this means that there can be distinctively political obstacles to parity, not reducible to maldistribution or misrecognition, although (again) interwoven with them. Such obstacles arise from the political constitution of society, as opposed to the class structure or status order. Grounded in a specifically political mode of social ordering, they can only be adequately grasped through a theory that conceptualizes representation, along with distribution and recognition, as one of three fundamental dimensions of justice.

If representation is the defining issue of the political, then the characteristic political injustice is *misrepresentation*. Misrepresentation occurs when political boundaries and/or decision rules function to wrongly deny some people the possibility of participating on a par with others in social interaction – including, but not only, in political arenas. Far from being reducible to maldistribution or misrecognition, misrepresentation can occur even in the absence of the latter injustices, although it is usually intertwined with them.

At least two different levels of misrepresentation can be distinguished. Insofar as political decision rules wrongly deny some of the included the chance to participate fully, as peers, the injustice is what I call *ordinary-political* misrepresentation. Here, where the issue is intraframe representation, we enter the familiar terrain of political science debates over the relative merits of alternative electoral systems. Do single-member-district, winner-take-all, first-past-the-post systems unjustly deny parity to numerical minorities? And if so, is proportional representation or cumulative voting the appropriate remedy (Guinier 1994; Ritchie and Hill 2001)? Likewise, do gender-blind rules, in conjunction with gender-based maldistribution and misrecognition, function to deny parity of political participation to women? And if so, are gender quotas an appropriate remedy (Phillips 1995; Rai 2002; Gray 2003; Htun 2004)? Such questions belong to the sphere of ordinary-political justice, which has usually been played out within the Keynesian-Westphalian frame.

Less obvious, perhaps, is a second level of misrepresentation, which concerns the boundary-setting aspect of the political. Here the injustice arises when the community's boundaries are drawn in such a way as to wrongly exclude some people from the chance to participate *at all* in its authorized contests over justice. In such cases, misrepresentation takes a deeper form, which I shall call *misframing*. The deeper character of misframing is a function of the crucial importance of framing to every question of social justice. Far from being of marginal importance, frame setting is among the most consequential of political decisions. Constituting both members and nonmembers in a single stroke, this decision effectively excludes the latter from the universe of those entitled to consideration within the community in matters of distribution, recognition, and ordinary-political representation. The result can be a serious injustice. When questions of justice are framed in a way that wrongly excludes some from consideration, the consequence is a special kind of meta-injustice, in which one is denied the chance to press first-order justice claims in a given political community. The injustice remains, moreover, even when those excluded from one political community are included as subjects of justice in another – as long as the effect of the political division is to put some relevant aspects of justice beyond their reach. Still more serious, of course, is the case in which one is excluded from membership in any political community. Akin to the loss of what Hannah Arendt called 'the right to have rights', that sort of misframing is a kind a 'political death' (Arendt 1973). Those who suffer it may become objects of charity or benevolence. But deprived of the possibility of authoring first-order claims, they become non-persons with respect to justice.

It is the misframing form of misrepresentation that globalization has recently begun to make visible. Earlier, in the heyday of the postwar welfare state, with the Keynesian-Westphalian frame securely in place, the principal concern in thinking about justice was distribution. Later, with the rise of the new social movements and multiculturalism, the center of gravity shifted to recognition. In both cases, the modern territorial state was assumed by default. As a result, the political dimension of justice was relegated to the margins. Where it did emerge, it took the ordinary-political form of contests over the decision rules internal to the polity, whose boundaries were taken for granted. Thus, claims for gender quotas and multicultural rights sought to remove political obstacles to participatory parity for those who were already included in principle in the political community.[11] Taking for granted the Keynesian-Westphalian frame, they did not call into question the assumption that the appropriate unit of justice was the territorial state.

Today, in contrast, globalization has put the question of the frame squarely on the political agenda. Increasingly subject to contestation, the Keynesian-Westphalian frame is now considered by many to be a major vehicle of injustice, as it partitions political space in ways that block many who are poor and despised from challenging the forces that oppress them. Channeling their claims into the domestic political spaces of relatively powerless, if not wholly failed, states, this frame insulates offshore powers from critique and control (Pogge 1999, 2002; Forst 2001, 2005). Among those shielded from the reach of justice are more powerful predator states and transnational private powers, including foreign investors and creditors, international currency speculators, and transnational corporations (Harris and Seid 2000). Also protected are the governance structures of the global economy, which set exploitative terms of interaction and then exempt them from democratic control (Cox 1996, 1997; Gill 1998; Helleiner 1994; Boyce 2004; Storm and Rao 2004). Finally, the Keynesian-Westphalian frame is self-insulating; the architecture of the interstate system protects the very partitioning of political space that it institutionalizes, effectively excluding transnational democratic decision-making on issues of justice (Bohman 1999; Dryzek 1999; Held 1995, 1999, 2000).

From this perspective, the Keynesian-Westphalian frame is a powerful instrument of injustice, which gerrymanders political space at the expense of the poor and despised. For those persons who are denied the chance to press transnational first-order claims, struggles against maldistribution and misrecognition cannot proceed, let alone succeed, unless they are joined with struggles against misframing. It is not surprising, therefore, that some consider misframing the defining injustice of a globalizing age.

Under these conditions of heightened awareness of misframing, the political dimension of justice is hard to ignore. Insofar as globalization is politicizing the question of the frame, it is also making visible an aspect of the grammar of justice that was often neglected in the previous period. It is now apparent that no claim for justice can avoid presupposing some notion of representation, implicit or explicit, insofar as none can avoid assuming a frame. Thus, representation is always already inherent in all claims for redistribution and recognition. The political dimension is implicit in, indeed required by, the grammar of the concept of justice. Thus, no redistribution or recognition without representation.[12]

In general, then, an adequate theory of justice for our time must be three-dimensional. Encompassing not only redistribution and recognition, but also representation, it must allow us to grasp the question of the frame as a question of justice. Incorporating the economic, cultural, and political dimensions, it must enable us to identify injustices of misframing and to evaluate possible remedies. Above all, it must permit us to pose, and to answer, the key political question of our age: How can we integrate struggles against maldistribution, misrecognition, and misrepresentation within a *post-Westphalian* frame?

On the politics of framing: from state-territoriality to social effectivity?

So far I have been arguing for the irreducible specificity of the political as one of three fundamental dimensions of justice. And I have identified two distinct levels of political injustice: ordinary-political misrepresentation and misframing. Now, I want to examine the politics of framing in a globalizing world. Distinguishing affirmative from transformative approaches, I shall argue that an adequate politics of representation must also address a third level: beyond contesting ordinary-political misrepresentation, on the one hand, and misframing, on the other, such a politics must also aim to democratize the process of frame setting.

I begin by explaining what I mean by 'the politics of framing'. Situated at my second level, where distinctions between members and nonmembers are drawn, this politics concerns the boundary-setting aspect of the political. Focused on the issues of who counts as a subject of justice, and what is the appropriate frame, the politics of framing comprises efforts to establish and consolidate, to contest and revise, the authoritative division of political space. Included here are struggles against misframing, which aim to dismantle the obstacles that prevent disadvantaged people from confronting the forces that oppress them with claims of justice. Centered on the setting and contesting of frames, the politics of framing is concerned with the question of the 'who'.

The politics of framing can take two distinct forms, both of which are now being practiced in our globalizing world.[13] The first approach, which I shall call the *affirmative* politics of framing, contests the boundaries of existing frames while accepting the Westphalian grammar of frame setting. In this politics, those who claim to suffer injustices of misframing seek to redraw the boundaries of existing territorial states or in some cases to create new ones. But they still assume that the territorial state is the appropriate unit within which to pose and resolve disputes about justice. For them accordingly, injustices of misframing are not a function of the general principle according to which the Westphalian order partitions political space. They arise, rather, as a result of the faulty way in which that principle has been applied. Thus, those who practice the affirmative politics of framing accept that the principle of state-territoriality is the proper basis for constituting the 'who' of justice. They agree, in other words, that what makes a given collection of individuals into fellow subjects of justice is their shared residence on the territory of a modern state and/or their shared membership in the political community that corresponds to such a state. Thus, far from challenging the underlying grammar of the Westphalian order, those who practice the affirmative politics of framing accept its state-territorial principle.[14]

Precisely that principle is contested, however, in a second version of the politics of framing, which I shall call the *transformative* approach. For proponents of this approach, the state-territorial principle no longer affords an adequate basis for determining the 'who' of justice in every case. They concede, of course, that that principle remains relevant for many purposes; thus, supporters of transformation do not propose to eliminate state-territoriality entirely. But they contend that its grammar is out of synch with the structural causes of many injustices in a globalizing world, which are not territorial in character. Examples include the financial markets, 'offshore factories', investment regimes, and governance structures of the global economy, which determine who works for a wage and who does not; the information networks of global media and cybertechnology, which determine who is included in the circuits of communicative power and who is not; and the bio-politics of climate, disease, drugs, weapons, and biotechnology, which determine who will live long and who will die young. In these matters, so fundamental to human well being, the forces that perpetrate injustice belong not to 'the space of places', but to 'the space of flows' (Castells 1996: 440–460). Not locatable within the jurisdiction of any actual or conceivable territorial state, they cannot be made answerable to claims of justice that are framed in terms of the state-territorial principle. In their case, so the argument goes, to invoke the state-territorial principle to determine the frame is itself to commit an injustice. By partitioning political space along territorial lines, this principle insulates extra- and non-territorial powers from the reach of justice. In a globalizing world, therefore, it is less likely to serve as a remedy for misframing than as means of inflicting or perpetuating it.

In general, then, the transformative politics of framing aims to change the deep grammar of frame setting in a globalizing world. This approach seeks to supplement the state-territorial principle of the Westphalian order with one or more *post-Westphalian* principles. The aim is to overcome injustices of misframing by changing not just the boundaries of the 'who' of justice, but also the mode of their constitution, hence the way in which they are drawn.[15]

What might a post-Westphalian mode of frame setting look like? Doubtless it is too early to have a clear view. Nevertheless, the most promising candidate so far is the 'all-affected principle'. This principle holds that all those affected by a given social structure or institution have moral standing as subjects of justice in relation to it. On this view, what turns a collection of people into fellow subjects of justice is not geographical proximity, but their co-imbrication in a common structural or institutional framework, which sets the ground rules that govern their social interaction, thereby shaping their respective life possibilities, in patterns of advantage and disadvantage.

Until recently, the all-affected principle seemed to coincide in the eyes of many with the state-territorial principle. It was assumed, in keeping with the Westphalian world picture, that the common framework that determined patterns of advantage and disadvantage was precisely the constitutional order of the modern territorial state. As a result, it seemed that in applying the state-territorial principle, one simultaneously captured the normative force of the all-affected principle. In fact, this was never truly so, as the long history of colonialism and neocolonialism attests. From the perspective of the metropole, however, the conflation of state-territoriality with social effectivity appeared to have an emancipatory thrust, as it served to justify the progressive incorporation, as subjects of justice, of the subordinate classes and status groups who were resident on the territory but excluded from active citizenship.

Today, however, the idea that state-territoriality can serve as a proxy for social effectivity is no longer plausible. Under current conditions, one's chances to live a good life do not depend wholly on the internal political constitution of the territorial state in which one resides. Although the latter remains undeniably relevant, its effects are mediated by other structures, both extra- and non-territorial, whose impact is at least as significant (Pogge 2002, especially sections on 'The causal role of global institutions in the persistence of severe poverty', pp. 112–116, and 'Explanatory nationalism: the deep significance of national borders', pp. 139–144). In general, globalization is driving a widening wedge between state territoriality and social effectivity. As those two principles increasingly diverge, the effect is to reveal the former as an inadequate surrogate for the latter. And so the question arises: Is it possible to apply the all-affected principle directly to the framing of justice, without going through the detour of state-territoriality?[16]

This is precisely what some practitioners of transformative politics are seeking to do. Seeking leverage against offshore sources of maldistribution and misrecognition, some globalization activists are appealing directly to the all-affected principle in order to circumvent the state-territorial partitioning of political space. Contesting their exclusion by the Keynesian-Westphalian frame, environmentalists and indigenous peoples are claiming standing as subjects of justice in relation to the extra- and non-territorial powers that impact their lives. Insisting that effectivity trumps state-territoriality, they have joined development activists, international feminists, and others in asserting their right to make claims against the structures that harm them, even when the latter cannot be located in the space of places. Casting off the Westphalian grammar of frame-setting, these claimants are applying the all-affected principle directly to questions of justice in a globalizing world (Castells 1996; Guidry *et al.* 2000; Khagram *et al.* 2002; Keck and Sikkink 1998; St. Clair 2000).

In such cases, the transformative politics of framing proceeds simultaneously in multiple dimensions and on multiple levels.[17] On one level, the social movements that practice this politics aim to redress first-order injustices of maldistribution, misrecognition, and ordinary-political misrepresentation. On a second level, these movements seek to redress meta-level injustices of misframing by reconstituting the 'who' of justice. In those cases, moreover, where the state-territorial principle serves more to indemnify than to challenge injustice, transformative social movements appeal instead to the all-affected principle. Invoking a post-Westphalian principle, they are seeking to change the very grammar of frame setting – and thereby to reconstruct the meta-political foundations of justice for a globalizing world.

But the claims of transformative politics go further still. In addition to appealing to a post-Westphalian principle, this politics is also inaugurating a post-

Westphalian *process* of frame setting. Above and beyond their other claims, these movements are also claiming a say in the process of frame setting. Rejecting the standard view, which deems frame setting the prerogative of states and transnational elites, they are effectively aiming to democratize the process by which the frames of justice are drawn and revised. Asserting their right to participate in constituting the 'who' of justice, they are simultaneously transforming the 'how' – by which I mean the accepted procedures for determining the 'who' (see Fraser 2005, forthcoming). At their most reflective and ambitious, accordingly, transformative movements are demanding the creation of new democratic arenas for entertaining arguments about the frame. In some cases, moreover, they are creating such arenas themselves. In the World Social Forum, for example, some practitioners of transformative politics have fashioned a transnational public sphere where they can participate on a par with others in airing and resolving disputes about the frame (Bohman 1998; Guidry *et al.* 2000; Pomiah 2004; Lara 2003; Fraser 2007). In this way, they are prefiguring the possibility of new institutions of *post-Westphalian democratic justice.*[18]

The democratizing dimension of transformative politics points to a third level of political injustice, above and beyond the two previously discussed. Previously, I distinguished first-order injustices of ordinary-political misrepresentation from second-order injustices of misframing. Now, however, we can discern a third-order species of political injustice, which corresponds to the question of the 'how'. Exemplified by undemocratic processes of frame setting, this injustice consists in the failure to institutionalize parity of participation at the meta-political level, in deliberations and decisions concerning the 'who'. Because what is at stake here is the process by which first-order political space is constituted, I shall call this injustice *meta-political misrepresentation.* Meta-political misrepresentation arises when states and transnational elites monopolize the activity of frame setting, denying voice to those who may be harmed in the process, and blocking creation of democratic fora where the latter's claims can be vetted and redressed. The effect is to exclude the overwhelming majority of people from participation in the meta-discourses that determine the authoritative division of political space. Lacking any institutional arenas for such participation, and submitted to an undemocratic approach to the 'how', the majority is denied the chance to engage on terms of parity in decision-making about the 'who'.

In general, then, struggles against misframing are revealing a new kind of democratic deficit. Just as globalization has made visible injustices of misframing, so transformative struggles against neoliberal globalization are making visible the injustice of meta-political misrepresentation. Exposing the lack of institutions where disputes about the 'who' can be democratically aired and resolved, these struggles are focusing attention on the 'how'. By demonstrating that the absence of such institutions impedes efforts to overcome injustice, they are revealing the deep internal connections between democracy and justice. The effect is to bring to light a structural feature of the current conjuncture: struggles for justice in a globalizing world cannot succeed unless they go hand in hand with struggles for *meta-political democracy*. At this level too, then, no redistribution or recognition without representation.

Paradigm shift: post-Westphalian democratic justice

I have been arguing that what distinguishes the current conjuncture is intensified contestation concerning both the 'who' and the 'how' of justice. Under these conditions, the theory of justice is undergoing a paradigm shift. Earlier, when the Keynesian-Westphalian frame was in place, most philosophers neglected the political dimension. Treating the territorial-state as a given, they endeavored to ascertain the requirements of justice theoretically, in a monological fashion. Thus, they did not envision any role in determining those requirements for those who would be subject to them, let alone for those who would be excluded by the national frame. Neglecting to reflect on the question of the frame, these philosophers never imagined that those whose fates would be so decisively shaped by framing decisions might be entitled to participate in making them. Disavowing any need for a dialogical democratic moment, they were content to produce monological theories of social justice.

Today, however, monological theories of social justice are becoming increasingly implausible. As we have seen, globalization cannot help but problematize the question of the 'how', as it politicizes the question of the 'who'. The process goes something like this: as the circle of those claiming a say in frame setting expands, decisions about the 'who' are increasingly viewed as political matters, which should be handled democratically, rather than as technical matters, which can be left to experts and elites. The effect is to shift the burden of argument, requiring defenders of expert privilege to make their case. No longer able to hold themselves above the fray, they are necessarily embroiled in disputes about the 'how'. As a result, they must contend with demands for meta-political democratization.

An analogous shift is currently making itself felt in normative philosophy. Just as some activists are seeking to transfer elite frame-setting prerogatives to democratic publics, so some theorists of justice are proposing to rethink the classic division of labor between theorist and *demos*. No longer content to ascertain the requirements of justice in a monological fashion, these theorists are looking increasingly to dialogical approaches, which treat important aspects of justice as matters for collective decision-making, to be determined by the citizens themselves, through democratic deliberation. For them, accordingly, the grammar of the theory of justice is being transformed. What could once be called the 'theory of social justice' now appears as the 'theory of *democratic justice*'.[19]

In its current form, however, the theory of democratic justice remains incomplete. To complete the shift from a monological to dialogical theory requires a further step, beyond those envisioned by most proponents of the dialogical turn.[20] Henceforth, democratic processes of determination must be applied not only to the 'what' of justice, but also to the 'who' and the 'how'. In that case, by adopting a democratic approach to the 'how', the theory of justice assumes a guise appropriate to a globalizing world: dialogical at *every* level, meta-political as well as ordinary-political, it becomes a theory of *post-Westphalian democratic justice*.

The view of justice as participatory parity lends itself easily to such an approach. This principle has a double quality that expresses the reflexive character of democratic justice. On the one hand, the principle of participatory parity is an outcome notion, which specifies a substantive principle of justice by which we may evaluate social arrangements: the latter are just if, and only if, they permit all the relevant social actors to participate as peers in social life. On the other hand, participatory parity is also a process notion, which specifies a procedural standard by which we may evaluate the democratic legitimacy of norms: the latter are legitimate if, and only if, they can command the assent of all concerned in fair and open processes of deliberation, in which all can participate as peers. By virtue of this double quality, the view of justice as participatory parity has an inherent reflexivity. Able to problematize both substance and procedure, it renders visible the mutual entwinement of those two aspects of social arrangements. Thus, this approach can expose both the unjust background conditions that skew putatively democratic decision-making and the undemocratic procedures that generate substantively unequal outcomes. As a result, it enables us to shift levels easily, moving back and forth as necessary between first-order and meta-level questions. Making manifest the co-implication of democracy and justice, the view of justice as participatory parity supplies just the sort of reflexivity that is needed in a globalizing world.

Let me conclude by recalling the principal features of the theory of justice that I have sketched here. An account of post-Westphalian democratic justice, this theory encompasses three fundamental dimensions: economic, cultural, and political. As a result, it renders visible, and criticizable, the mutual entwinement of maldistribution, misrecognition, and misrepresentation. In addition, this theory's account of political injustice encompasses three levels. Addressing not only ordinary-political misrepresentation, but also misframing and meta-political misrepresentation, it allows us to grasp the problem of the frame as a matter of justice. Focused not only on the 'what' of justice, but also on the 'who' and the 'how', it enables us to evaluate the justice of alternative principles and alternative processes of frame setting. Above all, as I noted before, the theory of post-Westphalian democratic justice encourages us to pose, and hopefully to answer, the key political question of our time: How can we integrate struggles against maldistribution, misrecognition, and misrepresentation within a post-Westphalian frame?

Notes

1 This text is a revised and expanded version of my second Spinoza Lecture, delivered at the University of Amsterdam, December 2, 2004. The lecture was drafted during my tenure there as Spinoza Professor in spring 2004 and revised during my subsequent fellowship year at the Wissenschaftskolleg zu Berlin, 2004–2005. My

warmest thanks to both institutions for their generous support of this work. Special thanks to Yolande Jansen and Hilla Dayan for selfless and good-natured assistance in a time of great need and to James Bohman for expert bibliographical advice. Thanks, also, to Amy Allen, Seyla Benhabib, Bert van den Brink, Alessandro Ferrara, Rainer Forst, Stefan Gosepath, John Judis, Ted Koditschek, María Pía Lara, David Peritz, Ann Laura Stoler, and Eli Zaretsky for thoughtful comments on earlier drafts. Thanks, finally, to Kristin Gissberg and Keith Haysom for expert research assistance.

2 The phrase 'Keynesian-Westphalian frame' is meant to signal the national-territorial underpinnings of justice disputes in the heyday of the postwar democratic welfare state, roughly 1945 through the 1970s. In this period, struggles over distribution in North America and Western Europe were premised on the assumption of state steering of national economies. And national Keynesianism, in turn, was premised on the assumption of an international state system that recognized territorial state sovereignty over domestic affairs, which included responsibility for the citizenry's welfare. Analogous assumptions also governed disputes about recognition in this period. The term 'Westphalian' refers to the Treaty of 1648, which established some key features of the international state system in question. However, I am concerned neither with the actual achievements of the Treaty nor with the centuries-long process by which the system it inaugurated evolved. Rather, I invoke 'Westphalia' as a political imaginary that mapped the world as a system of mutually recognizing sovereign territorial states. My claim is that this imaginary undergirded the postwar framing of debates about justice in the First World. For the distinction between Westphalia as 'event', as 'idea/ideal', as 'process of evolution', and as 'normative scoresheet', see Richard Falk (2002).

3 It might be assumed that, from the perspective of the Third World, Westphalian premises would have appeared patently counterfactual. Yet it is worth recalling that the great majority of anti-imperialists sought to achieve independent Westphalian states of their own. In contrast, only a small minority consistently championed justice within a global frame, for reasons that are entirely understandable.

4 This situation is by no means unprecedented. Even the most cursory reflection discloses historical parallels – for example, the period leading up to the Treaty of Westphalia and the period following World War I. In these moments, too, not just the substance of justice, but also the frame, was up for grabs.

5 I have discussed the elision of the problem of the frame in mainstream theories of justice in my first Spinoza Lecture, 'Who counts?' Thematizing the question of the frame'. See also Fraser (2005a).

6 This 'status model' of recognition represents an alternative to the standard 'identity model'. For a critique of the latter and a defense of the former, see Nancy Fraser (2000).

7 Here I assume quasi-Weberian conceptions of class and status. See Max Weber (1958).

8 For the full argument see Fraser (2003).

9 The neglect of the political is especially glaring in the case of theorists of justice who subscribe to liberal or communitarian philosophical premises. In contrast, deliberative democrats, agonistic democrats, and republicans have sought to theorize the political. But most of these theorists have had relatively little to say about the relation between democracy and justice; and none has conceptualized the political as a dimension of justice. Deliberative democratic accounts of the political include Jürgen Habermas (1996), and Amy Gutmann and Dennis Thompson (1996). Agonistic accounts of the political include William Connolly (1991), Bonnie Honig (1993), Chantal Mouffe (1993), and James Tully (1995). Republican accounts of the political include Philip Pettit (1996), and Quentin Skinner (1990). In contrast to these thinkers, a handful of others have linked the political directly to justice, although not in the way that I do here. See, for example, Michael Walzer (1983), Iris Marion Young (1990), Amartya Sen (1999), and Seyla Benhabib (2004).

10 Classic works on representation have dealt largely with what I am calling the decision-rule aspect, while ignoring the membership aspect. See, for example, Hannah Fenichel Pitkin (1967) and Bernard Manin (1997). Works that do treat the membership aspect include Walzer (1993) and Benhabib (2004). However, both Walzer and Benhabib arrive at conclusions that differ from the ones I draw here.

11 Among the best accounts of the normative force of these struggles are Will Kymlicka (1995) and Melissa Williams (1998).

12 I do not mean to suggest that the political is the master dimension of justice, more fundamental than the economic and the cultural. Rather, the three dimensions stand in relations of mutual entwinement and reciprocal influence. Just as the ability to make claims for distribution and recognition depends on relations of representation, so the ability to exercise one's political voice depends on the relations of class and status. In other words, the capacity to influence public debate and authoritative decision-making depends not only on formal decision rules but also on power relations rooted in the economic structure and the status order, a fact that is insufficiently stressed in most theories of deliberative democracy. Thus, maldistribution and misrecognition conspire to subvert the principle of equal political voice for every citizen, even in polities that claim to be democratic. But of course the converse is also true. Those who suffer from misrepresentation are vulnerable to injustices of status and class. Lacking political voice, they are unable to articulate and defend their interests with respect to distribution and recognition, which in turn exacerbates their misrepresenta-tion. In such cases, the result is a vicious circle in which the three orders of injustice reinforce one another, denying some people the chance to participate on a par with others in social life. In general, then, the political is not the master dimension. On the contrary, although they are conceptually distinct and mutually irreducible, the three sorts of obstacles to parity of participation are usually intertwined. It follows that efforts to overcome injustice cannot, except in rare cases, address themselves to one such dimension alone. Rather, struggles against maldistribution and misrecognition cannot succeed unless they are joined with struggles against misrepresentation, and vice-versa. Where one puts the emphasis, of course, is both a tactical and strategic decision. Given the current salience of injustices of misframing, my own preference is for the slogan, 'No redistribution or recognition without representation'. But even so, the politics of representation appears as one among three interconnected fronts in the struggle for social justice in a globalizing world.

13 In distinguishing 'affirmative' from 'transformative' approaches, I am adapting termi-nology I have used in the past with respect to redistribution and recognition. See Nancy Fraser (1995, 2003).

14 For the state-territorial principle, see Thomas Baldwin (1992). For doubts about the state-territorial principle (among other principles), see Frederick Whelan (1983).

15 I owe the idea of a post-territorial 'mode of political differentiation' to John G. Ruggie. See his immensely suggestive essay: 'Territoriality and beyond: problematiz-ing modernity in international relations' (Ruggie 1993). Also suggestive in this regard is Raul C. Pangalangan (2001).

16 Everything depends on finding a suitable interpretation of the all-affected principle. The key issue is how to narrow the idea of 'affectedness' to the point that it becomes a viable operationalizable standard for assessing the justice of various frames. The problem is that, given the so-called butterfly effect, one can adduce evidence that just about everyone is affected by just about everything. What is needed, therefore, is a way of distinguishing those levels and kinds of effectivity that are sufficient to confer moral standing from those that are not. One proposal, suggested by Carol Gould, is to limit such standing to those whose human rights are violated by a given practice or institution. Another proposal, suggested by David Held, is to accord standing to those whose life expectancy and life chances are significantly affected. My own view is that the all-affected principle is open to a plurality of reasonable interpretations. As a

result, its interpretation cannot be determined monologically, by philosophical fiat. Rather, philosophical analyses of affectedness should be understood as contributions to a broader public debate about the principle's meaning. (The same is true for empirical social-scientific accounts of who is affected by given institutions or policies.) In general, the all-affected principle must be interpreted dialogically, through the give-and-take of argument in democratic deliberation. That said, however, one thing is clear. Injustices of misframing can be avoided only if moral standing is not limited to those who are already accredited as official members of a given institution or as authorized participants in a given practice. To avoid such injustices, standing must also be accorded to those nonmembers and non participants significantly affected by the institution or practice at issue. Thus, sub-Saharan Africans, who have been involuntarily disconnected from the global economy, count as subjects of justice in relation to it, even if they do not participate officially in it. For the human-rights interpretation, see Carol C. Gould (2004). For the life expectancy and life-chances interpretation, see David Held (2004: 99). For the dialogical approach, see below, as well as Fraser (2005a, forthcoming). For the involuntary disconnection of sub-Saharan Africa from the official global economy, see James Ferguson (1999).

17 For a useful account, which differs from the one presented here, see Christine Chin and James H. Mittelman (1997).

18 For the time being, efforts to democratize the process of frame setting are confined to contestation in transnational civil society. Indispensable as this level is, it cannot succeed so long as there exist no formal institutions that can translate transnational public opinion into binding, enforceable decisions. In general, then, the civil-society track of transnational democratic politics needs to be complemented by a formal-institutional track. For further discussion of this problem, see Fraser (2005a, forthcoming), also James Bohman (1999).

19 The phrase comes from Ian Shapiro (1999). But the idea can also be found in Habermas (1996), Benhabib (2004), and Forst (2002).

20 None of the theorists cited in the previous note has attempted to apply the democratic justice approach to the problem of the frame. The thinker who comes closest is Rainer Forst, as he appreciates the importance of framing. But even Forst does not envision democratic processes of frame setting.

References

Arendt, H. (1973) *The Origins of Totalitarianism*, New York: Harcourt Brace.

Baldwin, T. (1992) 'The territorial state', in H. Gross and T.R. Harrison (eds) *Jurisprudence: Cambridge Essays*, Oxford: Clarendon Press.

Benhabib, S. (2004) *The Rights of Others: Aliens, Residents, and Citizens*, Cambridge: Cambridge University Press.

Bohman, J. (1998) 'The globalization of the public sphere: cosmopolitanism publicity and cultural pluralism', *Modern Schoolman* 75, 2: 101–117.

—— (1999) 'International regimes and democratic governance', *International Affairs* 75, 3: 499–513.

Boyce, J.K. (2004) 'Democratizing global economic governance', *Development and Change* 35, 3: 593–599.

Castells, M. (1996) *The Power of Identity*, Oxford: Blackwell.

Chin, C. and Mittelman, J.H. (1997) 'Conceptualizing resistance to globalisation', *New Political Economy* 2, 1: 25–37.

Connolly, W. (1991) *Identity/Difference: Negotiations of Political Paradox*, Ithaca: Cornell University Press.

Cox, R.W. (1996) 'A perspective on globalization', in J.H. Mittelman (ed.) *Globalization: Critical Reflections*, Boulder, CO: Lynne Rienner.

—— (1997) 'Democracy in hard times: economic globalization and the limits to liberal democracy', in A. McGrew (ed.) *The Transformation of Democracy?* Cambridge: Polity Press.

Dryzek, J. (1999) 'Transnational democracy', *Journal of Political Philosophy* 7, 1: 30–51.

Falk, R. (2002) 'Revisiting Westphalia, discovering post-Westphalia', *Journal of Ethics* 6, 4: 311–352.

Ferguson, J. (1999) 'Global disconnect: abjection and the aftermath of modernism', in Ferguson, *Expectations of Modernity: Myths and Meanings of Urban Life on the Zambian Copperbelt*, Berkeley: University of California Press, 234–254.

Forst, R. (2001) 'Towards a critical theory of transnational justice', in T. Pogge (ed.) *Global Justice*, Oxford: Oxford University Press.

—— (2002) *Contexts of Justice: Political Philosophy Beyond Liberalism and Communitarianism*, trans. J.M.M. Farrell, Berkeley: University of California Press.

—— (2005) 'Justice, morality and power in the global context', in A. Follesdal and T. Pogge (eds) *Real World Justice*, Dordrecht: Springer.

Fraser, N. (1995) 'From redistribution to recognition? Dilemmas of justice in a "postsocialist" age", *New Left Review* 212: 68–93.

—— (2000) 'Rethinking recognition: overcoming displacement and reification in cultural politics', *New Left Review* 3: 107–120.

—— (2003) 'Social justice in the age of identity politics: redistribution, recognition and participation', in N. Fraser and A. Honneth, *Redistribution or Recognition? A Political–Philosophical Exchange*, trans. J. Golb, J. Ingram, and C. Wilke, London: Verso.

—— (2005) 'Democratic justice in a globalizing age: thematizing the problem of the frame', in N. Karagiannis and P. Wagner (ed.) *Varieties of World-Making: Beyond Globalization*, Liverpool: Liverpool University Press.

—— (2007) 'Transnationalizing the public sphere: on the efficacy of public opinion in a post-Westphalian world', *Theory, Culture and Society* 24, 4: 1–24.

—— (forthcoming) 'Abnormal justice', *Critical Inquiry*.

Gill, S. (1998) 'New constitutionalism, democratisation and global political economy', *Pacific Review* 10, 1: 23–38.

Gould, C.C. (2004) *Globalizing Democracy and Human Rights*, Cambridge: Cambridge University Press.

Gray, T. (2003) 'Electoral gender quotas: lessons from Argentina and Chile', *Bulletin of Latin American Research* 21: 52–78.

Guidry, J.A., Kennedy, M.D. and Zeld, M.N. (2000*) Globalizations and Social Movements: Culture. Power and the Transnational Public Sphere*, Ann Arbor: University of Michigan Press.

Guinier, L. (1994) *The Tyranny of the Majority*, New York: The Free Press.

Gutmann, A. and Thompson, D. (1996) *Democracy and Disagreement*, Cambridge: Belknap Press.

Habermas, J. (1996*) Between Facts and Norms: Contributions to a Discourse Theory of Law and Democracy*, Cambridge, MA: The MIT Press.

Harris, R.L. and Seid, M.J. (2000) *Critical Perspectives on Globalization and Neoliberalism in the Developing Countries*, Boston: Leiden.

Held, D. (1995) *Democracy and the Global Order: from the Modern State to Cosmopolitan Governance*, Cambridge: Polity Press.

—— (1999) 'The transformation of political community: rethinking democracy in the context of globalization', in I. Shapiro and C. Hacker-Cordón (eds) *Democracy's Edges*, Cambridge: Cambridge University Press.

—— (2000) 'Regulating globalization?' *International Journal of Sociology* 15, 2: 394–408.

—— (2004) *Global Covenant: the Social Democratic Alternative to the Washington Consensus*, Cambridge: Polity Press.

Helleiner, E. (1994) 'From Bretton Woods to global finance: a world turned upside down', in R. Stubbs and G.R.D. Underhill (eds) *Political Economy and the Changing Global Order*, New York: St. Martin's Press.

Honig, B. (1993) *Political Theory and the Displacement of Politics*, Ithaca: Cornell University Press.

Htun, M. (2004) 'Is gender like ethnicity? The political representation of identity groups', *Perspectives on Politics* 2, 3: 439–458.

Keck, M.E. and Sikkink, K. (1998) *Activists Beyond Borders: Advocacy Networks in International Politics*, Ithaca: Cornell University Press.

Khagram, S., Sikkink, K. and Riker, J.V. (2002) *Restructuring World Politics: Transnational Social Movements, Networks, and Norms*, Minneapolis: University of Minneapolis Press.

Kymlicka, W. (1995) *Multicultural Citizenship: a Liberal Theory of Minority Rights*, London: Oxford University Press.

Lara, M.P. (2003) 'Diasporic global spheres', in R.N. Fiore and H.L. Nelson (eds) *Recognition, Responsibility and Rights: Feminist Ethics and Social Theory*, Towata, NJ: Rowman and Littlefield.

Manin, B. (1997) *The Principles of Representative Government*, Cambridge: Cambridge University Press.

Mouffe, C. (1993) *The Return of the Political*, London: Verso.

Pangalangan, R.P. (2001) 'Territorial sovereignty: command, title, and expanding the claims of the commons', in D. Miller and S.H. Hashmi (eds) *Boundaries and Justice: Diverse Ethical Perspectives*, Princeton: Princeton University Press.

Pettit, P. (1996) 'Freedom as antipower', *Ethics* 106, 3: 576–604.

Phillips, A. (1995) *The Politics of Presence*, Oxford: Clarendon Press.

Pitkin, H.F. (1967) *The Concept of Representation*, Berkeley: University of California Press.

Pogge, T.W. (1999) 'Economic justice and national borders', *Revision* 22, 2: 27–34.

—— (2002) *World and Poverty and Human Rights: Cosmopolitan Responsibilities and Reforms*, Cambridge: Polity Press.

Pomiah, T. (2004) 'Democracy vs. empire: alternatives to globalization presented at the world social forum', *Antipode* 36, 1: 130–133.

Rai, S.M. (2002) 'Political representation, democratic institutions and women's empowerment: the quota debate in India', in J.L. Parpart, S.M. Rai and K. Staudt (eds) *Rethinking Empowerment: Gender and Development in a Global/Local World*, New York: Routledge, 133–145.

Ritchie, R. and Hill, S. (2001) 'The case for proportional representation', in R. Ritchie and S. Hill (eds) *Whose Vote Counts?* Boston: Beacon Press, 1–33.

Ruggie, J.G. (1993) 'Territoriality and beyond: problematizing modernity in international relations', *International Organization* 47: 139–174.

St. Clair J. (2000) 'Seattle Diary', in A. Cockburn and J. St. Clair (eds) *Five Days that Shook the World: the Battle for Seattle and Beyond*, London: Verso.

Sen, A. (1999) *Development as Freedom*, New York: Anchor Books.

Shapiro, I. (1999) *Democratic Justice*, New Haven: Yale University Press.

Skinner, Q. (1990) 'The republican ideal of political liberty', in G. Bock, Q. Skinner and M. Viroli (eds) *Machiavelli and Republicanism*, Cambridge: Cambridge University Press.

Storm, S. and Rao, J.M. (2004) 'Market-led globalization and world democracy: can the twain ever meet?' *Development and Change* 35, 5: 567–581.

Tully, J. (1995) *Strange Multiplicity: Constitutionalism in an Age of Diversity*, Cambridge: Cambridge University Press.

Walzer, M. (1983) *Spheres of Justice*, New York: Basic Books.

Weber, M. (1958) 'Class, status, party', in Hans H. Gerth and C. Wright Mills (eds) *From Max Weber: Essays in Sociology*, Oxford: Oxford University Press.

Whelan, F. (1983) 'Democratic theory and the boundary problem', in J.R. Pennock and R.W. Chapman (eds) *Nomos XXV: Liberal Democracy*, New York and London: New York University Press.

Williams, M. (1998) *Voice, Trust, and Memory: Marginalized Groups and the Failings of Liberal Representation*, Princeton, NJ: Princeton University Press.

Young, I.M. (1990) *Justice and the Politics of Difference*, Princeton: Princeton University Press.

3 Justice and the public sphere

The dynamics of Nancy Fraser's critical theory

María Pía Lara and Robert Fine

Introduction

The conception of justice as fairness put forward in John Rawls' *Theory of Justice* (Rawls 1971) established the importance of a focus on justice and on how our views of justice need to change in the context of plural modern societies. In a way, Rawls' *Theory* restored important moral questions to the status of serious philosophical research. Rawls concentrated on our need to think about the organization of society that could validly be described as a just society. He returned to the idea of the social contract to redesign it in an intersubjective mode. His view of the social contract differed from preceding views in that he sought to generate basic political principles of 'pure procedural justice'. He highlighted the idea that rights do not belong to the state of nature but to a political order, and that there are moral elements in the contract procedure that are best represented by the idea of the 'veil of ignorance' to secure moral impartiality. Later, Rawls pursued the premise of political autonomy to define how we could find a translation of the concept of justice into the political realm. *Political Liberalism* (Rawls 1993) is the work in which Rawls established the idea of a political concept of justice in a plural society. His paradigm of justice, because it defined fairness in terms of certain procedures that generate an adequately just outcome, entailed not just an idea of moral equality but a rough equality of powers and resources.

If Rawls defined justice as fairness, Habermas redefined it as a decentered process of deliberative measures, shifting focus from the social contract to the social institutions and actual practices through which deliberation takes place. With this move Habermas articulated the notion that justice is an ongoing deliberative process of social inclusion, instantiated in his reconstruction of the idea of the public sphere. This is the reason why solidarity plays a major role in his definition of justice. Cooperation and dialogue – rather than the founding moment that is usually the case with social contract theories – serve as the basic premises on which the legitimating processes of political authority are articulated through the exercise of deliberation. Instead of resorting to the device of a social contract, as Rawls had done, Habermas took up the Kantian premises apparent in Rawls' project and turned them into the communicative premises of his own discourse theory. They became the rules of the legitimizing processes required for the building up of collective authority. Instead of a veil of ignorance Habermas proposed a principle of universalization that defines impartiality as a procedure of 'ideal role taking' and thus moved to an embodied, decentered idea of justice. Habermas' pragmatic presuppositions articulated the idea that there are possibilities of an inclusive, non-coercive rational discourse between free and equal participants where everyone is required to take the perspective of everyone else. In this way, Habermas connected his earlier conception of the public sphere to the sphere of justice and thus made rational discourse the device needed to find the generalizable interests that would emerge step by step with collective deliberations. Contrary to Rawls' translation of the social contract, Habermas no longer needed to define principles of justice prior to the deliberating processes by which societies ordered their interests. Instead, he sought to find a more open procedure of argumentative praxis without giving up the Kantian idea of the public use of reason or the pluralist view of modern societies.

Nancy Fraser has undertaken the challenge left by Rawls' and Habermas' theories of justice to develop further the complex and dynamic view of justice they advanced. The aim of this paper is to present how this has been achieved, the significance of her position in the wider debate about justice and the possibilities it offers when viewed in the light of recent debates about globalization and cosmopolitanism. The historical context out of which her work and this larger theoretical project evolved had to do with the emergence during the 1960s of struggles for civil rights, of emancipatory social movements against racism, of peace movements and of feminism both as a form of activism and as a theoretical position. It also had to do with the emergence of new social movements which, in reaction to the earlier ones, began to question the idea of justice more exclusively in terms of identity politics and social recognition.

Introducing politics into the schema of justice

It was not a coincidence that Fraser turned her interest in justice to explore the role of power. Indeed, as a feminist, she questioned why the role of power did not appear as a basic premise in Habermas' discourse theory. In 'What's critical about critical theory?' (Fraser 1988) Nancy Fraser questioned Habermas' theory of communicative action for not paying attention to the important criticisms coming from feminism. Focusing on the Habermasian distinction between the symbolic and material aspects of reproduction in modern societies, Fraser showed how women's activities are considered under a questionable patriarchal design. Fraser's interpretations of the symbolic contents of women's labor, and of the ways in which economic injustice is hidden through its symbolic content, led her to point out the limitations of the Habermasian distinction between system and the life-world. The most important question, however, that Fraser was able to illuminate was that actions related to the nuclear family are regulated by power and that Habermas's earlier conception of power reduces it to its bureaucratic dimension. Fraser showed how far male dominance is intrinsic to the ways in which institutions are designed. She understood that the meanings we give to our actions, the expression we give to our needs and the interpretations we make of how things are, are all sites of political struggles. She targeted the double dimension of Habermas's conception of reproduction – system and life-world – precisely because it missed how the struggle for meanings is also a struggle of power.

In a second stage of her criticism of Habermas, the target of her thinking was Habermas' notion of the public sphere. In her famous essay, 'Rethinking the public sphere' (1988), Fraser criticized Habermas for defining the idea of the public sphere in a narrow way, as if it were one, compact, singular entity. Fraser demonstrated that in Habermas's description of the public sphere, we find accessibility to the public sphere to be a given. For Fraser, by contrast, the exclusion of women and of other groups of people was central to the whole process of constituting a bourgeois public sphere. She observed that: 'it was the arena, the training ground, and eventually *the power base of a stratum of bourgeois men*, who were coming to see themselves as a "universal class"' (Fraser 1997). In 'preparing themselves to assert their fitness to govern' (Fraser 1988: 73) men excluded women from active citizenship. According to Fraser, Habermas' view of the public sphere was idealized because it gave no account of this structural exclusion and gave no space to thinking about reactions from other 'competing publics'. By erasing the site of the power struggles in the public sphere, Habermas had been blinded to the efforts of counterpublics to question the processes of social inclusion and deliberation itself. Competing publics are a crucial part of an emancipatory concept of the public sphere and as counterpublics they react against exclusion and develop their claims for social inclusion precisely because they are not considered capable of being part of the more general public sphere.

With the aid of the concept of publics and counterpublics, Fraser was able to develop a more dynamic idea of social struggles for inclusion in modern plural societies and at the same time to add a more political dimension to the notion of the public sphere. She was arguably one of the first social theorists to develop a decentered notion of the public sphere and address its dynamics as a political site of struggle. She was also capable of defining this process with new terms that helped us understand the different levels in which publics gain some kind of authority. By distinguishing between weak publics (civil society) and strong publics (parliament), Fraser could locate the territory of a decentered notion of authority and of the influence of different social actors in political terms; that is, as a struggle for hegemony. For Fraser, the importance of the public sphere as a site of domination as well as solidarity lies in how processes of hegemony effectively unfold. Fraser insisted on the need to understand such strategies of power as political; for example, how cultural processes of legitimation in public debates bracket inequalities in the status of women (and of other groups) as if we were all equal. In our empirical experiences of the public sphere, Fraser concluded, these processes mask how in stratified societies 'unequally empowered social groups tend to develop unequally valued cultural styles' (ibid.: 79) and accordingly do not foster what she was to call the right to participatory parity. Fraser's achievement was to situate power in relation to struggles around meanings that we associate with life-world actions and social institutions.

This criticism made a major impact on Habermas's own understanding of the public sphere and led him to redefine his own initial conception of it. Habermas now acknowledged that 'a different picture emerges if from the beginning one admits the coexistence of competing public spheres and takes account of the dynamics of those processes of communication that are excluded from the dominant public sphere' (Habermas 1992: 425). Responding to Fraser's focus on processes of exclusion and domination, he added:

> we may use 'excluded' in Foucault's sense when we are dealing with groups that play a *constitutive* role in the formation of a particular public sphere. 'Exclusion' assumes a different and less radical meaning when the same structures of communication simultaneously give rise to the formation of several arenas where, beside the hegemonic bourgeois public sphere, additional sub-cultural or class-specific public spheres [Fraser's counterpublics] are constituted on the basis of their own and initially not easily recognizable premises. The first case I did not consider at all at the time; the second I mentioned in the preface but left it at that.
>
> (Ibid.: 425)

Habermas now recognized how such processes of inclusion and exclusion are constitutive of the public sphere.

Just as Fraser needed to reframe Habermas's original conception of the public sphere to expand its emancipatory scope, she also needed to address how his idea of justice fits into feminist foci on systemic relations of inequality, given that the feminist literature was more inspired by ideas of domination and resistance than those of justice. For Fraser, these two different starting points could be addressed critically by reconfiguring our understanding of them in terms of their respective political frames. To be sure, she argued, power strategies are needed to transform societies. However, power unfolds into two different strands: one that connects to the Foucauldian idea of practices of domination in the cultural domain; the other, the more Marxist strand, which focuses on class and what we need to do in terms of political participation. Fraser uses Habermas's progressive approach to justice and deliberation to address the dilemmas arising between these two potentially conflicting dimensions of domination and class struggle.

Thus, though Fraser emphasized the contestatory function of counterpublics, she did not view them (to employ a double negative) as processes that could not entail claims of inclusion. She maintained that separatist groups which envision themselves as forming enclaves of resistance, still need to have a political program with emancipatory goals in order to transform their societies. Fraser explains how the Gramscian notion of hegemony fits with this idea because 'to interact discursively as a member of a public – subaltern or otherwise – is to aspire to disseminate one's discourse into ever-widening arenas' (Fraser 1988: 82). She argues that in stratified societies counterpublics have a dual character: 'On the one hand, they function as spaces of withdrawal and regroupment; on the other hand, they function as a basis and training ground for agitational activities directed toward wider publics.' It is 'precisely in the dialectic between these two functions that their emancipatory potential resides' (ibid.: 82).

From politics to reframing justice

It was in response to the problems that emerged in the political arena with particularistic identity groups that Fraser developed her critique of them. Her intuition was that social movements and identity politics have become so self-interested in their own theoretical debates that they have forgotten that justice needs to contemplate a broader axis. In developing novel ideas about recognition, Fraser maintained that we have left behind other important issues that relate to how societies should grapple with violations of justice, and in particular that questions of distributive justice need our continuing attention. We cannot subsume all violations of justice to the spectrum of recognition. Fraser accordingly proposed her now well-known perspectival dualism between recognition and redistribution as two conceptual axes of justice.

Fraser was preoccupied with the problem of the fragmentation of the public sphere: namely, that the mere generalization of particulars makes identity politics lose sight of the political strategies needed to transform societies. Fraser developed her dual notion of justice based on questioning the theoretical separation between the paradigms of recognition and redistribution. Habermas's intuition about configuring a de-centered notion of justice through processes of deliberation (as legitimizing devices) was rearticulated in Fraser's view on the decoupling of claims about cultural politics (recognition) from claims of social politics (redistribution). The division of feminism into two theoretical aspects, one based on the politics of difference and the other on the politics of equality, became the target of Fraser's arguments inasmuch as they present themselves as either/or positions. Fraser was able to show how these two claims – recognition and redistribution – are both claims about social inclusion that have become historically cogent in the context of social movements. We need to consider them in their relation to one another. The binary opposition between class politics *versus* identity politics and multiculturalism *versus* social democracy is too often presented as if their claims belong to two different paradigms: the redistribution paradigm focusing on injustices defined as socio-economic; and the recognition paradigm focusing on injustices understood as cultural patterns of representation, interpretation and communication. In the first paradigm we seek the remedy for injustice in restructuring economic relations; in the recognition paradigm we seek a remedy for social injustice in cultural or symbolic exchange. In the first paradigm we search for equality, while in the second we search for difference. If we understand gender injustice in a larger normative context, we can relocate distribution and recognition as configuring two different kinds of claims that are part and parcel of one paradigm of justice. Economic demands can be seen from this perspective as a basic organizing principle of restructuring capitalist societies and the moral wrongs they seek to redress are located in different forms of distributive injustice, such as gender-based exploitation, marginalization and deprivation. In the other aspect, that is, in terms of how gender lines have been drawn according to andromorphous designs, we need to focus on institutional patterns of cultural valuation. These moral wrongs constitute violations of justice in terms of social relations, institutional designs and cultural practices.

In developing this position Fraser's main addressee was not Habermas but thinkers preoccupied with developing theories of recognition, notably Charles Taylor (1994) and Axel Honneth (Fraser and Honneth 2003). Both developed a Hegelian perspective on recognition, though it was in collaboration with Honneth that Fraser's ideas have taken shape. Taylor and Honneth tie the concept of recognition to questions about self-realization and maintain that it is in the quest for recognition by another subject that we seek to fulfill our own identity. To deny someone recognition is to deprive her of human flourishing. Fraser argues that Taylor and Honneth place the concept of recognition in the paradigm of self-realization because they pose questions in terms of 'the good life' rather than justice. She proposes that we conceive of recognition as belonging to the paradigm of *justice* and treat moral wrongs as questions related to social status: 'This means examining institutionalized patterns of cultural value for their effects on the *relative standing* of social actors' (ibid.: 29). Understanding how patterns of cultural valuation are built in which some people appear inferior, excluded or invisible, allows us to speak of misrecognition or status subordination. Fraser wishes to escape the pitfalls of thinking about recognition in terms of psychological ideas about self-realization and stresses instead that we should conceive of recognition as belonging to institutionalized patterns of cultural valuation. Her insight is into how practices of subordination are related to violations of justice.

Fraser was able to develop this important amplification of the paradigm of justice by connecting its sociological and philosophical sides, that is, by showing how we are dealing with a problem of rights that she identifies under the register of 'parity of participation'. By treating misrecognition as a matter of an externally manifested violation of justice, we understand that what we need to do is to change social practices 'by deinstitutionalizing patterns of cultural value that impede parity of participation and replacing them with patterns that foster it' (ibid.: 31). Fraser conceptualizes the philosophical problem of recognition under a scenario of social injustice related to patterns of cultural value, institutional forms of interaction and the ways in which we can change both. Instead of speaking of recognition in terms of needs, she highlights the idea that justice is related to practices that change reality.

At the same time, Fraser introduces a meta-level of deliberation which reconstructs Habermas' original idea of justice as a reflexive concept. She conceives of this meta-level of deliberation about processes of deliberation as the legitimating device of genuine democratic arguments. In so doing, she gives a new political twist to the idea of the legitimating practices of deliberation as inclusive and democratic. The principle of participatory parity presupposes that all (adult) human beings should be conceived as partners of interaction who possess equal moral worth. On the other hand, in relation to redistribution, Fraser conceives of the institutional economic mechanisms by which resources are systematically denied to excluded groups as a violation of justice. Instead of the Marxist understanding of class in terms of ownership of means of production, Fraser understands class as an order of objective subordination derived from economic arrangements that deny some actors the means and resources they need in order to have participatory parity.

Justice in a post-Westphalian frame

In his critical review of Nancy Fraser and Axel Honneth's book, Thomas McCarthy points out an important problem related to Fraser's paradigm of justice constructed under the two axes of redistribution and recognition (McCarthy 2005). He writes that Fraser's double axis design reminds him of the Habermasian separation between system and life-world, which Fraser earlier criticized in her essay 'What's critical about critical theory?'. McCarthy points out that when pressed by Honneth (Fraser and Honneth 2003: 156) on why she adopts only two perspectives, economic and cultural, to the apparent exclusion of the legal and political, Fraser falls back on the two basic forms of societal integration, 'social' and 'systemic', which play such a central role in Habermas' construction (McCarthy 2005: 399). Perhaps in response to such criticism, Fraser has revised her approach to the question of the political in her later work on 'Redefining justice in a globalizing world' (Fraser 2005). We need to see first how she accomplishes this redefinition and then discuss what is still missing despite her new efforts.

Many of the important struggles of our times relate to legal discrimination and political domination, and what exactly we mean when we speak of legal equality and political democracy. Furthermore, if we seek to leave behind the Westphalian frame of analysis and turn to a global scenario, as Fraser among many now argues, then politics and law not only appear as vital dimensions of justice but dimensions we would have to comprehend in close connection with one another, since the rights of individuals, regardless of citizenship, are secured in part through the mediation of international law.

Needless to say, this interrelationship also lies at the core of Habermas' concerns in *Between Facts and Norms* (Habermas 1996). At first, Habermas dealt with the interrelationship between law and politics under the scenario of the nation-state. His basic idea, which he referred to as 'the co-originality of rights and democracy', is that individual autonomy and political power can only be secured through the mediation of law and that it is the procedure of lawmaking as a collective exercise that begets legitimacy for the rule of law. In this work Habermas differentiates between communicative power (in Arendtian terms) and administrative power. His view of power as the associational ways in which societies transform their self-regulating practices is embedded in a decentered notion of the public sphere and its dynamics. With the principle of popular sovereignty, Habermas argued:

> [all] governmental authority derives from the people, the individual's right to an equal opportunity to participate in democratic will formation is combined with legally institutionalized practice[s] of self-determination ... and ... this principle forms the hinge between the system of rights and the construction of a constitutional democracy.
>
> (Ibid.: 169)

Habermas sees the existence of rights as institutionalizing the communicative conditions for reasonable political will-formation. He recognized that the nation-state once represented a response to the historical challenge to find a functional equivalent for earlier forms of social integration; yet when we move beyond the nation-state to the processes of globalization, as we must, we are left with a void. The question is how to fill the mediating role of the rule of law in the schema of global politics and this is where Fraser steps in.

To fill this void, Fraser centre-stages the idea of 'participatory parity' at the most abstract level of a theory of justice. In her *Spinoza Lectures*[1] she places the political dimension of representation firmly alongside that of redistribution and recognition. She acknowledges that in her previous work she did not see that she needed to introduce this third dimension more integrally into her paradigm of justice, and that to do so she has to return to the meta-level of the framework of justice. The intuition she articulates is that the political is about 'establishing criteria of social belonging' as well as processes of 'establishing decision rules' and that questions of representation constitute the third dimension of justice alongside those of redistribution and recognition. If we now face the challenge of thinking about justice in a global frame, we need to address normative standards of representation and misrepresentation to deal with the people's right to participate in political arenas on a par with others. With predatory states, transnational private powers, transnational corporations, international speculators and the way the global economy dictates systems of social interaction, the participatory imparity of more than half of the world population has now become a stark and devastating reality. In order to address and redress this injustice, Fraser focuses on struggles against restrictive framing. By extending and radicalizing the demands of justice, she finds the means to bring the political back into the conceptualization of global democracy.

Fraser uses her well-established idea of 'participatory parity' to confront problems of misrepresentation at this global level. It allows her to face questions of substance and procedure at the same time while making apparent the mutual entwinement of these two aspects. As a form of political authority it offers a substantive principle of justice that helps us evaluate existing social arrangements; as a procedural standard it enables us to evaluate the democratic legitimacy of norms. From the methodological point of view, it allows us to go back and forth from first order to second order questions, and these dialogical moves articulate the need to strengthen the interrelationship between democracy and justice in a radically reflexive template.

The transition from thinking about justice in the frame of the modern territorial state to that of a global order is not easy to accomplish. The political dimension of representation has been as crucial a dimension of justice in the national framework as it is in the global and reflecting on the meta-issue of the frame does not begin with the global. The nation was never as naturalized as it normally appears in retrospect and the dismantling of institutionalized obstacles to the participation of some people on a par with others has been a recurrent feature of past struggles. The question of who is included and who excluded from the circle of those entitled to make justice claims on one another, and the meta-question of the procedures which structure such public processes of frame setting and misframing, have been the stuff of political argument from the start of the modern era, even if it is true that globalization makes this aspect of the grammar of justice more visible. We do not have to go along with Fraser's ultimatist slogan, 'no redistribution or recognition without representation', to see the close connections between these dimensions of justice.

Fraser's 'transormative approach' seeks both to change the boundaries of the 'who' of justice in the light of the fact that many injustices in a globalizing world are not territorial in character, and to democratize the ways in which these frames are constructed and boundaries are drawn. Fraser's tentative solution to post-Westphalian frame setting, the 'all-affected principle', holds that all those *affected* by a given social structure or institution have moral standing as subjects of justice in relation to it. The principle of doing justice to those affected contrasts with a liberal conception of the public sphere in which the right to express a view upon an issue is not conditional upon one's direct interest in it. However, it leads to problems of determining who is affected and how claims to be affected are assessed. We expect further deliberations around this thorny question of applying democratic processes of determination to the 'who' of justice claims.

Conclusion: critical theory, the public sphere and global justice

In a further essay, 'Transnationalizing the public sphere: on legitimacy and efficacy of public opinion in a post-Westphalian world' (2007), Fraser returns to her initial concerns about the political character of the public sphere. She acknowledges that this concept was first introduced to give an account of how our communicative practices contribute to a decentered normative notion of justice. It matters, accordingly, 'who participates and on what terms'. As a mechanism for holding state officials accountable for their actions, the public sphere should somehow 'correlate with sovereign power'. When dealing with transnational public spheres, it is no longer adequate to associate the notion of communicative power with sovereign states, but it is a complicated question to figure out how persons who are not considered members of concrete political communities could have equal rights to participate in political life. To address this problem, Fraser argues against both an 'empiricist' approach that sacrifices normative force and an 'externalist' approach that sacrifices critical traction. The alternative she puts forward is to design a critical-theoretical approach that 'seeks to locate normative standards and emancipatory political possibilities precisely within the historically unfolding constellation' (Fraser 2007). It is on this basis that Fraser begins to rethink the relationship between politics and law in the global context.

To be sure, we need to understand how rights have become a space of meanings about wider inclusion than can be seen in a strictly national frame of analysis. A more sociological approach, like that adopted in T.S. Marshall's theory of democratic rights, could offer Fraser some resource to think of sovereignty beyond the constraints of the nation-state. The principle of 'parity of participation' would need to be developed in connection with two differentiated notions of sovereignty. On the one hand, there is the institutional frame of international law designed as a process of social inclusion to protect individuals beyond the scope of the nation-state. This might be thought of as an external concept of sovereignty. On the other hand, the mediating role of international law deals with how nation-states themselves need to comply with agreements about what needs to be done to solve issues of internal justice. This would be an internal concept of sovereignty. That sovereignty is empirically changing should give us some hope as we start imagining new ways of conceptualizing it. Think of the case when even a superpower cannot guarantee the security and welfare of its own population except with the help of other nations. It would appear that in such a case sovereignty is losing its classical meaning. The maintenance of law and order within the nation-state needs now to be re-conceptualized to see how the global demands of justice cope with the protection of the rights of world citizens. This is because at the global scale, one crucial institutional protection persons can have as individuals lies in how their claims for new rights of inclusion should be protected by international law and by agreements among nation-states to enforce it.

The authoritative source of legitimation lies in the idea of a world public sphere. Consider, for example, how the US and UK sought the cooperation of other countries in their decision to go to war in and against Iraq. Few countries were on their side, most were against. The moral authority behind the critique of unilateralism derived from the many expressions of dissent developed in different public spheres. What was most interesting was the process of decoupling political authority from this exercise of force and its connection instead with the legitimating processes of deliberation in a world society. Spain, whose civil society was in the main against the decision of former Prime Minister Aznar to support the invasion of Iraq, saw the government lose power in the elections that followed. The contradictory ways in which public opinion recovered from the marginalization of opposition to the war has led the international press (and more slowly the internal American press) to publish widely on the lack of legitimacy behind the US and UK decision to go to war. It was in relation not only to international law as such (with all its ambiguities of interpretation and application) but also to normative standards developed within an international public sphere that the moral and political authority of this act of force has been critically evaluated.

Fraser does not have a particularly optimistic view of the normative role of the public sphere in transforming classical political concepts. The key issue is whether the public sphere has the capacity to be a site in which new meanings and new articulations of political practices are generated. The institutional basis of a world public sphere needs the mediation of a reconstructive process that can show us how international law can become a legitimate order when its *reflexivity* becomes the condition of its institutionalization.[2] Fraser's own account of justice would have to integrate the idea of a world public sphere to explain how the concept of 'parity of participation' could be considered as a new stage in the development of the right of political participation and a new dimension of human rights for world citizens. Fraser argues that because we do not possess a vision of the role of the public sphere, 'we have lost the capacity to use that category critically – in a way that has political bite' (Fraser 2007). However, the most important question about the space of a world public sphere is whether actors can acquire the capacity to act politically within it and how in turn these performances can lead to new processes of lending authority to the world community. Claims of inclusion and considerations of how new processes of inclusion could take shape, need the participation of those excluded actors who possess the imagination to make us look at things through alternative perspectives.

If we go back to Habermas's interest in how certain practices provide new clues as where to go from here, we would argue that we cannot dispense with the category of the world public sphere in thinking about any possible transformation. Even though we do not know how this could be accomplished, it is clear that we would have to revisit most of our political categories and see the new forms and shapes they take as they articulate around the idea of world political authority. If it is true that constitutional norms and legal constructs were first introduced by elites, as Habermas has argued, then his commentary about the kind of law making which anticipates the change in the state of consciousness that is triggered among the addressees in the course of its implementation (Habermas 2006), is highly pertinent to this conception of the world public sphere as a sphere that relates to rights. A reflexive internalization takes place when innovatory legal propositions are put into public debate. These processes entail a learning process in which nations, as it were, change their view of themselves and reconstructed practices of sovereignty allow independent actors to discover the benefit of acting as world citizens and members of an international cooperative community.

Arguably this has already happened in certain Latin American countries where it was only through forced agreements with previous authoritarian regimes that they could undergo political transition into democratic regimes.

The internal contradiction the new regimes had was how they could understand the importance of abiding by the rule of law when previous authoritarian regimes violated norms of law or transformed them into their opposite. The key to solving this contradiction was the transformation of views made possible by looking outside their national communities. They related to countries in which law was interpreted in the context of the larger paradigm of international law and in which processes of law making were reinforced by mutual agreements with other democracies. Excluded subjects from Latin American countries had more opportunity to seek justice in international arenas than in the internal arenas of their nation-state. The former was better equipped to meet the challenge of confronting serious violations of human rights. The Pinochet case is only one of those cases that have allowed international justice to enter into the realms of sovereign states: it has impelled Chilean society to undo previous institutional arrangements and prosecute those individuals who committed state crimes. This is one way in which sovereign nations are learning to subordinate national interests to the obligations they have taken on as members of the international community and in which, by relating the nation-state to the requirements of international justice, support from the international community triggers new possibilities of reshaping transitions to democracy. Those citizens who have reacted against this history of forced agreements have been deeply influenced by how institutions of international law have interpreted their rights internationally and this has enabled them to start reopening the requirements of transitional justice.

The defence of the concept of a world public sphere may be considered along the lines of developing a decentered notion of political authority. This means decoupling the conceptual linkage between national law and the state's monopoly on legitimate force in favour of a supranational law that still gets its force by means of the sanctions monopolized by nation states, but is now given authority by the way citizens recognize themselves as authors of international laws. It would certainly be difficult to imagine a new political constitution of a world society without some normative idea of a world public sphere providing the mediation between international law and world politics. This is one way, we think, in which Fraser's abiding concerns with the politics of the public sphere might be integrated with her more recent thinking about post-Westphalian democratic justice.

Notes

1 University of Amsterdam, 2004 and 2005. Fraser's contribution to this collection is a revised and expanded version of her second Spinoza lecture (Fraser 2005).
2 A further of this issue is offered by Habermas when he comments in *Between Facts and Norms* that both Weber and Parsons operated with a notion that ideas and interests (Weber) or cultural values and motives (Parsons) 'interpenetrate in social orders' through certain collective practices. The reason why Habermas follows Parsons in particular is because Parsons was concerned with the evolution of law in terms of its function of securing solidarity. According to Habermas:

Parsons understands modern law as a transmission belt by which solidarity – the demanding structures of mutual recognition we know from face to face interaction – is transmitted in abstract but binding form to the anonymous and systematically mediated relationship of a complex society.

(Habermas 1996: 76)

Parsons relied heavily on Marshall's account of the gradual extension of rights of inclusion in order to understand how collective institutions fostered practices of solidarity.

References

Fraser, N. (1988) 'What's critical about critical theory?' in Benhabib, S. and Cornell, D. (eds) *Feminism as Critique*, Minneapolis: University of Minnesota Press.

—— (1997) 'Rethinking the public sphere', *Justice Interruptus: Critical Reflections on the "Post-socialist" Condition*, New York and London: Routledge.

—— (2005) 'Reframing justice in a globalizing world', *New Left Review*, 36: 69–88.

—— (2007) 'Transnationalizing the public sphere: on the legitimacy and efficacy of public opinion in a post-Westphalian world', *Theory, Culture and Society* 24, 4: 1–24.

Fraser, N. and Honneth, A. (2003) *Redistribution or Recognition? A Political-Philosophical Exchange*, London and New York: Verso.

Habermas, J. (1992) 'Further reflections on the public sphere' in Calhoun, C. (ed.) *Habermas and the Public Sphere*, Cambridge, Massachusetts: MIT Press.

—— (1996) *Between Facts and Norms: Contributions to A Discourse Theory of Law and Democracy*, trans. William Rehg, Cambridge: Massachusetts: MIT Press.

—— (2006) *The Divided West*, trans. Cronin, C., Cambridge: Polity Press.

McCarthy, T. (2005) 'Review of Fraser and Honneth', *Ethics*, January: 397–402.

Rawls, J. (1971) *A Theory of Justice*, Cambridge, Massachusetts: Harvard University Press.

—— (1993) *Political Liberalism*, 2nd edition, New York: 1996.

Taylor, C. (1994) 'The politics of recognition' in Gutmann, A. (ed.) *Multiculturalism: Examining the Politics of Recognition*, Princeton, NJ: Princeton University Press.

4 Sexuality, subjectivity and … economics?

Mandy Merck

Where lesbian and gay studies was pioneered in Anglo-American departments of history and sociology, its queer successor's poststructuralist turn was driven by critical theorists in literature, visual culture, media studies and rhetoric.[1] This produced crucial new attention to the 'cultural' constitution of the sexual subject, but in other respects it constrained the theory's analytical reach and capacities. Such failings did not go wholly unremarked in the development of the field, and as early as 1993 Cindy Patton complained of the political limits of queer '"reading" techniques' – 'the logics of homosexual construction/disappearance uncovered as formal operations of literary (or popular) texts' (Patton 1993: 166). But the misgivings she expressed in *Fear of a Queer Planet* were largely ignored by those relying on such methods (11 literary scholars among 15 contributors to a collection subtitled *Queer Politics and Social Theory*). As the collection's other dissident, Steven Seidman, observed: 'Institutional and historical analysis and an integrative political vision seem to have dropped out' (Seidman 1993). Less than a decade later Dennis Altman would count the cost of these omissions for any attempt to understand sexuality under globalization. All too often, he complained, the consequence of queer culturalism was the neglect of 'conventional sources of political and economic power' (Altman 2001: 158) in favour of the particular symbolic phenomena that it had evolved to investigate.

In 1997, the economic relations of sexuality were addressed in a volume of essays analysing phenomena ranging from the gentrification of gay neighbourhoods to campaigns for domestic partner benefits. But, significantly, queer theory is hardly mentioned in *Homo Economics*, with the exception of Richard Cornwall's attempt to articulate interrelations between a property-owning individualism and both the proscription and the defence of homosexuality, via theories of consumer preferences and readings of Wilde and Genet (Cornwall 1997). In the two writers' celebrations of a perverse individuality, Cornwall perceived a Bersanian 'betrayal' of the social relations of the market system. If his speculations suggested that a 'queer political economy' might be possible, an exchange published that same year debated its desirability.

'Heterosexist capitalism?' The question on the cover of the *New Left Review* may have lured older readers down memory lane, but it also signalled a new development on the sexual political agenda not widely anticipated in 1998 –

what Nancy Fraser announced inside as 'reclaiming the best elements of socialist politics ... and integrating them with the best elements of the politics of the "new social movements"' (Fraser 1998: 149). Fraser's announcement came at the end of a debate which had also appeared during the previous year in the US journal *Social Text* in response to her reflections on the 'post-socialist condition', *Justice Interruptus* (Fraser 1997). In that study she addresses the much-heralded turn in left politics from an emphasis on the redistribution of resources to a stress on identity focussing on cultural recognition. Arguing for a strategy aimed at 'transforming the deep structures of both political economy and culture', she distinguishes claims for cultural or symbolic justice, which she terms 'recognition', and claims for socio-economic justice, or 'redistribution'. To illustrate this difference, she provocatively positions various social groups along a continuum, separating those who seek economic justice, at one end, from those who seek cultural recognition, at the other. In the middle she places groups who might claim both – notably those who experience ethnic or gender subordination. At the extreme end of economic oppression she locates the working class, and at the far end of stigma, those whose sexualities are 'despised'. This opposition of lesbians and gay men to victims of economic exploitation is qualified by Fraser's own admission that most oppressed groups suffer both maldistribution and misrecognition, indeed that 'economic justice and cultural justice are usually interimbricated'. But her schematic assignment of heterosexism to cultural politics and class exploitation to political economy drew a critical response.

Judith Butler opens her argument with Fraser by challenging two positions – the complaint that the new social movements (feminism, anti-racism, environmental struggles and – most nefarious of all – queer politics) ignore 'the interrelatedness of social and economic conditions' and the accusation that 'the cultural focus of left politics has abandoned the material project of Marxism' (Butler 1998: 34). As she and Fraser agree, the belief that social theory has taken such a 'cultural turn' was by then widespread. Witness Richard Rorty's 1998 declaration that 'the cultural left thinks more about stigma than money, more about deep and hidden psychosexual motivations than about shallow and evident greed' (Rorty 1998: 77). Or the elegiac 1999 collection of sociological essays entitled *Culture and Economy after the Cultural Turn*, with its jacket copy proclaiming 'the decline of interest in economic aspects of society'. Inside, Harriet Bradley and Steve Fenton chart the transformation of gender studies from a concern with 'material factors' to those of – in Michèle Barrett's phrase – 'sexuality, subjectivity and textuality' (Bradley and Fenton 1999: 120).[2]

In their attempt to historicize this shift, Bradley and Fenton cite five key developments:

1   The collapse of Marxism after the fall of Soviet communism.
2   The rise of postmodernist approaches to cultural theory and cultural studies.
3   An increased scholarly interest in psychoanalytic theory.
4   Critiques of racism within feminism and their challenge to the notion of a unified category 'women'.

5   The influence of poststructuralist and deconstructionist theories of discourse
      as constituting rather than merely reflecting gendered subjectivities.

The resulting impetus, to a cultural definition of gender and to cultural analysis
in feminist studies, is not one which Bradley and Fenton celebrate. Like many of
the collection's contributions, theirs is an attempt to combine the ostensibly
opposing frameworks of culture and economy, rather than to abandon the investigation of economic interests and influences. Thus, the pair insist upon the
integration of textual, archival, institutional and ethnographic studies with
broader statistical indices of economics and demography when analysing 'any
social phenomenon'. And in passing they make what now seems a prescient
argument for contextualizing cultural analyses of the re-assertion of Islam,
notably that by young British women of South Asian descent:

> in terms of the global economic and political hierarchies which portrayed
> Middle Eastern societies as subordinate and inferior to the west; and to the
> conditions of economic deprivation and inequality in many Muslim soci-
> eties, such as Egypt, Turkey and Algeria, which increased the support
> among the rural and industrial proletariats for Islamic parties.
>
> (Bradley and Fenton 1999: 129)

In seeking to elude the abstractions of both economism and culturalism,
Bradley and Fenton refuse to divide their purviews between global and local,
structural and experiential. At the same time, they insist upon the mutually inter-
rogating engagements of differing methodologies rather than a hierarchy or conflation of analyses. But where they argue the need for a proliferation of
contending perspectives on gender and ethnicity, Butler answers Fraser by refusing her differentiation 'between material and the cultural life' (Butler 1998: 36).
Replying to Fraser's claim that lesbian and gay politics stand outside those of
political economy – since homosexuality is neither a class-specific condition nor
the basis for a division of labour – Butler invokes a socialist tradition that
stretches back to Engel's *The Origin of Family, Private Property and the State*
(1968). There Engels declares the production of human beings and their means
of existence the ultimate factor in history – 'according to the materialist conception' (p. 449). As Butler stresses, Engels' argument became central to socialist
feminist accounts of the family as part of the mode of production in the 1970s
and 1980s. And despite Engels' own naturalization of heterosexuality in that
study, his emphasis on the production of human beings offered an entrée for
psychoanalytic speculations on the constitution of sexual subjectivities in the
service of capital.
     Repeating these arguments, Butler acknowledges her debts to left cultural
theorists such as Raymond Williams and Stuart Hall, as well as to the philosopher whose work had hitherto offered the most consistent Marxist reference in
her repertoire, Louis Althusser. It is his essay claiming the material existence of
'Ideological State Apparatuses' that enables her to argue that matter exists in

different modalities in *Bodies That Matter* (1993), and the same essay's concept of interpellation through which she develops the relation between ideology and subject formation in *The Psychic Life of Power* (1997a) and *Excitable Speech* (1977b). There too Althusser argues for the efficacy of institutions such as the family in reproducing the skills and disciplines of labour power, while elsewhere refusing determinist representations of the social formation as a mere superstructure of an economic base. But if his work underwrote the socialist feminist position Butler espouses some 20 years after it was initially formulated (and long after its abandonment by so many of those who originally employed it), it is Gayle Rubin's pioneering 1975 essay on 'The traffic in women' that most influences her response to Fraser.

Again, Butler's enthusiasm for what some others have disdained as a rather dated attempt to propose 'gender, obligatory heterosexuality and the constraint of female sexuality' (Rubin 1975: 179) as requirements of contemporary capitalism might seem surprising – not least to its author, who famously revised her position in the 1980s, and who attempted to persuade Butler to do likewise in a fascinating discussion published in the 1990s. But, like that of Rubin and her socialist feminist contemporaries of the 1970s, and Althusser before them, Butler's challenge to a distinction between sexual and economic oppression relies upon a political economy of kinship. Indeed, she takes up the position of her predecessors to invoke a very particular theory of kinship, the structural anthropology of Claude Lévi-Strauss. Following Rubin's initial essay, she cites the anthropologist's observations that in pre-state cultures the exchange of women enforced by the incest taboo ensures political, economic and symbolic alliances between social groups, for whom intermarriage fosters peace, trade relations and communication – the creation of 'society'. Here too Butler points out that the symbolic function of women in such exchanges provides an avenue to Lacanian accounts of the role of signification in the constitution of gendered subjectivity. But against the 'universalizing pathos' of both Lacan and Lévi-Strauss's hypostasis of female subordination, she argues for an historicized account of kinship, 'socially contingent and socially transformable' (Butler 1998: 44) which would recognize the counter-normative sexual arrangements in contemporary alternatives to the patriarchal family.

Butler does not win this debate. Certainly Fraser's argument is troubled by its tendency to reify identity categories even as it questions identity politics, separating 'women, racialized peoples, and/or gays and lesbians' from each other and their mutual conditions of historical constitution while failing to consider the inter-relationships of their 'status injuries' – the abjectifying feminization of both homosexuality and certain ethnicities in men, the still prevalent attempts to stigmatize the women's movement with accusations of lesbianism. Nevertheless, she persuasively argues that such heterosexism – socially imbricated though it is – need not be, and increasingly is not, a requirement of capital accumulation. As she succinctly demonstrates, Butler's assignment of sexual regulation to the economic structure alternately proceeds by definition – simply equating the economic with the cultural since the latter includes the reproduction of goods and people – or by functionalist claims that capitalism 'needs' heterosexuality. The effect is to divest capitalism (a term Butler indicatively eschews in favour of 'political economy' or 'the economic') as well as kinship of the historicity she finds missing in the works of Lacan and Levi-Strauss. In response to Butler's illustrations of 'the normative heterosexuality of the economy' – the exclusion of homosexuals from partnership rights in property, taxation and inheritance; as well as the economic disadvantages suffered by lesbians and people with AIDS – Fraser counters with contemporary corporations' 'gay-friendly' policies, notably the extension of partnership benefits to lesbian and gay employees in the face of religious opposition. More provocatively, she challenges the grounds of her opponent's theory, agreeing that the economic and the cultural are equally 'material', while insisting that they are no longer integrated as they once were in the kinship systems of the pre-capitalist societies studied by Lévi-Strauss.

In describing the attenuation of the link between accumulation and the regulation of kinship, Fraser is only echoing the lesbian and gay historians who had argued the case against capitalism's 'hard-wired heterosexism' long before she took it up: John d'Emilio, who claimed that capitalism commodified the economic functions that previously promoted familiar dependency even as it 'enshrined the family as the source of love, affection and emotional security' (d'Emilio 1984: 148) – with the result that both homosexuality, and the scapegoating of homosexuals for threatening family values, became increasingly widespread; Jeffrey Weeks, who traced the extensive development of metropolitan male prostitution to late nineteenth-century capitalism's incorporation of sexuality into the cash nexus (Weeks 1979); Lillian Faderman, who argued that middle-class women's entry into the professions gave them the financial means to make life partnerships with one another (Faderman 1991); and Gayle Rubin, who memorably revised her kin-based analysis of erotic organization to incorporate Foucault's theory of a system of sexual stratification superimposed from the eighteenth century on the earlier regulation of marriage (Rubin 1984).

Defending that revision in her discussion with Butler, Rubin distinguishes contemporary gay kinship, as a voluntary system of association and intimacy, from the regulation of marriage:

> Levi-Strauss is talking about societies in which those relations of marriage and descent *are* the social structure. They either organize almost all of the social life, or they are the most important and visible institutional apparatus. In modern systems, kinship is already a structure that is much reduced in institutional importance. It is not radical to say, in anthropology, that kinship doesn't do in modern urban societies what it used to do in premodern cultures. Furthermore, gay kinship closely resembles what anthropologists would call 'fictive' or 'informal kinship'. Such systems of informal or fictive kinship are even less institutionalized and structurally stable than those relationships which are reinforced by state authority.
>
> (Rubin with Butler 1994: 60)

Butler replies with examples of the continued idealization of the traditional family in the policing of child abuse, public sex and prostitution, as well as restrictions on lesbian and gay parenting and partnership rights (Butler 1994). And although she concurs with Rubin that 'kinship can't possibly be the predominant way in which we try to take account of the complexity of contemporary social or sexual life' (Rubin with Butler 1994: 60), it remains the focus of her subsequent study, *Antigone's Claim* (2000). There, despite her estimable challenge to structural anthropology's foundational heteronormativity, her reading of Sophocles' tragedy and its commentaries reinstate kinship as the site integrating the subject's sexual and social existence. To do so she extends its domain to 'any number of social arrangements that organize the reproduction of material life, that can include the ritualization of birth and death, that provide bonds of intimate alliance both enduring and breakable, and that regulate sexuality through sanction and taboo' (Butler 2000: 72). But what of the social arrangements that organize the reproduction of material life outside the family, enforced or elective? Whether we pursue that reproduction in terms of its instrumental forces in the workplace, its ideological relations in the schools, churches, political parties, trade unions and media, or the repressive apparatus of army, police, courts and prisons – to invoke Althusser's categories – none of these institutions are in themselves those of kinship, however much they govern our intimate lives.

Although *Antigone's Claim* again proposes a 'socially alterable' understanding of kinship – including in its contemporary manifestations not only homosexual parenting but black urban families headed by groups of mothers, aunts and grandmothers, other parenting arrangements shared by more than two adults and voluntary single parenting – it is in Butler's recent dialogues with Ernesto Laclau and Slavoj Zizek that her historicization of the structuralist 'law' opens (however briefly) to a parallel treatment of 'the economic'. Under the heading *Contingency, Hegemony, Universality* (Butler *et al.* 2000), she returns to the work of Zizek and Laclau first employed in *Bodies That Matter* to develop her theory of the phantasmatic investment in identity. But the Gramscian derivation of these dialogues, as well as their direct debt to Laclau and Mouffe's *Hegemony and Socialist Strategy* (2001), enforces at least nominal attention to the mode of production as an element of the hegemonic formation under discussion. Again, particularly in her discussion of Lacanian psychoanalysis, kinship is a central issue, but here it is mobilized against the transcultural imperative of (hetero)sexual difference reiterated by Zizek. Challenging this model (and its incongruity with his historical Marxism), Butler posits an avowedly dynamic notion of subjectivity. Insofar as it retains psychoanalysis, it does so largely to account for the unconscious registration of – or resistance to – social norms and identifications, albeit in ways that may involve instability, failure or contradiction. And if, in her argument, the Lacanian 'symbolic' and even the supposedly non-symbolizable 'real' are socially transformable, so the 'economic' of the Fraser debate is historicized into 'capitalism', and granted some possible relation to the psychic processes of subjectification: 'It is unclear', Butler writes, 'that the subject is not, for instance, from the start, structured by certain general features of capitalism, or that capitalism does not produce certain quandaries for the unconscious and, indeed, the psychic subject more generally' (Butler *et al.* 2000: 139).

But this highly qualified hypothesis – hedged in by its characteristically Butlerian double negatives – is never developed. Although she insists that struggles over sexual difference, like those over class and nation, have a contingent historical character, she suggests no points of contact or communality, let alone the functionalist integration previously criticized by Fraser. Nor, in what proves to be a highly abstract discussion of politics and subject formation, does she pursue her speculations on capitalism's relation to psychic life. But then, responding to Zizek's complaint that neither she nor Laclau challenge the fundamentals of the capitalist market economy and the liberal-democratic political regime, she retorts that no contribution to their dialogues offers 'a critique of the market economy' nor really asks what 'the economic' might mean (Butler *et al.* 2000: 277–288). Her final questions, of our a priori understandings of economic equality and its relation to political enfranchisement, are characteristically suggestive and characteristically unanswered. She takes them no further than to propose a genealogical rethinking of the separation of the cultural from the economic in the academic disciplines of anthropology and political theory. Which is, of course, where her polemic against Fraser began.

In a subsequent defence of lesbian and gay kinship relations, Butler questions gay marriage, and even domestic partnership contracts, as appropriate bases for the allocation of health care, asking why there should not 'be ways of organizing health care entitlements such that everyone, regardless of marital status, has access to them?' But despite her challenge to the extension of marital normativity and its nexus of property relations, despite her acknowledgement of international adoption and donor insemination in a global economy, the focus of her discussion remains kinship, and the state as the agent of its legitimation. Indeed, she retains the structuralist conflation of psychical and political 'law' to declare the state 'the means by which a fantasy becomes literalized: desire and sexuality are ratified, justified, known, publicly instated, imagined as permanent, durable' (Butler 2002: 21–22).

But, as Brett Levinson has asked of Butler, what happens 'when we move from a world in which the highest political institution is the state, to one in which the state must compete for its sovereignty with global movements (including AIDS), above all the market ...?' (Levinson 1999: 94–95). Whether, as Stephen Shapiro argues, this attention to global markets proceeds from queer theory's failure to establish itself in its own academic market, or from perceived limits in its political purview, a new economic dimension is increasingly evident in its studies (Shapiro 2004). Addressing the academy's role in the globalization of such identities, a Call for Papers from the Queer Caucus of the 2001 Society for Cinema Studies conference notes that:

In contemporary academic discourse, 'queer' has come to signify a particularly postmodern mode of socio-cultural subversion .... At the same time, however, the political, economic and ideological contexts and determinants of 'queer' moving-image culture have not generally been acknowledged, much less challenged …. How does the marketability of 'global queer' and its purported creative difference satisfy the assimilationist and ideological dreams of liberal humanism and (post) western imperialism?

(Gerstner and Ginsberg 2001)

In an ambitious attempt to answer this question, Rosemary Hennessy has written a political economy of 'queer' identity which posits it as both an expression and an instrument of globalization. *Profit and Pleasure: Sexual Identities in Late Capitalism* argues that while that mode of production continues to make use of heteronormativity to enforce a gendered division of labour, neither those norms, nor gender subordination per se, are required for accumulation. What capitalism 'does require', Hennessy claims, 'is an unequal division of labor' (Hennessy 2000: 105). Here she outlines the familiar story of post-Fordism's search for cheap and politically defenceless labour markets, dispersing production across the globe, transforming the patterns of employment, family life, sexual practice, national identity, social migration and production itself – now accelerated, decentralized, deregulated and made 'flexible'. Within the same logic, commodification has been both extended and intensified, colonizing the individual's physical and psychological existence as new markets for self-improvement, its ideal form 'attuned to freeing up the previously static and relatively fixed spatial and temporal dimensions of daily life' (ibid.: 107) (the Walkman and the microwave in the 1980s; the 'mobile', as it is so rightly called, in the 1990s).

Hennessy calls the structure of consciousness characteristic of these changes 'postmodernism', but, unlike Fredric Jameson, she does not ignore or deny its specifically sexual aspects. For Jameson, the psycho-logic of late capitalism involves a schizophrenic breakdown of temporality and a free-floating euphoria, a hallucinatory delight in simulation whose only sexual attribute is a certain 'camp' or 'hysterical' exhilaration. For Hennessy, writing some 15 years later, the mode of production finds its subjective equivalent in the disciplined flexibility of the middle-class professional service worker: 'habitual mobility, adaptability in every undertaking, the ability to navigate among possible alternatives and spaces, and a cultivation of ambivalence as a structure of feeling' (ibid.: 108). And who better to represent this cultivated ambivalence than that anti-identitarian identity 'queer' – free-floating, self-fashioning, apparently autonomous?

Hennessy's suspicions recall a related critique from another quarter, Biddy Martin's concerns about the construction of queerness as a sexually mobile vanguard superseding the outmoded physicality of old-fashioned gender politics. The effect, she warns, is to detach queer politics from corporeality and reassign that domain to the supposedly fixed identities and interests represented by women and people of colour. In consequence, Martin concludes, queerness is awarded a mobility that is decidedly upward, that of the white male (Martin 1996). Subsequently, Regenia Gagnier (2000) has argued that post-industrial societies tend to detach sexuality from both biological reproduction and social role and assign it to pleasure – in consumerist discourses – or pain – in Dworkinite polemic. Although Hennessy does not discuss these arguments, one of the merits of her own is the attention she draws to the economic character of queerness and how its unstated dependence on wealth and education secures its transitivity 'beyond' racial and gender identities.

But as Hennessy acknowledges, this queer ideal is not evenly dispersed across the globe, nor unchallenged by state and cultural heteronormativity. Indeed, in her conception, neoliberalism's employment of this subjectivity, like the commodification of desire that it represents and intensifies, is often at odds with specific enterprises' continued reliance on compulsory heterosexuality to organize exploitation. Nevertheless, the increasing accommodation of the 'global gay', as middle-class professional and consumer, challenges functionalist assumptions of an intrinsically heterosexist capitalism. What then of the relation between sexual politics and those of redistribution?

To pursue this question, it is worth considering Hennessy's own analyses of the positions discussed earlier. Returning to Gayle Rubin's early attempt to develop Engels' *Origin of the Family* into an enlarged theory of sexuality and social production, she argues that her anthropological focus on the premodern kin group as the site of subjectification precludes more than passing attention to subsequent influences, such as the organization of work and childcare outside its domain – let alone the gendered and racialized divisions of labour, changing patterns of commodification, state formations and so on of contemporary existence. (Moreover, Rubin's attempt to attribute gender subordination to social exchange is critiqued for neglecting the importance of production to economic analysis.) Nor does Rubin's revised position receive her approval, since its Foucauldian history of the proliferation and regulation of modern sexualities is judged to detach their development from both kinship and the economy in the autonomy it grants to normative practices.

Similarly, Hennessy questions the limits of Butler's analysis of sex as the materialization of norms. While acknowledging that law, culture, ideology and symbolization materially produce social life, she distinguishes what she calls cultural materialism from the historical materialism that emphasizes the production of social life by people making what is needed 'to survive' (Hennessy 2000: 85). Furthermore, she complains that Butler's attempt to incorporate all these practices into a single materiality under the heading of kinship fails to connect sexual subordination to relations of labour or exploitation.

Not even Nancy Fraser's project for 'transforming the deep structures of both political economy and culture' (Fraser 1997: 32) escapes this censure, since its schematic division of economic, racial, gender and sexual subordination, however overlapping, is argued to forestall consideration of their historical interrelation within production and consumption. In making class a mere analogue of other categories of social oppression, Hennessy maintains, Fraser's theoretical edifice risks collapsing back into the identity politics she sets out to transform. And her redistributive politics are far too reformist for the radical anti-capitalism *Profit and Pleasure* espouses.

Such a project leaves Hennessy with precious few allies outside classical Marxism, and having pronounced her qualified endorsement of Althusser's theory of over-determination, which supports her own attempt to demonstrate how a variety of social factors derive from and contribute to economic contradiction, she punctuates her study with brief sorties at other feminist and lesbian positions. Thus, Teresa de Lauretis's psychoanalytic approach to lesbian subjectivity is criticized – predictably – for privatizing accounts of psychological development within the nuclear family and dehistoricizing its relation to changing modes of production and political domination. Less predictably, she also condemns de Lauretis's *The Practice of Love* (1994) for its biographical (and autobiographical) characterization of sexual orientation as a narrative of lifelong consciousness. The effect, she declares – in a surprisingly Foucauldian aside – is to produce object choice not as practice but as identity, one more of the exclusionary identities argued to cripple collective resistance.

As for the anti-psychoanalytic arguments of critics like Elizabeth Grosz, formulated via Deleuze and Guattari in response to de Lauretis, these too are given short shrift, condemned – as Hennessy condemns 'sex radicalism' in general – for abstracting desire from material or affective need and reifying it as an autonomous and insatiable drive or energy. In a parallel argument, poststructuralist accounts of identity's inherent instability are reinterpreted as economically-grounded struggles over meaning:

> the constitutive inability of any identity to secure its referent or to capture what it names – whether that identity be woman, homosexual, heterosexual, or queer – is not the result of an instability inherent in signification, but of the social contradictions on which capitalism is premised and which are condensed in the struggles over naming.
>
> (Hennessy 2000: 68)

Where Hennessy does find corroboration, it is in commentaries which historicize their psychic modelling within such patterns. Thus she cites Lauren Berlant and Wendy Brown's explanations for the depoliticizing of capitalism in American life via the rhetoric of intimacy and identity which structure so much of sexual politics – rhetoric which, as Brown points out, is nonetheless fuelled by an unconscious resentment and idealization of class power.

It is unlikely that the latter two would sign up to the more flagrantly contentious elements of Hennessy's argument – its head banging reduction of all contests over meaning to those of resources; the refusal to recognize a register of unsatisfiable demand beyond that of gratifiable need; or the conviction that an interest in style, textuality or performative play necessarily precludes attention to divisions of wealth and labour, a conviction that gainsays the entire history of Marxist cultural criticism, as well as the textual, indeed performative, character of economic practices such as contract, wages and the money form itself. Then there are the occasional caricatures of opponents' positions: to say that queer theory can be unwittingly complicit with globalization is hardly grounds for declaring its proponents architects of neoliberal public intellectual discourse. As for Hennessy's ludicrous attempt to link the rise of 'bad girl' lesbian sex radicalism to the reduction of welfare rights, this ignores the frequency with which exponents of the former position are opponents of the latter, as well as the historical alliance between socialism and sexual libertarianism in Anglo-American feminism. For these reasons, despite its global perspective, *Profit and Pleasure* has thus far exerted little influence on the analysis of sexuality and globalization emerging in lesbian and gay scholarship.

Here two recent titles divide the field between a 'queer' approach and one that is expressly critical of it. In *Global Sex*, Dennis Altman (2001) espouses a self-consciously retro Marxist-Freudianism to survey the international transformation of sexual practices and identities ranging from non-marital cohabitation to sex tourism to militarized machismo. But his attempt to describe the vast nexus of connections linking them with globalized capitalism takes neither analysis much further than to stress the intersection of economic and psychological forces in such changes. Despite an approving citation of Aijaz Ahmad's complaint that postcolonial theory evades questions of determination by reducing Marxism to only one element of textual analysis, Altman's own adherence to Fraser's distribution/recognition dualism precludes much pursuit of determinate mediations. Moreover, his psychoanalysis is largely deployed in an admittedly commonsensical discussion of displaced desires and gendered phobias. But if this 'Marxist-Freudianism' is really a global social constructionism, Altman's knowledgeable synthesis of economic forces, political institutions and social movements, both internationally and in over 100 named countries, is a valuable counterpart to *Queer Globalizations*.

Like *Global Sex*, *Queer Globalizations* is a First-World production, whose multiethnic contributors teach in the US, and its 13 articles are narrower in their focus and far more preoccupied by their site of enunciation. This critical attention to western hegemony in arenas ranging from coming-out narratives to human rights rhetoric usefully challenges the aggrandizing analogies attributed to globalizing discourses, including Altman's own; but it also has the paradoxical effect of referring everything back to the hegemon. Even more problematically, the editors' declared emphasis on 'subjective mediation and agency' is initially opposed to a highly mechanical socio-economism, a sort of straw 'facticity' (Cruz-Malavé and Manalansan IV 2002: 7–8). Happily this warning is often ignored, as in Janet Jakobsen's illuminating analysis of the links between the supposedly 'value free' US economy and the 'family values' of the US state – to the advantage of US corporations who simultaneously export their employees' jobs to cheaper labour markets abroad and equalize partnership benefits for the lucky remainder at home, while campaigning against the tax-funded provision of any such entitlements to others (Jakobsen 2002). As Jakobsen provocatively argues, gay American appeals to a secular market mistake the continuing Protestant character of its capitalism, however global its dominance.

Elsewhere in this collection, queer kinship and queer neoliberalism are also reconsidered – in an essay which remarks on the recent address of US household advertising to male couples and one which asks how far queer criticism is itself implicated in 'neoliberal visions of freedom, desire, value and profit?'(Maurer 2002: 102). But unlike Hennessy, Bill Maurer's alternative to postmodern globalization is not Marxism but the elegantly regulated capitalism of the gay modernist John Maynard Keynes. And unlike Butler, Miranda Joseph concludes that homosexual kinship is increasingly compatible with capitalist consumption in the US, but not with those goods' production in the patriarchally disciplined maquilas of Mexico (Joseph 2002). In Maurer's view, Keynes' recommendations for international instruments to equalize balances of payments, stabilize commodity prices and finance postwar relief were informed by a Bloomsbury cosmopolitanism which might have restrained both global dominance and its conservative local oppositions. Joseph concludes that Latin American sweatshops have to be a queer issue, not least because the commodities of our commercially recognized relationships are constructed in them by workers denied such recognition. Her impassioned final appeal – to refuse gay marriage to the market and join anti-capitalist campaigns – might not be Maurer's style. But their increasingly shared opposition to the economic order from which queer theory has arguably both emerged and departed signals a significant turn in sexual scholarship.

Afterword

Figure 4.1 Cartoon by David Austin from the *Guardian*, 27 November 2003.

The first version of this article was completed in early 2003 for publication in 2004. Since then same-sex marriage and civil unions between homosexual couples have been legalized in some local US jurisdictions, although the legitimacy of these initiatives is now subject to the deliberation of the higher courts. In the UK, civil partnerships for homosexual couples became legal nationally at the end of 2005. With them came parity with married couples' tax, inheritance, state pension, immigration and next-of-kin rights. These rights augment earlier measures permitting the adoption of children and prohibiting discrimination on grounds of sexual orientation in employment. Legislation outlawing discrimination in regard to sexual orientation in the provision of goods and services has now come into effect. In a country which retains an established church whose bishops sit in the upper chamber of its legislature some anomalies persist, such as the designation 'partnership' protecting the religious exclusion of homosexuals from marriage.[3] And, of course, the success of legislation in preventing discrimination against homosexuals remains to be seen. Nevertheless, British lesbians and gays, like many of their counterparts elsewhere in Europe, can be said to have achieved near formal equality with heterosexuals. How might these developments affect our understandings of the relationship between sexuality, subjectivity and economics?

First, it must be admitted that Nancy Fraser's argument against the functionalist assumption that capitalism requires homosexual subordination seems, so far at least, to be borne out. Britain continues as a capitalist country, indeed one with record-setting disparities between the incomes of the richest and the poorest of its citizens. Moreover, it could be argued that awarding homosexual equality is not at odds with the current government's management of this economy. Not only do such measures underwrite New Labour's support for the 'meritocratic' accumulation of wealth, they may actually contribute to its attempts to privatize state welfare provisions. Such an argument was made quite succinctly in a cartoon published in the *Guardian* on 27 November 2003 (Figure 1), the day after the government announced its forthcoming parliamentary agenda. Among the measures proposed was the recognition of same-sex partnerships. Also announced was a bill allowing most of the country's universities (the Scottish parliament chose otherwise) to raise their domestic tuition fees from £1,125 per year to £3,000, 'topping up' a shortfall in tax funding then running at an estimated £2.5 billion per year.

In the cartoon, two frowning middle-aged men sit together as one complains: 'We get hitched, adopt a kid, get stuck with its top-up fees ...'. But the gay dads in the cartoon, or more likely their child – who will be 'permitted' to pay for university tuition after graduation – can anticipate much higher fees in the future. As soon as the figure of £3,000 was announced, it was derided by the heads of the nation's leading universities, who pointed out that even these increases would fail to restore funding per student to 1989 rates – and demanded that they be uncapped as soon as possible to permit the imposition of £10,000 or £15,000 or more in annual tuition fees to compete with their US competitors.

Such privatization is an increasing feature of British life, from care for the elderly to education at secondary as well as tertiary levels. Not only has new infrastructure investment in schools and hospitals been transferred to private finance initiatives (on lucrative terms for investors) but the cherished principle that health care should be free at the point of demand is now under attack. In these circumstances, the costs of caring will increasingly fall to the family, including the newly recognized homosexual family. As the website of the lesbian and gay lobbyists Stonewall warns readers: 'You get every right – and every responsibility – straight couples get when they marry'. For surviving partners attempting to escape the 40 per cent inheritance tax on estates valued in 2007 at more than £300,000 (the price of a two-bedroom flat in London) that may be a bargain. For those who discover that they will lose their disability benefits or be charged for their partner's child maintenance obligations from a previous relationship, it may not be. (The income of the *Guardian*'s gay dads will also be taken into account should their child apply for a government grant or university bursary towards maintenance costs during enrolment.)

In these circumstances, postponing marriage and childbearing has increasingly become the norm in the UK, with the new homosexual familialism often remarked ironically as the sole countervailing trend. (Thus the comically 'clone' styling of the gay couple in the cartoon, whose shaved heads and moustaches now identify them not as sexual outlaws but as the only men likely these days to want marriage and children.) Given all this, it might not seem surprising if the government sought to extend the recognition of partnership as widely as possible. At present Labour continues to refuse such rights to unmarried heterosexual couples – a position variously attributed to a residual deference to religious marriage traditions and to the costs of granting spousal pension rights to millions of potential beneficiaries (as opposed to many fewer lesbians and gays) at a time when the state pension system is critically underfunded. If there are financial as well as political calculations here, they may be different for heterosexuals and homosexuals, because the latter's minority status is assumed.

Whether this anomaly can legally continue in the face, for example, of possible *heterosexual* appeals to the European courts, remains to be seen. In May 2006, the Law Commission launched a review of the legal rights of the country's estimated two million cohabiting couples. It will consider formalizing the division of assets on separation, as well as the inheritance of property after death. Financial support for the children of such relationships will also be examined. This initiative was predictably decried by the Archbishop of Canterbury, Dr Rowan Williams, who argued that such provisions could compete with marriage. But his warning that the term 'cohabitation' currently includes a vast variety of arrangements may be a salient consideration if the government elects to enforce financial dependency as its definitive condition.

Meanwhile in the US, federal policy in regard to economic incentives for marriage is far less ambiguous, with the Bush administration's 'Healthy Marriage Initiative' diverting funds from programmes for refugees, Native Americans and disabled people to sponsor marital propaganda and training for high school students and cohabiting couples, while promoting a constitutional amendment against homosexual wedlock (Lerner 2004). In the face of both this initiative and the rainbow weddings industry that has sprung up in liberal cities like Boston and San Francisco, queer theorists in the US have become increasingly vocal in their opposition to what Miranda Joseph describes as 'wedding ourselves to capitalism' (Joseph 2002: 93). Thus, expanding her more tentative argument for the provision of health care regardless of marital status, Butler considers the likely exclusion of 'vulnerable populations: genderqueer and trans people, youth and the aging' from the financial succour of conjugal partnership. Here, as she points out, the issue becomes not only one of extended definitions of kinship, but also that of broader community alliances, such as those pioneered across racial, sexual and economic divisions by AIDS activists before the arrival of antiretrovirals 'ended' the health crisis for those who had access to them. In the name of such alliances, Butler proposes the disaggregation[4] of economic benefits from marital status and a counter agenda of universal health care, collective housing, restrictions on drug profiteering and the forging of global coalitions to combat the devastation of HIV (Butler 2004: 20–21). Such proposals, in response to the privatizing impetus of both traditional marriage and 'marriage lite', offer new approaches to an economically responsible sexual politics and a socially articulated theory of queer subjectivity.

Notes

1 An earlier version of this article appeared in 'Cultures and economies', *new formations* 52, Spring 2004.
2 See also Michèle Barrett (1992).
3 In June 2006 lawyers acting for a British lesbian couple married in British Columbia began a High Court challenge to the Civil Partnership Act, seeking legal recognition of their marriage under the European Convention of Human Rights and the UK Human Rights Act. The interim High Court ruling allowing the case of British academics Celia Kitzinger and Sue Wilkinson to proceed declared that the current requirement that a marriage between same-sex partners abroad be treated as a civil partnership in Britain constituted prima facie discrimination on the grounds of sexual orientation. However, in August 2006 the president of the High Court's Family Division ruled that their Canadian marriage could be recognized in the UK only as a civil partnership.
4 I use the term 'disaggregation' in reference to the UK feminist campaign in the late 1970s and early 1980s for women's financial independence. Although tax provisions have changed since that period, the aggregation of a couple's income in regard, for example, to the calculation of benefit entitlement has been retained. See Michèle Barrett and Mary McIntosh (1982: 150–151).

References

Altman, D. (2001) *Global Sex*, Chicago: University of Chicago.
Barrett, M. (1992) 'Words and things: materialism and method in contemporary feminist analysis', in Barrett, M. and Phillips, A. (eds), *Destabilizing Theory*, London: Polity.
Barrett, M. and McIntosh, M. (1982) *The Anti-Social Family*, London: Verso.
Bradley, H and Fenton, S. (1999) 'Reconciling culture and economy', in Ray, L. and Sayer, A. (eds), *Culture and Economy after the Cultural Turn*, London: Sage.

Butler, J. (1993) *Bodies That Matter*, New York: Routledge.
—— (1994) 'Against proper objects', *differences*, 6, 2–3: 13–15.
—— (1997a) *The Psychic Life of Power*, Stanford: Stanford University Press.
—— (1997b) *Excitable Speech*, New York: Routledge.
—— (1998) 'Merely cultural', *New Left Review*, 227: 33–44.
—— (2000) *Antigone's Claim: kinship between life and death*, New York: Columbia University Press.
—— (2002) 'Is kinship always already heterosexual?', *Differences*, 13, (Spring): 14–44.
—— (2004) 'Can marriage be saved?', *The Nation*, July 5: 20–21.
Butler, J., Laclau, E. and Zizek, S. (2000) *Contingency, Hegemony, Universality*, London: Verso.
Cornwall, R.R. (1997) 'Queer political economy', in Gluckman, A. and Reed, B. (eds), *Homo Economics: Capitalism, Community and Lesbian and Gay Life*, New York: Routledge.
Cruz-Malavé, A. and Manalansan IV, M.F. (2002) 'Introduction: dissident sexualities/alternative globalisms', in Cruz-Malave, A. and Manalansan IV, M.F. (eds), *Queer Globalizations*, New York: New York University Press.
De Lauretis, T. (1994) *The Practice of Love: Lesbian Sexuality and Perverse Desire*, Bloomington: Indiana University Press.
d'Emilio, J. (1984) 'Capitalism and gay identity', in Snitow, A., Stansell, C. and Thompson, S. (eds), *Desire: the Politics of Sexuality*, London: Virago.
Engels, F. (1968) 'Preface to the first edition: the origin of the family, private property and the state', in Marx, K. and Engels, F., *Selected Works*, London: Lawrence and Wishart, 449.
Faderman, L. (1991) *Odd Girls and Twilight Lovers: a History of Lesbian Life in Twentieth-century America*, New York: Columbia University Press.
Fraser, N. (1997) *Justice Interruptus: Critical Reflections on the 'Postsocialist' Condition*, New York: Routledge.
—— (1998) 'Heterosexism, misrecognition and capitalism: a response to Judith Butler', *New Left Review*, 228: 140–149.
Gagnier, R. (2000) *The Insatiability of Human Wants: Economics and Aesthetics in Market Society*, Chicago: University of Chicago.
Gerstner, D. and Ginsberg, T. (2001) 'Conference notes' co-chairs of the Society for Cinema Studies Queer Caucus.
Hennessy, R. (2000) *Profit and Pleasure: Sexual Identities in Late Capitalism*, New York: Routledge.
Jakobsen, J.R. (2002) 'Can homosexuals end western civilization as we know it? Family values in a global economy', in Cruz-Malavé, A. and Manalansan IV, M.F. (eds), *Queer Globalizations*, New York: New York University Press.
Joseph, M. (2002) 'Family affairs', in Cruz-Malave, A. and Manalansan IV, M.F. (eds), *Queer Globalizations*, New York: New York University Press.
Laclau, E. and Mouffe, C. (2001) *Hegemony and Socialist Strategy*, London: Verso.
Lerner, S. (2004) 'Marriage on the mind', *The Nation*, July 5: 40–42.
Levinson, B. (1999) 'Sex without sex, queering the market, the collapse of the political, the death of difference, and AIDS', *Diacritics*, 29, 3: 94–95.
Martin, B. (1996) 'Sexualities without genders and other queer utopias', in *Femininity Played Straight*, New York: Routledge, 71–94.
Maurer, B. (2002) 'Redecorating the international economy: Keynes, Grant, and the

queering of Bretton Woods', in Cruz-Malavé, A. and Manalansan IV, M.F. (eds), *Queer Globalizations*, New York: New York University Press.

Patton, C. (1993) 'Tremble, Hetero Swine!', in Warner, M. (ed.), *Fear of a Queer Planet*, Minneapolis: University of Minnesota Press.

Rorty, R. (1998) *Achieving Our Country*, Cambridge, MA: Harvard University Press.

Rubin, G. (1975) 'The traffic in women: notes on the "political economy" of sex', in Reiter, R.R. (ed.), *Toward an Anthropology of Women*, New York: Monthly Review Press.

—— (1984) 'Thinking sex: notes for a radical theory of the politics of sexuality', in Vance, C.S. (ed.), *Pleasure and Danger: Exploring Female Sexuality*, Boston: Routledge & Kegan Paul.

Rubin, G. with Butler, J. (1994) 'Sexual traffic', *Differences*, 6, 2–3. Reprinted in Merck, M., Segal, N. and Wright, E. (eds), *Coming Out of Feminism?*, Oxford: Blackwell 1998.

Seidman, S. (1993) 'Identity and politics in a "postmodern" gay culture', in Warner, M. (ed.), *Fear of a Queer Planet*, Minneapolis: University of Minnesota Press.

Shapiro, S. (2004) 'Marx to the rescue! Queer theory and the crisis of prestige', *New Formations*, 53: 77–90.

Weeks, J. (1979) *Coming Out: Homosexual Politics in Britain, from The Nineteenth Century to the Present*, New York: Quartet Books.

5 Nancy Fraser's integrated theory of justice

A 'sociologically rich' model for a global capitalist era?

Terry Lovell

Introduction

The aim of a series of exchanges between Nancy Fraser and Axel Honneth was to delineate, in the spirit of critical social theory, 'a sociologically rich interpretation of the normative claims implicit in the social conflicts of the present' (Honneth, in Fraser and Honneth 2003: 110), that draws therefore on sociology as well as normative theory. Honneth's chief sociological recourse in this exchange is to the empirical study conducted by Pierre Bourdieu and a team of researchers on social suffering in contemporary society among marginalized working-class communities on the fringes of Paris and elsewhere (Bourdieu *et al.* 1999), of the kind that witnessed the upsurge of angry, violent demonstrations across France in the autumn of 2005. Fraser had herself drawn upon aspects of Bourdieu's conceptual frame in the early stages of the development of her integrated theory of justice, the central concern of this paper, which suggests that this point of reference lends itself to further consideration in assessing the exchange.

Although feminist issues are not at the centre of her exchange with Honneth, Fraser's feminism marks all that she writes, as is clear in many of the vivid examples with which her theory is furnished. One prominent resource for feminist theory in the 1970s was the Marxism that circulated in sociology and many other disciplines. The famous cultural or linguistic turn that subsequently affected so many of the disciplines on which feminist scholarship had drawn, gave greater prominence to philosophy and to textual studies, even to the point of reducing 'the social' to 'the textual'. The turn of the twenty-first century has witnessed a 'return to the social'[1], restoring attention to causal/structural sociological analysis, but this project is no simple turning back. The cultural turn was no cul-de-sac. 'The cultural' retains the place it has won in feminist theorizing in which 'the social' had been temporarily eclipsed.[2]

The history of feminism in the second half of the twentieth century has been one of development, contestation and transformation. Fraser's early contributions came from a socialist feminist perspective, and many who aligned themselves with this approach were hostile to 'the cultural turn' and to postmodernism. But Fraser holds together in critical synthesis the legacy of socialist feminism, aspects of postmodernism, and finally and perhaps most significantly, critical theory. Her approach is dialogical.

Her characteristic strategy in response to those who would set these feminisms in opposition to one another has been 'the finesse'. She seeks out, through critique, defensible versions of each that may then be reconciled.[3] Her theory of justice is built in the context of 'the post-socialist condition' (Fraser 1997), and it holds together another dichotomous opposition between 'the politics of equality' and 'the politics of difference'. In characteristic fashion she accords privilege to neither one against the imperatives of the other, arguing the case that justice requires, and can integrate, valid forms of both.

Bourdieu's is a complex sociology of domination. One of its principal lines of articulation distinguishes social structure from habitus, although these are intimately linked.[4] Habitus is a powerful yet elusive concept, and is significant in the sociological underpinnings sought for Fraser's and Honneth's rival socio-normative theories of justice. It makes of Bourdieu a tacit third party to their exchange. All three have positioned themselves in relationship to Habermas over the manner in which the sphere of public debate, within which injustice claims circulate and are assessed, systematically disadvantages dominated social and reference groups.[5]

Honneth's critique and Bourdieu's sociology of domination provide two pressure points on Fraser's theory. But the third and most urgent challenge lies in the project of interpreting and adapting the theory to the exigencies of global capitalism, a challenge which Fraser has addressed in her recent work, including her contribution to this volume. I shall begin with a brief account of her theory of justice.

Fraser's integrated theory of justice

Fraser's early framing of her theory is concerned primarily with inequality and injustice in the context of global capitalism and the increase in cultural diversity in modern society that it carries in its train. She argues for a 'dual perspectival' approach that distinguishes two types of injustice, those of misrecognition and maldistribution, rooted respectively in the cultural domination that is perpetuated through the status order and the economic system of modern capitalism. She identifies three types of socio-economic injustice:

1 Exploitation (appropriation of fruits of labour).
2 Economic marginalization (restriction to undesirable or poorly paid work, or denial of access to incomes).
3 Denial of an adequate material standard of living.

Her three types of 'cultural or symbolic' injustice rooted in 'social patterns of representation etc.' (Fraser 1997: 14) are:

1 Cultural domination (subjection to alien standards of judgement).
2 Non-recognition (subjection to cultural invisibility).
3 Disrespect (routine subjection to malign stereotypes and disparagements).

Fraser is interested in systematic injustices that affect those occupying particular positions within the social relations of the class and status orders. To be sure, socio-cultural groups and categories are not mutually exclusive. But Fraser argues that they may be classified according to their primary roots and their attendant vulnerability to one or another type of injustice. She places them along a continuum; at one extreme are those groups that are rooted primarily in the economic order, most vulnerable to maldistribution; at the other end are clustered those that are defined within the matrix of status distinction and who are particularly vulnerable to misrecognition. If the subaltern social class – the working (but not always employed) class – provides the paradigm case with regard to economic injustice, Fraser's examples of groups that suffer primarily from cultural injustice include those whose sexualities place them outside the hierarchies and values of the dominant culture, including homosexuals. At the centre point we find what Fraser terms 'bivalent' groups that are equally vulnerable to both types of injustice. The two examples she uses are those of gender and 'race', both identified as culturally rather than economically grounded, but she argues that these distinctions have become sufficiently deeply embedded in, and structuring of, the inequalities of the economic order to merit this bivalent status. Dalits in India would serve as a powerful example (Chigateri 2004). Their oppression is at one and the same time rooted in the (cultural) status order that defines caste (for Max Weber, castes were status groups) and deeply embedded in an economic order that perpetuates them.

Bivalent groups are presented as special cases, but it is not always easy to distinguish them from groups grounded more fully in the economic or status orders. The dominated, or subaltern class was never homogeneous; but in a variety of contexts and forms, it developed distinctive social and cultural institutions and practices, and a habitus that was marked in terms of class. Wherever subaltern groups are culturally distinct, they may attract disparagement, cultural misrecognition. On the other hand, *pace* Judith Butler (1998), homosexuals, insofar as they are culturally visible, may pay severe economic penalties, and suffer physical as well as what Bourdieu terms symbolic violence (Bourdieu 2000). But whether injustices are principally generated in the economic system or the cultural/status order, or whether they are fully bivalent, Fraser's dual perspectival approach carries the imperative that analysis must always examine all cases and all proposed remedies in terms of both, and it is this that serves to protect against any given categories being seen as 'merely cultural' or exclusively 'economic'.

Fraser is indeed concerned, alongside philosophical/political analysis, to offer *guidelines* for a more practical, pragmatic task: to identify modes of intervention that are, in a given conjuncture and a particular case, likely to have some success in remedying the injustice suffered, or at least reducing it, but above all, that will not exacerbate it (Fraser 1997). Interventions that focus exclusively on remedying economic disadvantage (certain types of ameliorative redistribution for example) may deepen the injustices of misrecognition that these groups simultaneously suffer. There is a parallel risk in addressing the injustices of misrecognition solely by the politics of 'difference' or 'recognition'. The example that Fraser uses is that of 'cultural feminism', in which culturally produced and structurally instituted gender characteristics are celebrated and affirmed, and thereby risk being reinforced, naturalized and reproduced. The key political task therefore always is to identify strategies and tactics that combine positively, without allowing one to, as it were, unpick or aggravate the other.

In the elaboration of her model of justice in her exchange with Honneth, Fraser brings to the foreground the more inclusive moral category of *participatory parity* – her defining criterion of justice. Injustice claims of whatever kind are to be validated only if the practices they target can be shown to diminish or obstruct the possibilities for equal participation in social life and in the discourses of the democratic public sphere.

The exchange with Honneth: enter Bourdieu

The main thrust of Honneth's critique of Fraser targets her dualism. He argues that while redistribution may be essential to remedy injustice, it can be subsumed under a suitably calibrated category of recognition. Thus the marginalized groups that are the subject of Bourdieu *et al.*'s research (1999) manifestly suffer distributive injustice, and because their predicament is rooted in the dislocations of social class and the global economic order, presumably would be placed by Fraser towards the maldistribution end of her continuum. But Honneth, who draws attention to this research in mounting his disagreement with Fraser, identifies their suffering in terms of his broader, encompassing category of misrecognition. Bourdieu's empirical example was chosen to provide something of a test case. Honneth aims to show that even at this end point of Fraser's continuum, the felt injustice expressed in such communities is, above all, the injustice of disrespect – the violation of legitimate normative expectations promised by a complex societal recognition order. If we do not need a separate category of specifically economic injustice even in this extreme case, then Fraser's dualism falls. Second, and drawing on the same example, Honneth accuses Fraser of over-reliance upon those recognition struggles that have been articulated through new social movements and that have therefore found a voice within the discourses of the public domain.[6] He argues, drawing on the research interviews, that: 'the overwhelming share of cases of everyday misery are still to be found beyond the perceptual threshold of the political public sphere' (Honneth, in Fraser and Honneth 2003: 118). Finally, it should be noted that Honneth is concerned with injustice in order to redress the 'deeper' levels of harm that misrecognition causes in terms of *human flourishing*, and the opportunity to develop 'intact selves', the primary condition for participating in the social world and pursuing 'the good life'. Manifestly, the conditions under which the people of the communities studied in the research were placed do not lend themselves to human flourishing, however defined.

Fraser argues that what constitutes human flourishing and 'the good life', is a judgement that is not universally shared among competing but 'reasonable' visions of modern multicultural society (Fraser, in Fraser and Honneth 2003: 223). Fraser describes her position as one of 'non-sectarian thick deontological liberalism' (ibid.: 230). But her concern is to keep her model of justice general enough, 'thin' enough, to avoid sectarianism and thereby navigate the rapids of cultural relativism, yet 'thick' enough to offer substantive guidelines at a pragmatic level. This concern motivates her distinction between the binding *moral* imperatives of justice, and culturally relative *ethical* imperatives that bind only those that adhere to them. These ethical norms include (variable) conceptions of the good life, whereas for Honneth no adequate account of justice is possible that does not incorporate at the very least a 'weak conception' of the good life, such as he himself proposes (Honneth, in Fraser and Honneth 2003: 114). In this paper I shall stay close to the particular example raised by Bourdieu's research.

Dualism and recognition

Dualist approaches that distinguish between 'the economic/material' and 'the cultural' have proved contentious within feminism in response to dual systems theory[7], and within the form of cultural studies named by Raymond Williams as cultural materialism rather than the study of a separate realm of culture (Williams 1977). Cognizant of both, Fraser yet offers an unashamedly dualist account of justice, and this aspect of her work came under criticism from Iris Marion Young (1997) as well as Butler and Honneth. Fraser mounts a robust, unapologetic rejoinder; her dualism of the economic and the cultural is, first, an *analytical* rather than a substantive distinction, and she argues against identifying the economic per se with the economic *system* of modern society, the cultural with either its *status order*, or, in the manner of feminist dual systems theory, with institutions and practices defined as 'ideological', including sexuality and the family, as was clear in her exchange with Butler (Butler 1998; Fraser 1998); second, she names it a *perspectival dualism* and in this aspect it is political and strategic as well as analytical; third, Fraser shares Honneth's wish to form a *unitary* account of justice, but argues that this goal is aided and not impeded by her analytical perspectival dualism. All claims, whether the injustice in question is grounded in the capitalist economic system or the dominant status order, must be brought before the bar of participatory parity.

For Honneth, by contrast, the unifying concept is that of a (thick, multilayered and historically developed) recognition order, one whose claims extend over social relations generally, including economic relations and practices. The 'so-whatness' of this claim lies in his identification of a deep (psychic) level of affect, 'structurally directed against the unreasonable demands of society' that permits us to speak of 'the necessity of a practice of transgression' (Honneth, in Fraser and Honneth 2003: 243). For, like Fraser, his concern is with social transformation in the direction of social justice.

Honneth disputes Fraser's claim that her categories are analytical. Despite her disclaimers to the contrary, he argues that they designate two substantive areas of the socio-cultural world. This gives them some resemblance to the sociological opposition between 'system integration' and 'social integration' (Lockwood 1964), towards which Honneth takes an ambivalent stance (Fraser and Honneth 2003: 156). He denies the very existence of a systemic, self-reproducing economic system that is outside the purview of, or may flout with impunity, even the 'deep grammar' of a normative order that demands respect across the whole of social space. The economic system, as well as all kinds of social relations and practices, is normatively bound. Honneth distances himself from Lockwood's distinction, then, but with a hint of kettle logic, argues that were he to use it, it would be necessary to concede 'a certain primacy to social integration' (ibid.: 250), or in his own terms, to the broad normative recognition order that would have to be classified as 'cultural' (if we had to choose!). Economic injustices are experienced as breaches of the social recognition order: 'the economic' and 'the cultural' is, he claims, an opposition that 'designates the respects in which disrespect is experienced' (ibid.: 157). A separate category of specifically economic injustice is not required.

What light does Bourdieu's approach throw on this dispute? Recognition and misrecognition are key concepts in his sociology of domination; the power to dominate is held by social actors by virtue of their location in a complex social space of positions that are relationally defined, and their (positional) holdings of two types of capital: cultural and economic (Bourdieu 1984). Fraser's opposition resembles, and may even have been influenced by Bourdieu's frame. Bourdieu nowhere unequivocally reduces or subordinates one to the other.[8] 'Economic capital' and 'cultural capital' are related through the concept of 'capital composition' (the particular mix that is characteristic of given positions in social space – see Bourdieu 1984), and more importantly, as we shall see, through 'symbolic capital'. He has been accused of quasi-Marxist economic reductionism – among others, interestingly, by Honneth (who levels the same charge against Fraser)[9] – but some defences of Bourdieu against this recurrent charge might suggest that he should rather be read as attaching the greater significance to the *symbolic violence* of misrecognition (Wacquant 2005: 20), and this concept is critical to the present discussion.

For Bourdieu, misrecognition is pervasive and complex. Misrecognition of the dominated by the dominant takes the form of a (*legitimated*) refusal to grant any but inferior standing to the dominated or to recognize them other than on the terms of the dominant culture on which their own claims to distinction are based. The recognition and respect that the dominant require of their 'inferiors', in addition to that secured from their peers, may also yield them rich symbolic profits. But the misrecognition and disrespect inflicted on the dominated is deeply harmful to them and it constitutes symbolic violence *in proportion to its legitimacy* (Bourdieu 2000: 240 *passim*).

Symbolic capital is not, Bourdieu argues, 'a particular kind of capital but what every kind of capital becomes when it is misrecognized as capital, that is, as force, a power or capacity for (actual or potential) exploitation, and therefore recognized as legitimate' (ibid.: 242). The emphasis on legitimacy is nowhere more evident than in his description of the state as 'the central bank of symbolic capital' (ibid.: 240). As the state claims a monopoly on the legitimate use of force, it is possession of this state-sanctioned symbolic capital through the offices of a 'state nobility' generated and reproduced through the educational system, that confers the power both to recognize others and to withhold recognition: 'To be known and recognized also means possessing the power to recognize, to state, with success, what merits being known and recognized' (ibid.: 242).

It is a sociological, and indeed a literary truism (hammered home, for example, in Jane Austen's novels) that access to _economic_ capital does not in and of itself command recognition. 'New money' may be discounted within traditional status orders; and on the other hand a lessening of inequality through measures of redistribution to individuals and communities may not on its own secure the ability among the dominated to command respect, but may provoke resentment and a deepening of misrecognition. However, this can be made to cut both ways, so far as Fraser and Honneth's argument over dualism or monism is concerned, since each recognizes that redistribution alone rarely secures justice, especially where economic injustice is intercalated with misrecognition, as with Fraser's bivalent groups, and as they are in the communities of Bourdieu's research.

Fraser's account of 'cultural or symbolic injustice' is very close to Bourdieu's concepts of misrecognition and symbolic violence. But where there is a significant difference is, first, in her argument that the conditions of modern global capitalism bring a greater degree of cultural pluralism in their train that alters the cultural/status order of earlier periods of capitalism. The global capitalist economy disrupts the _symbolic_ order that sanctioned traditional claims of status. As we shall see, Bourdieu agrees that this order has been radically affected, though not in the direction of multicultural pluralism but rather through the erosion of the autonomy of certain key fields of cultural and intellectual production that have been sources of opposition to dominant values.

But modern multiculturalism means, for Fraser, that there no longer exists any single all-powerful and _legitimate_ value _system_ able to draw on the crushing symbolic authority that leads Bourdieu to declare that 'one of the most unequal of all distributions, and probably, in any case, the most cruel, is the distribution of symbolic capital, that is, of _social importance and of reasons for living_, (Bourdieu 2000: 241, emphasis added). In other words, for Fraser there is no longer a central bank: cultural capital in modern society is held in diverse currencies.

Within Fraser's perspectival dualism, subaltern social groupings in specific socio-historical circumstances may and usually do suffer from some admixture of economic and cultural injustice, and this is certainly true of those groups that are the points of reference in Bourdieu's remarks in _Pascalian Meditations_ (2000) and in _The Weight of the World_. Most certainly their acute social suffering encompasses at least two, and for those in employment, all three of Fraser's types of socio-economic injustice: economic marginalization and denial of an adequate material standard of living, and exploitation. They also suffer all three types of 'cultural or symbolic injustice: cultural domination, non-recognition and disrespect'. In these circumstances and in others economic injustice may indeed be *experienced* as misrecognition, as Honneth claims. But little follows from this in terms of the superior purchase that is claimed by Honneth's (complex) recognition monism or Fraser's perspectival dualism. In analysing the social suffering in question, Honneth would be obliged to consider each of what he claims are 'the respects in which disrespect is experienced' – the economic and the cultural – while Fraser's perspectival dualism requires no less, although at both the philosophical and pragmatic level, it is important for her to be free to distinguish the definition of injustice from any dependency upon the manner in which it is experienced.[10] However the case has a bearing upon the social/system integration distinction. The economic injustice that the groups in these communities suffer are rooted in the history of the formation of modern global capitalism and its effects in particular places and points in time, causes that are not necessarily transparent to the sufferers, whose complaints often target more immediately visible and diverse fellow-sufferers. These communities lack 'social integration'. And we may well wish, with Fraser, to distinguish between this level of social interaction, and a (more or less integrated) *system* that is economic, it is true, but whose transactions are nonetheless bound by system-specific norms.

Discourses and speakers do not command equal attention in the democratic public sphere. How do subaltern and counter-hegemonic discourses fare?

Can the subaltern speak? Can the subaltern be heard?

For Honneth, the reference point of injustice is experiential, and what is *experienced* as injustice, and *displayed* as 'psychic suffering', may not be articulated consciously, or very clearly in the words of the sufferers. It lies at the deep level at which Honneth locates 'a human psyche structurally directed against the unreasonable demands of society' (Honneth, in Fraser and Honneth 2003: 243). Bourdieu, in his methodological appendix to the research, appears to lend support to such a view, referring as he does in a passage cited by Honneth, to 'unexpressed and often inexpressible malaises' (Bourdieu *et al.* 1999: 627, cited in Fraser and Honneth 2003: 119); he distinguishes between 'what is expressed' and 'what is said':

> Social agents do not innately possess a science of what they are and what they do. More precisely they do not necessarily have access to the *core principles* of their discontent or their malaise, and, without aiming to mislead, their most spontaneous declarations may express something quite different from what they seem to say.
>
> (Bourdieu *et al.* 1999: 620, emphasis added)

Fraser's reply to Honneth's discussion of the subaltern speech of the dominated does not refer directly to *The Weight of the World*. Her rejoinder and his subsequent response establish that Honneth, too, recognizes the framing of all experiences of injustice by discourses that are normative and public, including Fraser's 'folk paradigms'. But Honneth draws on a distinction between 'language' and 'discourse' in order to privilege 'a repertoire of deeper normative principles that determine the linguistic horizons of socio-moral thoughts and feelings' (Honneth, in Fraser and Honneth 2003: 250). This distinction resembles Bourdieu's opposition between what is said and what is expressed, and his imputation of *core principles* to the latter. Why is it that Bourdieu, and following him, Honneth, believe that the very core of what is expressed may depart from what is said? The answer lies partly at least in Bourdieu's concept of habitus.

Habitus is not preconscious, nor unconscious, and does not lie outside the space of 'the social' – certainly not in any psychic level that precedes the formation of social actors. To draw on Lockwood's distinction, it is generated at the level of social interaction in the practical competence – ways of doing and being – that children learn in specific contexts. It is what is taken for granted, goes without saying. Habitus is dispositional and practical. It is expressed, but is not readily available to reflexive articulation. Habitus is read through what is said, but also through bodily hexis, bearing, manner of speech, accent, and so on.[11] Honneth is drawing on this concept when he observes that 'not everything that normatively underlies human communication ... can take linguistic form, since recognition is often tied first of all to physical gestures or mimetic forms of expression' (Honneth, in Fraser and Honneth 2003: 247). However, *The Weight of the World* is distinguished by the sheer amount of directly transcribed *speech* that it contains, and that makes it such a very long book. Fraser's emphasis is on the discursive rather than the experiential, but she is well aware that 'discourse' is by no means limited to what is consciously articulated. However, there are few examples in published research of even the type of speech that we find in *The Weight of the World*, let alone what is expressed through non-verbal aspects of habitus, something very difficult to capture in interview transcripts. Even Angela McRobbie, who is deeply critical of the research, concedes that 'the proliferation of voices in *The Weight of the World* does admittedly fill an absence in current sociological and also social policy writing' (McRobbie 2002: 131).

However, Bourdieu's claim of social agents' limited access to 'the core principles of their malaise' refers, in addition to the 'unsaid' of habitus, to the fact that the social structural conditions and relations that connect causally with the level of social practice and may disrupt or dislocate it, are not transparent to experience. The project of the research is to relate 'what is expressed' to social causal relations that can be known but not directly experienced, in order to place pervasive forms of social suffering and social injustice into the deliberations of the discursive public sphere in a form in which they are more likely to gain a hearing. This is why he attaches so much importance to the participation of intellectuals: they are enjoined to provide 'resources for rethinking and renewing democratic struggles' (Wacquant 2005: 4). Here he is at one with Fraser, insofar as she wishes to place among the repertoire of '*decentred discourses of social criticism*', alongside folk paradigms, 'the structural analysis of social subordina-tion and political sociologies of social movements' (Fraser, in Fraser and Honneth 2003: 205) that provide 'a moral grammar that social actors can ... draw on in *any* sphere to evaluate social arrangements' (ibid.: 208).

Fraser remains unwilling to cede the definition of injustice to the experience of suffering that is 'expressed, but unsaid', that requires interpretation to be 'unveiled', and that resides at deeper levels than the articulations that are expressed and that circulate in social movements. The problem lies in part at least in the grounds on which 'what is expressed but not said' is interpreted, in relation to the language of complaint on the one hand, and of sociological and political analysis on the other.

Gayatri Chakravorty Spivak famously argued, in the context of colonial and imperial dominion, that the subaltern could not speak. But the dispossessed and marginalized narrators of their miseries in *The Weight of the World* are loud in their complaints. They are not, like the dead Hindu widow immolated on her husband's funeral pyre, consigned to a profound silence on which interpretation may be overlaid at will (Spivak 1988). Nevertheless Bourdieu, like all researchers, must interpret the discourse, verbal and non-verbal, of his respon-dents, and the extent and nature of the interpretation used in the research has been the object of controversy. Objections have been raised on diametrically opposed grounds: under-interpretation of the lengthy interview transcripts (for discussion, see Boyne 2002; Schinkel 2004; Vitellone 2004), but also, by McRobbie, of what might be termed '(over)-interpretation by sleight of hand'. She complains of the absence of analysis of the social and cultural contexts of the interviews that has the result that the speakers seem to be using 'comparable discourse to his [Bourdieu's] own sociology, i.e. the respondents seem to be saying the same thing, but in their own words' (McRobbie 2002: 136). The accusation is that he closes the distance between two forms of discourse by overlaying 'what is said' with a sociologically informed discourse that interprets 'what is expressed', evading any tension between them by the elision of the two.

The terms which Bourdieu uses to describe his sociological method include some striking metaphors: he speaks of 'socio-analysis' (which echoes and dis-places 'psychoanalysis') and of the 'clinical sociologist', likened to the physi-cian who must 'uncover the structural causes that statements and apparent signs unveil only by veiling' (Bourdieu *et al.* 1999: 628). However, the distinction between what is said and what is expressed leaves room for troubling differ-ences of interpretation that reverberate in the history of feminism. It may be useful to step back here and draw some comparisons with these troubles – dis-putes over the terms in which complaints are expressed and those in which they are interpreted by feminists within the 'feminist counter-public sphere' (Felski 1989) and in the sociology of gender, feminist and otherwise.

In the period following the resurgence of the western women's movement in the 1970s, the popular forms of 'female complaint' that feminists interpreted in terms of feminist politics and theory began to be preceded by disclaimers: 'I am not a feminist [or a 'women's libber'], but ...'. Feminist scholarship in an academic setting was always vulnerable to the charge that was often laid against it by grassroots feminist activists that we spoke only for women like ourselves – middle class, white, educated, articulate, western: a charge that recurs. A succession of voices emerged along these and other lines of difference,[12] some refusing the feminist label altogether, but identifying themselves as working-class women, women of colour, disabled women, and in the political geography of international counter-hegemony, as subaltern women of the South: that is in terms of their position as women but not necessarily in terms of the politics of feminism.

This distinction has been closed over when convenient, in the history of colonial domination, and more recently, in defence of the invasion of Afghanistan and Iraq in the aftermath of 9/11. The 'feminist card' is freely used in the justification of war, as of imperial domination – the mission to 'save' subaltern women from myriad oppressions and violations.[13]

The opposition is opened up once more in a distinction that can be challenging to feminism between feminism and the sociology of women that may be detected in Bourdieu's stance towards feminism. His work on masculine domination (Bourdieu 1990, 2001) drew greater attention to his sociology amongst many feminists who had been more influenced by poststructuralism. Paradoxically however, it was his direct address to this issue, one that is simply not found in Foucault for example, that provoked feminist hostility, especially among French materialist feminists who are in many respects closer to Bourdieu than they are to feminist poststructuralism or postmodernism.[14] Bourdieu seemed to be claiming for his 'clinical sociology' the ability to read and interpret the habitus of *women*, against any conscious, verbal feminist stance, and with more accuracy than much feminist analysis had achieved. He analysed it in terms of the 'relative constancy' (Bourdieu 2001: 94) of the *feminine habitus* over against overt political and analytical beliefs.[15]

Bourdieu, like the various constituencies of women who refused the label, saw the dominance within feminism of what he might have termed the 'dominated sex of the dominant class': women relatively rich in holdings of cultural and social capital, able to profit from feminism in intra-class sectional struggles for greater equality. Gains of (middle-class) women in the era of contemporary feminism in terms of educational and employment opportunities may have been at the expense of the relative position of the working class as a whole, evidence of a change of class reproduction strategy among the dominant. Bridget Fowler takes this up in a paper on *Masculine Domination*: 'we have been slow to describe the *class consequences* of the increasing success of women as upwards invaders of 'service class (dominant class) jobs'. She adds that these class consequences are difficult to reconcile with 'programmes for reducing inequality' (Fowler 2003: 482).

Certainly it is no easy matter to separate class and gender inequality, as I have argued elsewhere (Lovell 2004). But Fraser's perspectival dualism offers strategies for attempting this, as may be seen in her essay 'Beyond the family wage' (Fraser 1997). And I believe it is precisely the danger of 'speaking for others' who are differently positioned within social space, for which second wave feminists were castigated in the 1970s and 1980s, that makes Fraser so very wary of claims to interpret, or to speak *for*, the needs or the speech of others, as her concept of 'needs talk' (1989) demonstrates. There is a fine balance to be struck between the 'decentred discourses' of critical sociology, and subaltern speech, when these discourses rearticulate that speech *in other words*.

Bourdieu's methodology is legitimated not only by the need to 'unveil' the speech of the dominated through its re-interpretation in terms of the social causes of the miseries suffered, the complaints laid, using the discourses of critical, 'clinical', 'reflexive' sociology, but also by the obstacles that impede the ability of subaltern speech to *gain a hearing*; that is to say, not (or not only) because of the obscurity *to the sufferers* of the causes of their discontents, but because their speech and its idioms is discounted as he indicates in his critique of Habermas:

> The representation of political life that Habermas proposes ... obscures and represses the question of the economic and social commitments that would have to be fulfilled in order to allow the public deliberation capable of leading to a rational consensus, that is a debate in which compelling particular interests *would receive the same consideration* and in which participants, conforming to an ideal model of 'communicative action', *would seek to understand the points of view of others and to give them the same weight as their own* .... Domination is never absent from social relations of communication.
>
> (Bourdieu 2000: 65, emphasis added)

Bourdieu makes a complex claim that legitimates the indirect transmission of the point of view of the dominated through the interventions within the public discursive sphere of the sociologist and others. Fraser's work has been deeply influenced by Habermas, but she, too, takes her critical distance. His concept of the public sphere – 'a theater in modern societies in which political participation is enacted through the medium of talk' (Fraser 1997: 76) – is her political/theoretical touchstone, but also her point of departure from Habermas: her touchstone because 'indispensable to critical social theory and democratic political practice', her point of departure insofar as this concept that emerged in liberal discourse and social practice and institutions over two hundred years ago, stands in need of a thorough reworking in relation to modern capitalism that Habermas has not fully effected. Fraser's critique raises difficulties that parallel those signalled by Bourdieu:

> We should question whether it is possible even in principle for interlocutors to deliberate *as if* they were social peers in specially designated discursive arenas, when these discursive arenas are situated in a larger societal context that is pervaded by structural relations of dominance and subordination.
>
> (Fraser 1997: 79)

The voices that compete for a hearing in the public discursive sphere, then, have greater and lesser degrees of success along various lines of domination, and this is Bourdieu's main concern and also that of Honneth – and of Fraser, who in addition, argues that these lines of domination include lines of cultural difference under the impact of global capitalism, migration and multiculturalism.

Competing discourses in the arenas of the public sphere

Bourdieu's model places great weight of emphasis on the power of the dominant symbolic order, but does not present it as entirely unitary. The fierce competition for 'distinction' within specialized fields has a dynamic of its own that generates the oppositional stance in the challenges of new intellectual and artistic generations. These fields are 'restricted', privileged: they have a high price of entry. But his first restricted oppositional field lies in the space between domination and submission. Above all it is identified, historically, in the institutions and practices of what has been termed 'the proletarian public sphere' (Negt and Kluge 1993.)[16] Bourdieu's restricted field of the subordinated class of capitalism includes both formal working-class organizations such as trades unions and informal practices such as those that governed exchanges in less formal contexts such as working-class bars and pubs (Bourdieu 1984: 183n), equivalent in some respects to the coffee-houses of the eighteenth century bourgeois public sphere (Habermas 1989). This sphere is restricted not in terms of the price of entry (although the distinctive nomos of the field certainly does not welcome all comers equally), but of its reach: the arenas of social and cultural life in which it commands recognition and respect.

The institutions and cultural practices of the working class found expression and a degree of at least counter-cultural legitimacy within a range of discursive arenas in the heyday of industrial capitalism in various contexts. But with the demise of heavy industry, this representation has been curtailed, transformed, diminished. Even where institutional and informal cultural practices survive, the cultural capital that is recognized and honoured in them is reduced in its reach, and lacks the power of more strategically positioned forms. It no longer circulates outside these rapidly shrinking fields. In 1987 Bourdieu characterized the (western) working class as 'a well-founded historical construction' (Bourdieu 1987: 9). By the close of the century, and as his death approached, he was increasingly anguished by the undermining of these foundations by global capitalism and neoliberalism. One of Bourdieu's 'resources for a journey of hope'[17] is undermined with the fragmentation of this particular restricted field.[18] This fragmentation has left in its wake a large and growing number of discarded communities (Santos 2001) of the type represented in *The Weight of the World*, across the globe. Part of Honneth's case, drawing on this research, rests upon the argument that such constituencies have on the one hand lost out with the fragmentation of the working class and its culture and institutions, without having found the means of commanding attention among the competing dissonant voices of multiculturalism and new social movements.

But Bourdieu is not only concerned with those whose access to full participation in the discursive public sphere is impeded by domination, cultural and economic, but also with some whose access is privileged. He views with dismay the erosion of the authority of at least one sector of the dominant class under the invasive hegemony of global capitalism. People who command *symbolic capital* have the power, as we have seen, to exercise *symbolic violence*. By the same token they are in a position to challenge such violence, to *accord recognition* against the grain of the established recognition order, to challenge dominant cultural values. There are positions within social space that not only authorize, but also require intellectual cultural production. Bourdieu's later, more polemical essays addressed with increasing urgency the obligations that fall upon those who are enjoined to speak, and who do so with the authority of science, to use that authority to 'unveil' the sufferings and injustices visited upon the dominated.[19] Bourdieu identifies the critical intellectual as one of the major sources of 'opposing critical powers that are essential to genuine democracy' (Bourdieu 1998) and this was to be a recurrent theme of his later work:

> I would like writers, artists, philosophers and scientists to be able to make their voice heard directly in all the arenas of public life in which they are competent. I think that everyone would have a lot to gain if the logic of intellectual life, that of argument and refutation, were extended to public life.
>
> (Bourdieu 1998: 9)[20]

These positions of symbolic power are found in the second of Bourdieu's types of restricted field, located in arenas of social space that admit only those who are able to compete effectively within them. Bourdieu follows the classical sociological account of differentiation and the emergence of (semi)-autonomous sub-fields with the development of capitalist modernity, to argue that some of these sub-fields institutionalize rules that not only challenge but also even reverse the norms that obtain in the economic and political fields of power: the field of art (Bourdieu 1996) and the field of science (Bourdieu 2004).

The autonomy of these fields is always more or less insecure, and it is *relative*. It is always possible to unpick the mediations that link these specialized cultural productions to the economic field, whose effects are never entirely absent. But nevertheless Bourdieu depended increasingly on this second type of restricted field for his slender resources for hope. They are cosmopolitan, culturally dominant and privileged. But Bourdieu's public intellectuals are honed within them. They are fields of privilege because of their relative insulation from the fields of power (economic and political), and because of the 'distance from necessity' of their players. Bourdieu defends the autonomy of these fields. For it is the distinction that they have won within them in terms of rules that are specific to them – that may, like the rules of art, reverse those of the fields of power – that makes it possible for those so distinguished to step into the role of (critical) 'public intellectual': 'The intellectual is constituted as such by intervening in the political field *in the name of autonomy*' (Bourdieu 1996: 129).

These restricted fields are threatened by marketization. They provide a problematic resource in the task of critical transformation whose value is the more apparent as its autonomy is threatened with its transformation into a market place. He is concerned above all with his own academic discipline: sociology. He validates its claim to objectivity to the extent that it practices a rigorous methodological reflexivity (Bourdieu 2004). Engaged publicly on their authority *as* autonomous scholars in the discursive public sphere to publicize the transformative social *criticism* that is immanent in their work, rather than in the service of public and private think tanks, the task of the public intellectual may be realized.

Bourdieu shares little of Fraser's optimism with regard to the manner in which global capitalism disrupts traditional status orders because it not only fragments subaltern class communities but also simultaneously erodes the relative autonomy of the intellectual field. His is a deep Gramscian pessimism of the intellect. It is true that we glimpse a certain, almost desperate, optimism of the will in his late essays that brings him closer to Fraser, as he looks towards the renewal of trade unionism, the mobilization of artists and intellectuals in civil society, and new global movements – a collaboration in Gramsci's terms of traditional and organic intellectuals – to counter the effects of a globalized economy, a globalized corporate/American culture (Bourdieu and Wacquant) 2005). The global capitalist system has a greater degree of freedom to neglect many of the problems of social disintegration it may occasion among the peoples it discards. But the limits to this freedom are marked by the strength and desperation of the resistance of these peoples, and by counter-hegemonic movements against globalization. This freedom may be greater, nevertheless, than that accorded earlier forms of capitalism more closely linked with the nation state, and it is to this issue that we turn in the concluding section of the paper.

Social justice and the system of global capitalism

Fraser and Honneth end the introduction to their political–philosophical exchange by agreeing to disagree over a large and fundamental question concerning the nature of global capitalism:

> Should capitalism, as it exists today, be understood as a social system that differentiates an economic order that is not directly regulated by institutionalized patterns of cultural value from other social orders that are? Or should the capitalist economic order be understood rather as a consequence of a mode of cultural valuation that is bound up, from the very outset, with asymmetrical forms of recognition?
>
> (Fraser and Honneth 2003: 5)

The second alternative is that of Honneth. He posits an emergent complex recognition order that has generated legitimate expectations, and feelings of injustice that are symptoms of disorder at Lockwood's level of 'social integration' that reside in the sense that may approach outrage, that these expectations have been violated. Expressed in a multitude of ways, there is an underlying 'unitary structure of feelings of illegitimately withheld recognition' (Honneth, in Fraser and Honneth 2003: 246) embedded at his deep moral/normative level: 'Only if the idea of a human psyche structurally directed against the unreasonable demands of society is added to ... the connection between social order and subversion can one speak of the necessity of a practice of transgression' (ibid.: 243). This approach posits, in the last resort, a commonality of 'truly universal ends', to borrow a phrase whose very use by Bourdieu indicates a certain degree of convergence with Honneth when he looks forward to 'the gradual emergence of political forces, themselves also global, capable of demanding the creation of transnational bodies entrusted with controlling the dominant economic forces so as to subordinate them to truly universal ends' (Bourdieu 2003: 96).

The first alternative is that of Fraser in her positing of 'the operation of impersonal system mechanisms' of modern global capitalism (Fraser and Honneth 2003: 214). Slavoj Zizek goes further: 'Capital is effectively a global machine blindly running its course' (Zizek 1997: 45). But Zizek ties his blind machine to the multiculturalism that Fraser valorizes; he argues, invoking Frederic Jameson, that multiculturalism is simply the 'cultural logic' of global capitalism. In a similar spirit, Bourdieu refers to the differences that capitalist multiculturalism tolerates as little more than cultural theme parks: cultures cannibalized and drained of any anchorage in any distinctive way of life.

This bleak vision is one in which high levels of social disintegration and attendant social conflict and human suffering can be contained for lengthy periods of time without leading to system disintegration. Fraser rarely strikes such a bleak note. However she recognizes, in her use of the concept of system integration, a not unrelated claim: movements and values that were transgressive when they challenged key institutions and practices that secured the reproduction of the capitalist system, may be accommodated at the present conjecture with little difficulty at the system level as against the social dynamics of particular communities and even nation-states. Her main point in her exchange with Butler was that socially transgressive sexualities are no longer per se subversive when normative heterosexuality is no longer 'hardwired' to the global capitalist system. Deviations from this norm are not a threat to a modern global capitalism, however they may disrupt and transgress particular communities or sensibilities (Butler 1998; Fraser 1998. See also Mandy Merck's contribution to this collection). Global capitalism can afford extensive cultural re-wiring.[21]

Counter-hegemonic groups and movements are notoriously diverse, in their aims, political commitments and composition. Fraser's concept of *participatory party* makes a virtue of diversity, envisaging a plurality of dialogic discourses that are *in principle* non-integrated, and in contestation, one with another.

Value-pluralism, where it is given a degree of legitimacy within the dominant culture, legitimates the right of groups and individuals to present and defend their values and practices, and to make injustice claims within the public sphere. In her critique of Habermas (Fraser 1997), Fraser argues the case for viewing a layered, plural, dispersed structuring of the public sphere in a positive light. Subaltern counterpublics would function for their members first, as 'spaces of withdrawal and regroupment' and as 'arenas of identity formation'. But the withdrawal is strategic. It precedes and presages broader engagement: 'To inter-act discursively as a member of a public ... is to aspire to disseminate one's dis-course into ever-widening arenas' (ibid.: 82). It allows space for a bottom up, dialogic, participative democracy.

Fraser's resistance to Honneth's wish to include within any model of justice at least a minimalist concept of 'the good life' is because she believes that this is not a question of justice but of 'relevance to value' and as such must remain, permanently, on the dialogical table, as it were, in the deliberations of the public sphere. She honours the substantive logic of 'thick liberalism' that she shares with Honneth – the identification of fundamental social conditions for participa-tory parity – so she is therefore no mere proceduralist, since this carries impera-tives for radical social transformation, including economic justice. But she honours at the same time a more general deontological logic that is 'thin' enough' not to be mortgaged to any single understanding of what constitutes 'the good life'. Justice does not require the affirmation of any particular set of (ethical) values. Critical sociological research helps to identify impediments to participatory parity as they are embedded in social structure and process; critical political theory and critical social policy aid the analysis of alternative political and policy interventions for their ability to best redress injustices in a given con-juncture; and to critical philosophical theory falls the task of providing guide-lines for the deliberations of the public sphere. Judgement and decision-making belongs, however, within the deliberative sphere itself, at a variety of levels from the local to the national and the transnational (Fraser 1997, 2005).

Candidates for the label of a (reasonable) concept of the good life will be exposed to critical scrutiny regarding their plausibility, and this scrutiny will draw upon opinions, argument, dramatization, evidence and the views of a variety of experts and competing discourses. What is absolute, for Fraser, is the right to participate in this process of defining, discovering, advancing, criticizing and judging the way that we live, the circumstances in which we do so, and the consequences that our practices have for ourselves and for others. For Fraser, this is a collective rather than an individual project insofar as it depends on a vigorous discursive process within a variety of active, democratic communities, groups, organizations and representative bodies: she concludes, with optimism: 'I see no reason to rule out the possibility of a society in which social equality and cultural diversity coexist with participatory democracy' (Fraser 1997: 84).

Conclusion

The debate between Fraser and Honneth necessarily leaves many of the issues which it touches and provokes tantalizingly unanswered, particularly those related to the shift to a transnational frame that she has begun to address more systematically in her recent work, including her contribution to this volume.

However, they stand together against discourses that dismantle 'structure' for 'flow' in their characterizations of modern global capitalism. Capitalism has never been fixed in stone, held within immovable, unchanging structures, certainly not in Marx's account. In its moving history, there have been periods of intensive transformation, of restructuring, which may be experienced as flux, in which, as Marx famously put it: 'all that is solid melts into air' (Berman 1983). Global capitalism is experiencing perhaps the most intensive capitalist restructuring to date – one that is very much ongoing at the present time. The discourses that valorize flux, flow, constant process, flourish in this experienced 'melting', and the vertiginous exciting possibilities it promises and even to a degree delivers. For it does not only deliver the radical dislocation and misery it inflicts on so many of the world's people. But that this is a re-*structuring* is clear in, for example, the negotiations of GATS, TRIPS and other trade agreements. Once in place, the emergent structures of global capitalism may prove extremely difficult to undo, for nation-states as well as for counter-hegemonic movements.

Fraser's concept of participatory parity has strong *prima facie* plausibility as a principle of justice in addressing a broad range of social conflicts, disputes and injustice claims in this newly emerging global order. Moreover, she is in a position to draw upon a rich legacy of feminist counter-hegemonic practices of long-standing. Two movements spring to mind here. First, the one generated in the UK in the course of negotiating often difficult relationships with the left, confronting institutionalized forms of political organization with the more decentred, participatory forms that arose in the Women's Liberation Movement. *Beyond the Fragments* (Rowbotham et al. 1979) was a tremendously influential text in the history of that troubled relationship and of the formulation of a different kind of political practice. The second is encapsulated in the concept of *transversal politics* that Cockburn ascribes to Italian feminism, and that Nira Yuval-Davis has developed (Yuval-Davis 1997).[22] Cynthia Cockburn drew on this idea in her study of four groups engaged in attempts to establish connections between women 'across the divide' in zones of bitter conflict: Northern Ireland, Israel and Palestine, and Bosnia-Hercegovina (Cockburn 1998).

The fabric of the interactive, inter-relational networks in such ventures is fragile, easily broken, and with no short route to radical social transformation on a broader scale. However, one interesting aspect is that it has built on the practice of creating bridges *across lines of inequality* between members of the different communities who engage in these links. Participatory parity is a principle that aims in the longer term to eliminate such inequality as impediments to its achievement. Meanwhile it has to work with and against them. Dependency, as she has also recognized (Fraser and Gordon, in Fraser 1997), is ubiquitous in social relations, endemic in human life. Not all inequalities can be entirely offset through democratic participatory politics. In any case, in the short to medium term we face the urgent requirement to develop practices that ensure equal moral respect across difference, and non-damaging means of handling dependency (Sennett 2004). Democratic communication, representation, dialogue, across lines of inequality and dependency, as Fraser fully recognizes, cannot wait.

Notes

1 In August 2005, the journal *Feminist Theory* included a special feature entitled '(Re) Claiming the social'.

2 In Andrew Sayer's critical realist perspective, we find a full acknowledgement of the importance of the textual/cultural is combined with a robust refusal of any positioning of 'the social' as exclusively textual (Sayer 2000).

3 One example must suffice. Seyla Benhabib (1995) identified 'strong' and 'weak' versions of postmodernism's theses in her critical engagement with Judith Butler. Fraser's contribution to the debate identified an intermediate 'medium strength' variant in order to avoid losing the value-pluralism and 'difference' of postmodernism without compromising those theoretical and political commitments that require defensible forms of universalism (Fraser 1995).

4 Too intimately, in Margaret Archer's critical realist critique of Bourdieu. She accuses him of 'central conflationism' of structure and social process (Archer 1983, 1993).

5 In a critique of Fraser, Sylvia Walby valorizes 'reference groups' over 'communities' (Walby 2001)

6 Fraser falls foul, he argues, of what Calhoun terms 'normative idealism': the airbrushing out of exclusionary, racist, violent 'recognition struggles' (Calhoun 1995, cited in Fraser and Honneth 2003: 120 *passim*). Yet Fraser, in her critique of Habermas, wrote: 'Let me not be misunderstood. I do not mean to suggest that subaltern counterpublics are always necessarily virtuous; some of them, alas, are explicitly antidemocratic and antiegalitarian' (Fraser 1997: 82).

7 Dual systems theory emerged with the 'psychoanalytic turn' in Marxist feminism in the 1970s. It posited the existence of two parallel, interconnected systems of domination, consisting of the social relations of production, and the sex/gender system. For a brief discussion, see the Introduction to Part IV on psychoanalysis and feminism in Lovell (1990: 187–195).

8 It is true that Young instances Bourdieu as exemplary in refusing to separate them, either substantively or analytically (Young 1997: 154).

9 Honneth pointed out in an earlier article (Honneth 1986), that Bourdieu proffers a more gently sloping relationship of domination across his 'map', between positions closer to 'the economic' and those closer to 'the cultural': 'the economic' has relative primacy, 'the cultural, only relative autonomy. Bourdieu's dominant regions of social space cross the whole range, but his 'cultural dominants' are 'dominated dominants'. In his discussions with Loic Wacquant that touch upon his relationship with British cultural studies, he explains that he was concerned 'to bend the stick a little' (Bourdieu and Wacquant 1992). But for Honneth this comes perilously close to quasi-Marxist reductionism.

10 Both Fraser and Honneth would offer very different analyses and political responses to those of Sarkozy, the then French Minister of the Interior. Yet even Sarkozy responds in terms of a double analysis that invokes both 'disrespect'– to be sure, not of the disrespect *suffered* (not least at the hands of Sarkozy in the terms in which he responded to the explosive events in cities across France in the autumn of 2005, but rather the disrespect *shown to others* by the angry demonstrators), and the need for interventions aimed at more sustained economic renewal. A similar disjunction underpins Tony Blair's 'respect agenda'. The work of Richard Sennett (2004) offers a more nuanced and subtle sociological account of 'respect'.

11 For an account by Bourdieu of this concept, see Bourdieu (1990, chapter 3).

12 For a useful discussion of the various forms that 'difference' took within feminism, see Barrett (1987).

13 This card is sometimes played within feminism. In an interview (*Guardian*, G2, 4 April 2006: 24–25) Phyllis Chesler argues that 'feminism has failed Muslim women by colluding in their oppression'.

14 For an example of this response in France, see Armengaud and Ghaïss (1993). For a useful introduction to materialist feminism, see Leonard and Adkins (1996).
15 Typically, those feminists in the UK who have been influenced by his work have drawn on his conceptual framework rather than on what he writes specifically on women and gender, see for example Adkins and Skeggs (2004).
16 Bourdieu does not use this Habermasian term, and his accounts of the working-class habitus cuts across public and domestic life.
17 Raymond Williams uses this phrase to title the concluding chapter of his book *Towards 2000* (Williams 1983).
18 Bourdieu's pessimism with respect to working-class culture has been resisted among those schooled in the tradition of British cultural studies and labour history, with its practice of seeking out oppositional values in working-class popular culture. But Bourdieu has rejected what he sees as an over-optimistic search for markers of resistance in popular forms, and especially where these are commercial. Bourdieu has been criticized by Bridget Fowler, among others, for this stance: she argues that he 'regards the linguistic "market" for popular speech as inherently weak and relegated to an unofficial existence, cut off from the places where decisions are made' (Fowler 2003: 476).
19 But Spivak's warning should be noted: 'the substantive concern for the politics of the oppressed ... can hide a privileging of the intellectual' (Spivak 1988: 292).
20 Bourdieu prefaces the English edition of a second set of occasional essays (2003), with 'A letter to the American reader'. In this he expresses the hope that American scholars, stepping into the role of 'public intellectuals', might 'strengthen the critique of and resistance to the neoliberal dogma by showing that this critique can strike at, and radiate from, its very nerve center and global hub' (2003: 10).
   This was written before the events of 9/11, but it is interesting to note that the membership of the American Sociological Association, alone among professional associations in the US, on the eve of the Iraq war in 2003, passed a resolution opposing it by a two-thirds majority. The ASA conference in 2004 was dominated by a debate on public sociology.
21 'Gay men in full-time jobs earn on average £34,000 a year, compared with the national average for men of £28,800. Lesbians earn £6,000 more than the national average for women ... according to the survey of readers of Diva and Gay Times by the marketing consultancy OUT Now' (*Guardian*, Monday 23 January 2006: 7). Of course these readers are hardly representative of the lesbian and gay population as a whole.
22 Cockburn draws on William Connolly's concept of 'agonistic democracy' (Connolly 1991) which 'breaks with the comfortable and dangerous illusion of "community" and the politics of communitarianism, that assumes consensus is (must be) possible. Instead it settles for the difficult reality of unavoidable, unending, careful, respectful struggle' (Cockburn 1998: 216).

References

Adkins, L. and Skeggs, B. (2004) *Feminism After Bourdieu*, Oxford: Blackwell.
Archer, M. (1983) 'Process without system: Bernstein and Bourdieu', *European Journal of Sociology*, xxiv, I: 196–221.
—— (1993) 'Bourdieu's theory of cultural reproduction: French or universal?', *French Cultural Studies*, iv: 225–240.
Armengaud, F. and Ghaïss, J. (1993) 'Pierre Bourdieu: Grand Temoin?', *Nouvelles Questions Féministes*, 14, 3: 83–88. Abridged English translation, with Christine Delphy: 'Liberty, equality ... but most of all fraternity', *Trouble and Strife*, 31, summer 1995.

Barrett, M. (1987) 'The concept of difference', *Feminist Review*, 26: 49–62.

Benhabib, S. (1995) 'Feminism and postmodernism', in S. Benhabib, J. Butler, D. Cornell and N. Fraser (eds) *Feminist Contentions*, New York and London: Routledge.

Berman, M. (1983) *All that is Solid Melts into Air: the Experience of Modernity*, London: Verso.

Bourdieu, P. (1984) *Distinction*, trans. R. Nice, London: Routledge.

—— (1987) 'What makes a social class? On the theoretical and practical existence of groups', *Berkeley Journal of Sociology*, 32: 1–17.

—— (1990) *The Logic of Practice*, trans. R. Nice, Cambridge: Polity.

—— (1996) *The Rules of Art*, Cambridge: Polity Press.

—— (1998) *Acts of Resistance*, trans. R. Nice, Cambridge: Polity.

—— (2000) *Pascalian Meditations*, trans. R. Nice, Cambridge: Polity.

—— (2001) *Masculine Domination*, trans. R. Nice, Cambridge: Polity.

—— (2003) *Firing Back*, trans. L. Wacquant, London and New York: Verso.

—— (2004) *Science of Science and Reflexivity*, trans. R. Nice, Cambridge: Polity.

Bourdieu, P. and Wacquant, L.J.D. (1992) *An Invitation to Reflexive Sociology*, Cambridge: Polity.

—— (2005) 'The cunning of imperial reason', in L.J.D. Waquant (ed.) *Pierre Bourdieu and Democratic Politics*, Cambridge: Polity.

Bourdieu, P. *et al.* (1999) *The Weight of the World*, trans. P.P. Ferguson, S. Emanuel, J. Johnson and S. Waryn, Cambridge: Polity.

Boyne, R. (2002) 'Bourdieu: from class to culture', *Theory, Culture and Society*, 19, 3: 117–128.

Butler, J. (1998) 'Merely cultural', *New Left Review*, 227: 33–44.

Calhoun, C. (1995) 'The politics of identity and recognition' in H. Calhoun, *Critical Social Theory*, Oxford: Blackwells.

Chigateri, S. (2004) *Uncovering Injustice: Towards a Dalit Feminist Politics in Bangalore*. Unpublished doctoral thesis, Warwick University.

Cockburn, C. (1998) *The Space Between Us: Negotiating Gender and National Identity in Conflict*, London: Zed.

Connolly, W. (1991) *Identity/Difference: Democratic Negotiations of Political Paradox*, Ithaca and London: Cornell University Press.

Felski, R. (1989) *Beyond Feminist Aesthetics*, London: Hutchinson.

Fowler, B. (2003) 'Reading Pierre Bourdieu's *Masculine Domination*: Notes towards an intersectional analysis of gender, culture and class', *Cultural Studies*, 17, 3/4: 468–494.

Fraser, N. (1989) *Unruly Practices*, New York and London: Routledge.

—— (1995) 'Pragmatism, feminism and the linguistic turn', in Benhabib *et al.*, *Feminist Contentions*, New York and London: Routledge.

—— (1997) *Justice Interruptus: Critical Reflections on the 'Postsocialist' Condition*, New York and London: Routledge.

—— (1998) 'Heterosexism, misrecognition and capitalism', *New Left Review*, 228: 140–149.

—— (2005) 'Reframing justice in a globalizing world', *New Left Review*, 36: 69–66.

Fraser, N. and Honneth, A. (2003) *Redistribution or Recognition? A Political-Philosophical Exchange*, London: Verso.

Habermas, J. (1989) *The Structural Transformation of the Public Sphere*, trans. T. Burger with F. Lawrence, Cambridge: MIT Press.

Honneth, A. (1986) 'The fragmented world of symbolic forms: reflections on Pierre Bourdieu's sociology of culture', *Theory, Culture and Society*, 3: 55–67.

Leonard, D. and Adkins, L. (eds) (1996) *Sex in Question: French Materialist Feminism*, London: Taylor and Francis.

Lockwood, D. (1964) 'Social integration and system integration', in G.K. Zollschan and H.W. Hirsch (eds) *Explorations in Social Change*, Boston: Houghton Mifflin.

Lovell, T. (1990) *British Feminist Thought*, Oxford: Blackwell.

—— (2004) 'Bourdieu, class and gender: "the return of the living dead"?', in L. Adkins and B. Skeggs (eds) *Feminism after Bourdieu*, Oxford: Blackwell.

McRobbie, A. (2002) 'A mixed bag of misfortunes? Bourdieu's *The Weight of the World*', *Theory, Culture and Society*, 19, 3: 129–138.

Negt, O. and Kluge, A. (1993) *Public Sphere and Experience*, trans. P. Labanyi *et al.*, Minneapolis: University of Minnesota Press.

Rowbotham, S., Segal, L. and Wainright, H. (1979) *Beyond the Fragments*, Newcastle Socialist Centre and Islington Community Press.

Santos, B. de S. (2001) '*Nuestra America*: reinventing a subaltern paradigm of recognition and redistribution', in *Theory, Culture and Society*, 18, 2–3: 185–217.

Sayer, A. (2000) *Realism and Social Science*, London: Sage.

Schinkel, W. (2004) 'Pierre Bourdieu's political turn?' *Theory, Culture and Society*, 20, 6: 69–93.

Sennett, R. (2004) *Respect*, London: Allen Lane.

Spivak, G.C. (1988) 'Can the subaltern speak?', in C. Nelson and L. Grossberg (eds) *Marxism and the Interpretation of Culture*, London: Macmillan.

Vitellone, N. (2004) 'Habitus and social suffering: culture, addiction and the syringe', in L. Adkins and B. Skeggs (eds) *Feminism After Bourdieu*, Oxford: Blackwell.

Wacquant, L. (ed.) (2005) *Pierre Bourdieu and Democratic Politics*, Cambridge: Polity.

Walby, S. (2001) 'From community to coalition: the politics of recognition as the handmaiden of the politics of equality in an era of globalization', *Theory, Culture and Society*, 18, 2–3: 113–135.

Williams, R. (1977) *Marxism and Literature*, Oxford: Oxford University Press.

—— (1983) *Towards 2000*, London: Chatto and Windus.

Young, I.M. (1997) 'Unruly categories: a critique of Nancy Fraser's dual systems theory', *New Left Review*, 222: 147–160.

Yuval Davis, N. (1997) *Gender and Nation*, London, Thousand Oaks, New Delhi: Sage.

Zizek, S. (1997) 'Multiculturalism, or the cultural logic of multinational capitalism', *New Left Review*, 225: 28–51.

6 Class, moral worth and recognition

Andrew Sayer

Introduction

Class, unlike, say, ethnicity, is not a social form or identity demanding recognition as legitimate (Coole 1986; Fraser 1999). Low income people are not disadvantaged primarily because others fail to value their identity and misrecognize and undervalue their cultural goods, or indeed because they are stigmatized, though all these things make their situation worse; rather they are disadvantaged primarily because they lack the means to live in ways which they as well as others value. Certainly, some may be consigned to the working class because of racism or other identity-sensitive forms of behaviour, but these are not necessary conditions of being working class. The lottery of the market and of birth and the intergenerational transmission of capitals can produce (and have widely produced) class inequalities even in the absence of these forms of discrimination.

Despite the fact that people inherit rather than deserve their natal class, they may feel class pride or shame and care a great deal about how they are positioned with respect to class and how others treat them. They are likely to be concerned about class in terms of recognition of their worth, and want to be respected or respectable. But recognition and valuation are in part conditional on what people do, how they behave and live, so 'class concern' is also about having access to the practices and ways of living that are valued, and class of course renders this access highly unequal. The inequalities in resources and opportunities themselves have little or nothing to do with the moral worth or merit of individuals but they have a major impact on the possibility of achieving valued ways of life that bring recognition and self-respect.

In this article I want to argue that we will better understand the implications of class if we probe lay normative responses to it, particularly as regards how people value themselves and others. If we are to understand the significance of class we need to take lay normativity, especially morality, much more seriously than sociology has tended to do; without this we are likely to produce bland, alienated accounts which fail to make sense of why class is a matter of concern and embarrassment to people, or as Savage *et al.* put it: 'a loaded moral signifier' (Savage *et al.* 2001; see also Lawler 2000; Reay 1998; Skeggs 1997, 2004; Sayer 2002). Sentiments such as pride, shame, envy, resentment, compassion and contempt are not just forms of 'affect' but are evaluative judgements of how people are being treated as regards what they value, that is things they consider to affect their well-being. They are forms of emotional reason. Such sentiments may vary in their distribution across the social field, but they can also be partly indifferent to social divisions, for they are responsive to – and discriminate among – standards, situations and behaviours which vary partly independently of class and other divisions. I shall argue that we cannot grasp the moral significance of class unless we take notice of this dual character of lay morality. We also need to deepen the analysis of relations between recognition and economic distribution by distinguishing between conditional and unconditional recognition and the different kinds of goods which people value, to take account of how their normative rationales differ. In all these matters, I believe that sociology can benefit from drawing upon certain concepts and analyses from moral philosophy.[1]

I begin with the neglect of lay normativity and especially lay morality in contemporary social science, and the consequent difficulty it has in understanding why social life is a matter of *concern* to people. Next I illustrate the dual differentiated and universalizing character of lay moral valuations by reference to the paradoxical example of 'moral boundary drawing'. I then comment on the moral sentiment of shame, this being a powerful element of the experience of class, and one that again depends on moral and other norms being partly shared across classes. In the final section I examine the relations between recognition and economic distribution with respect to class, in order to illuminate how and why class is associated with shame and pride, and then conclude.

Lay normativity and morality

With some partial exceptions[2], modern social scientists are trained to bracket out normative matters and adopt an exclusively positive (descriptive and explanatory)[3] approach to the world, rather than evaluating what is good or bad about it. This has had two unfortunate effects; first, that unless they also happen to have had some training in political and moral philosophy, social scientists lack expertise in normative thinking; and second, that in their positive studies, they often overlook the normative character of everyday experience, or at least fail to take it seriously as anything more than 'affect', or internalization of 'norms' as conventions regarding behaviour, or an expression of 'values', understood as subjective matters having no rational basis. Hence the scholastic fallacy goes beyond the tendency, identified by Bourdieu, for academics to project their discursive, contemplative orientation to the world onto those they study (Bourdieu 2000): it involves a failure to grasp not only the predominantly practical character of everyday life but its *normative* character. Actions are mainly explained externally, in the third person, as products of social position and influences, discourses, cultural norms or indeed habitus. But in their own lives, people, including off-duty sociologists, are *concerned* about what they do and what happens to them and *justify* their actions rather than explain them externally. Even sociologists do not explain their interventions in debates or committees by reducing them to functions of their position within the social field but according to what they think is the best thing to do or argue. Of course our justifications are indeed influenced by our social position and by wider discourses, but reflexivity is needed not only to examine such influences, but also to examine what they do *not* explain, that is how everyday situations often require us to make decisions and *justify* what we do, for the appropriate behaviour is not simply prescribed by external forces or cultural scripts.[4]

We are normative beings, in the sense that we are concerned about the world and the well-being of what we value in it, including ourselves. The most important questions people tend to face in their everyday lives are normative ones of how to act, what to do for the best, what is good or bad about what is happening, including how others are treating them. The presence of this concern may be evident in fleeting encounters and conversations, in feelings about how things are going, as well as in momentous decisions such as whether to have children, change job, or what to do about a relationship which has gone bad. These are things which people *care* about deeply. If we ignore this lay normativity, or reduce it to an effect of discourse or socialization, we produce an anodyne and alienated account of subjectivity which renders our evident concern about what we do and what happens to us incomprehensible.

We derive our concerns from culture but in relation to our capacity as needy beings for being encultured. As Kathryn Dean argues, following Arendt, our development as social actors from a state of radical incompleteness and indeterminacy as newborns depends on 'cultural parenting' which develops in us concerns (Dean 2003). But of course not just any object can be encultured or be concerned about anything.[5] To be capable of enculturation, and of having concerns and commitments, of worrying about what to do and what would be for the best, we must be particular kinds of being. We are concerned about things because we feel or believe them to have implications for our welfare or that of others that we care about. For this to be possible we must be the kind of beings which are capable of flourishing or suffering and of registering (albeit fallibly) how we are faring (Archer 2000; Nussbaum 2000, 2001). As Adam Smith argued, we are vulnerable, deeply social beings who are not only physically and economically dependent on others but psychologically dependent on them and in need of their recognition (Smith 1759). A purely one-sided explanation of this need that invokes just social relations or culture or discourse is itself radically incomplete.

One could try to use the category of 'affect' to identify concerns, but there is a danger that this may affirm an opposition of reason and emotion, and a disengagement of emotion from what happens to people, so that it becomes 'merely subjective' and lacking any rational content, and it becomes unclear how concerns can be *about* anything. It is perhaps significant that when we speak of 'affect*ations*' and 'affect*ing*' a certain manner, we mean precisely to draw attention to their simulated – or rather dissimulated and false – character. Rather I suggest that we need a more cognitive view of emotion as a form of evaluative judgement of matters affecting or believed to affect our well-being (Nussbaum 2001; see also Archer 2000; Barbalet, 2001; Helm 2001).[6] Emotions may be expressive but they are also about what we believe to be happening regarding things which we care about. Of course they are fallible judgements, but then so too are the judgements of unemotional kinds of reason. Their fallibility derives from the fact that they are about something which can exist or occur independently of them, and hence about which they can be mistaken. They are both subjective (a predicate of subjects) and (fallibly) objective. When someone says that they 'have good reason to be angry', they imply that someone has done something that objectively harms them, such as injuring them or slandering them. Likewise, feelings associated with class such as envy, resentment, compassion, contempt, shame, pride, deference and condescension are *evaluative* responses to particular properties of class inequalities and relations. They are influenced but not predetermined by position within the social field. Different cultures may give us different things to value, for example, different things to feel proud or ashamed of; this is demonstrated by Michèle Lamont's comparative studies of French and US middle- and working-class men with regard to their social positions (Lamont 1992, 2000). Nevertheless the capacity to feel pride and shame appears to be universal.[7]

Much of our normative orientation to the world is at the level of dispositions and emotions, indeed not only aesthetic but ethical dispositions can be part of the habitus, acquired through practice as intelligent dispositions which enable us often to react appropriately to situations instantly, without reflection (Sayer 2005).[8] In order to understand our normative orientation to the world we therefore need to avoid treating fact and value, reason and emotion, as opposed, and acknowledge that while emotions and values are fallible they are not irrational or 'merely subjective', but are often perceptive and reasonable judgements about situations and processes.

While normativity embraces aesthetics and functional valuation of things, for example regarding the efficiency of an organization, it is the moral dimension of lay normativity that I want to emphasize. By this I mean simply matters of how people should treat others and be treated by them, which of course is crucial for their subjective and objective well-being. It includes but goes beyond matters of justice and fairness, to relations of recognition, care and friendship, and it implies a conception[9] of the good life. Lay morality may be formalized in norms but it is more effective in influencing behaviour in the form of learned dispositions and moral sentiments, which are acquired through ongoing social interaction, as explored by Adam Smith in *The Theory of Moral Sentiments* (Smith 1759). It is important to note that to refer to such matters as moral is not necessarily to express approval of them; from a normative point of view, researchers may consider some norms and practices to be immoral that actors consider moral.

Insofar as sociologists have been interested in lay normativity, they have emphasized its social differentiation, that is how it how it is both sensitive to and influenced by social position. There is plenty of evidence of this for things like voting behaviour and taste – for example, in Bourdieu's analysis of aesthetic judgements and their relation to actors' habitus and position within the social field (Bourdieu 1984).[10] But in the case of morality I wish to argue that we cannot understand it unless we recognize that it also spills out beyond such divisions and sometimes ignores them. It is in virtue of this that moral sentiments can inform resistance as well as conformity to class and the normative valuations which commonly accompany it. Like Smith, I wish to argue that *moral* judgements are likely to be *less* sensitive to the social position of the valuer and the valued than is the case for aesthetic judgements (Smith 1759, vol. 2: 200). As we shall see, this has crucial implications for the experience of class that are likely to be missed if we just relate such matters to social position. The first reason why we might expect morality to be less socially variable than aesthetics is that morality is primarily about relations to others, about how people should treat one another in ways conducive to well-being. How you dress or whether you like tattoos or wallpaper make much less difference to the well-being of others than how you treat them – whether you are honest or deceitful, generous or selfish, respectful or contemptuous.[11] Thus it is therefore easier to be pluralist about aesthetics than about moral matters.

Second, moral understandings underpin all kinds of social interaction, both between members of different groups and among members of the same group. The informal moral education that we gain in early life teaches us that we can be well or badly treated by members of our own group, for example by our siblings, and sometimes that even members of stigmatized other groups may behave in ways we consider to be moral, contradicting negative stereotypes of them. The qualities we consider to be good and bad regarding behaviour do not correspond neatly with social divisions. The moral dispositions and sentiments that we develop have a generalizing or universalizing character. This derives not from Kantian deductions but, as Smith argued, from the ongoing mutual and self-monitoring that occurs in everyday interactions with others, imagining what our behaviour implies for others and how it will be viewed by others, and generalizing from one kind of moral experience to other situations which seem similar. In monitoring our own conduct according to its effects and the responses of others in different social situations we develop a complex set of ethical (and sometimes unethical) dispositions, partly subconsciously and partly through reflection and repeated practice. Of course, moral beliefs may sometimes endorse inequalities and relations of deference and condescension, but they also embody notions of fairness and conceptions of the good which can prompt resistance to domination. Moral systems usually have internal inconsistencies which can be exploited, for example by applying a norm of fairness which is common in one kind of practice to another where it is lacking. To imagine that morality was *never* indifferent to social divisions would be to imply that people only ever act with 'double standards', never consistently. Clearly they do sometimes use double standards, often in ways which tend to reproduce social inequalities, as is the case with gender, but some degree of consistency is intrinsic to morality insofar as it refers to people with similar capacities for flourishing and suffering, and often lay criticisms of inequalities appeal to these.[12]

I shall argue that although the fact that morality is sometimes indifferent to social distinctions may simply seem less interesting from a sociological point of view, it actually helps to explain the significance of such distinctions; that is why they are a matter of moral concern. The imagined or real challenge – 'think you're better than us, do you?' – both highlights and attacks double standards. I now want to discuss two examples of the moral experience of class which illustrate this dual quality.

Moral boundary drawing

One of the ways in which lay morality has been registered in recent sociology has been in relation to 'moral boundary drawing'. This term denotes the way in which social groups often distinguish themselves from others in terms of moral differences, claiming for themselves certain virtues which others are held to lack: we are down-to-earth, they are pretentious; we are cosmopolitan, they are parochial; we are hard-working, they are lazy; and so on (Lamont 1992, 2000; Southerton 2002). It is particularly strong in groups that are anxious about their position in terms of both how they are regarded from above and the risk of falling into the groups they despise and fear below them. It is evident in extreme form in the 'Beltway' community in Chicago studied by Maria Kefalas (Kefalas 2003). This consisted of white upper-working class and lower middle class residents who regarded themselves as honest, self-disciplined, self-reliant, hard-working people, taking pride in their houses, gardens and community. They saw and attempted to construct themselves in opposition to those poorer white and black residents of the inner city who they saw as feckless, ill-disciplined, immoral and involved in gangs and drug culture. On the face of it, this fits comfortably with sociology's interest in social differentiation, and might be taken to illustrate the way in which moral dispositions and norms vary according to social position.

However, first it is important to note that while the possession of the claimed virtues is held to be localized, the valued norms themselves are assumed to be *universally* applicable.[13] The working class do not say down-to-earthness is good only for their own class, the middle classes do not say cosmopolitanism is only a virtue in the middle classes. They claim that these things are good for everyone, only that they have them while their others unfortunately lack them. If the values were not believed to be universally applicable, the others could hardly be disparaged for allegedly failing to live up to them. Second, in virtue of this assumed universalism, moral boundary drawing is *open to falsification*. This was dramatically illustrated in the Beltway case, when two teenage girls were murdered. The trauma of this event for the community was greatly compounded by the discovery that their killers were not, as its members instantly assumed, black gang members from the inner city, but two white teenage boys from Beltway itself. One was the son of a police officer, the other the son of a fire fighter – archetypal respectable working-class occupations – and both were members of a local, Beltway gang. As Kefalas records, the residents went to considerable lengths to resist this threat to their identity, but the origin of the murderers was undeniable.

Shame

Shame is a particularly powerful emotion and one that is often associated with class (Skeggs 1997). While it is deeply social in that it is a response to the imagined or actual views of others, it is also a particularly private, reflexive emotion, in that it primarily involves an evaluation of the self by the self.[14] It is often regarded in sociology as an emotion which tends to produce conformity and social order (Barbalet 2001; Scheff 1990). Shame is evoked by failure of an individual or group to live according to their values or commitments, especially ones concerning their relation to others and goods which others also value. It is commonly a response to the real or imagined contempt, derision or avoidance of real or imagined others, particularly those whose values are respected (Williams 1993). To act in a shameful (or contemptible) way is to invite such contempt, including self-contempt. It may be prompted by inaction as well as action, by lack as well as wrongdoing. Particularly where it derives from lack rather than specific acts, shame may be a largely unarticulated feeling existing below the threshold of awareness – one that is difficult 'to get in touch with' – yet still capable of blighting one's life.

Like all emotions, shame is *about* something: it assumes referents in terms of failings, actual or imagined. Also, like other emotions, it is a fallible response in the sense that it can be unwarranted or mistaken.[15] The person who through no fault of their own has a despised body shape or who cannot afford fashionable clothing, has done nothing shameful, but might still feel shame. Equally, the complementary feeling of contempt may be unwarranted, if it is unrelated to any shameful or contemptible behaviour for which the despised can reasonably be held responsible. This is the case with class contempt.[16]

Shame is in some ways the opposite of self-respect and pride, but they are also related. To experience shame is to feel inadequate, lacking in worth, and perhaps lacking in dignity and integrity. Self-respect derives from a feeling that one is living a worthwhile life and a confidence in one's ability to do what one considers worthwhile. Thus, the chief sources of self-respect among the American working-class men interviewed by Lamont derived from their self-discipline, their ability to work hard, provide for and protect their families and maintain their values in an insecure environment (Lamont 2000). Although deeply private, self-respect is also an inescapably social emotion: it is impossible for us to maintain the conviction that how we live and what we do is worthwhile if there are no others who think so (Rawls 1971: 440–441).

It is therefore clear that, as the psychologist Sylvan Tomkins argued, the negative feeling of shame is dependent on a positive valuation of the behaviours, ideals or principles in question (Sedgwick and Frank 1995: 136; see also Nussbaum 2001: 196, and Probyn 2004). It is only if we have certain expectations of ourselves and our society that we can be shamed. This central feature of shame is commonly overlooked by sociological accounts whose disciplinary inclination to emphasize external social influence leads them to treat shame as merely the product of external disapproval (e.g. Scheff 1990). To fail to act or live in a way which one does not care about need not provoke shame. To be treated with contempt by others for whose values one has no respect might induce sadness and anger but it does not induce shame. The worst kind of disrespect, the kind that is most likely to make one feel shame, is that which comes from those whose values and judgements one most respects. Hence, the stronger the commonality of values, the greater the possibilities for shaming. Class inequalities mean that the 'social bases of respect' in terms of access to valued ways of living are unequally distributed, and therefore that shame is likely to be endemic to the experience of class. If there were not at least partial cross-class agreement on the valuation of ways of life and behaviour, there would be little reason for class-related shame, or concern about respectability.

The shame response is an important mechanism in the production of social order, indeed it is hard to imagine how there could be much social order without it, for through it people internalize expectations, norms and ideals, and discipline and punish themselves. The capacity for shame is one of the mechanisms by which people are ensnared by cultural discourses and norms, in all their diversity,[17] although the metaphor of being ensnared is also too passive, for the need for recognition, whose pursuit always carries the risk of failing and being shamed, drives us to seek out ways of acting virtuously from among the many possibilities. All this is not to deny the common presence of power in social settings involving shame, but on their own, concepts of power, whether in capillary or arterial form, cannot explain the internalized normative force and selectivity of shame responses (Foucault 1977). In this context, we might note that although not directly acknowledged by Bourdieu, a capacity for shame is a necessary but rarely acknowledged condition for symbolic domination, indeed the latter is scarcely intelligible independently of this emotion.

However, shame is not merely an emotion that produces social conformity, for sometimes it may promote *resistance*. Those who are fervently anti-racist, for example, may speak out against racism in situations where doing so might invite contempt. If we had no normative commitments, then it is hard to see why we would ever want to resist and how we would ever be shamed, because we would simply 'go with the flow', accepting whatever the pressures of the moment required. However, the anti-racist who keeps silent when others make racist remarks is likely to feel shame for conforming instead of resisting. Shame can therefore produce either conformity or resistance, but we cannot make sense of this if we reduce it to no more than a product of fear of external disapproval.

When faced with conditions which are shaming because they give people little alternative but to live in ways they do not consider acceptable, there is always a temptation to reconsider the valuations giving rise to the shame, devaluing what others value, and valuing what others despise. To the extent that the working class refuse what they are refused, as Bourdieu put it, they avoid the shame that accompanies lack, indeed this may be a motive for their refusal, though of course this involves refusing what may be valuable, and hence increasing their others' disdain for them (Bourdieu 1984). By contrast, the desire to be respectable and recognized as such is a shame response dependent on some degree of positive feeling towards what is lacked (Skeggs 1997).

Shame in response to inequalities is likely to be the stronger where actors have individualistic explanations of inequalities and where there are hegemonic norms rather than disputed ones. Thus, the more that working-class parents are ambitious for their children and the more they accept dominant values regarding education, the more vulnerable they become to shame if the school system rejects them.[18] The black working-class youths studied by Jay Macleod who believed in 'the American dream' of individual responsibility for one's own fortune were more vulnerable to shame than their white counterparts who rejected it (Macleod 1995). Similarly, the French working men studied by Lamont were less likely to feel shame than their US counterparts because they had a more structural and politicized understanding of class (Lamont 2000).

Recognition and distribution, internal and external goods

If we interpret recognition broadly as being about recognizing someone's moral worth as a person, rather than as a person of a particular identity, as has recently been common in discussions about the politics of recognition, then we can identify certain relations between recognition and distribution. First, in order to justify any particular moral-political stance on economic distribution, we have ultimately to appeal to matters of recognition; in the case of an egalitarian politics of distribution, a recognition of all as of equal moral worth, equally needy, equally deserving (with appropriate adjustments for unavoidable and benign forms of difference) (Honneth 1995). But there is also a relation in the opposite direction, from recognition to distribution, for recognition is a matter of deeds as well as words. If I were Prime Minister and told voters that my government viewed everyone as of equal worth, but then presided over a distribution of basic resources to those same people that was significantly unequal, they would be justified in saying that my fine words were contradicted by my deeds (Fraser 1999; Yar 2001). In this way, recognition and distribution can be mutually supportive or capable of contradicting one another.

In practice, economic distribution may bear little or no relation to moral worth or other forms of merit, although the rich may try to claim that they deserve their wealth, thus implying that unequal economic distribution follows proper recognition of unequal worth. A critic might reply that being wealthy does not indicate that one is a better person, and reject the assumption that economic worth is a measure of moral worth, i.e. that economic distribution is a measure of the recognition one deserves. Such an objection is ambiguous for it could be construed either as claiming that equal worth does not require confirmation by equal distribution of income or wealth, or that it does indeed deserve and require just that. New Labour would presumably deny that economic inequalities reflected different judgements of the moral worth of people, and argue (a) that inequalities are needed to give the price incentives allegedly required by a dynamic economy, and (b) that success should be rewarded. Interestingly, Hayek, the leading neoliberal theorist, argued that market outcomes were as much a product of luck (for example, due to differences in scarcity) as the merits of market actors (Hayek 1960). (In fact he worried about whether young people should be told this, lest it de-motivated them!). So instead of appealing, implausibly, to the alleged meritocratic character of the capitalist social order, one could say, like Hayek, that economic distribution is largely a matter of luck, for which no-one is responsible.[19]

This acknowledgement of moral luck is absent in a common false assumption that lies behind many lay reactions to class, namely 'the belief in a just world' (Lerner 1980). This is a belief in the 'moral well-orderedness' of the world, so that good intentions straightforwardly produce good actions with good effects, which in turn proportionately reward the actor, 'giving them their due'. Hence, the extent to which individuals' lives go well or badly is believed to be a simple reflection of their virtues and vices. It refuses to acknowledge the contingency and moral luck which disrupt such relations arbitrarily. Many things happen to us – good or bad – which we do not deserve, and they can not only influence specific outcomes of our actions but shape the kind of people we become: they happen regardless, driven by forces which have nothing to do with justice or human well-being (Nussbaum 1986; Smith 1759). While philosophers tend to portray these as random contingencies impacting on individuals and coming from nowhere in particular, they also include the largely unintended but systematic effects of major social structures such as those of capitalism and patriarchy. Under capitalism inequalities are not merely effects of trans-historical moral luck, or indeed of the lottery of the market, but of legally enforced unequal property rights. In other words, it is possible to identify structural features of society which add to the lack of moral well-orderedness of the world, and do so not merely randomly but systematically and recurrently, so that the goods and bads tend to fall repeatedly on the same people, creating continuities in the reproduction of class and geographical inequalities.

The world always seems fairer to the lucky, but even the unlucky may prefer to avoid the pain of resentment by being generous and saying things like: 'if they've earned it, they deserve it' about the rich (passing over the ambiguity of 'earned', which can mean either 'worked for and deserved something', or simply 'received payment'). Ironically, the belief in a just world motivates actors both to be moral and to blame the unfortunate and disregard injustice, by attributing disadvantage to personal failure. Thus, welfare benefits for the unemployed are unpopular with many US citizens because they believe in the particular version of the idea of a just world embodied in 'the American dream' (Gilens 1999; see also Kefalas 2003; Lamont 2000; Macleod 1995).

We can take the analysis of class and recognition further by using two distinctions. Charles Taylor distinguishes between two kinds of recognition: unconditional, where it is given to people by virtue of their humanity, equal worth, equal neediness, or more concretely by virtue of their standing as citizens; and conditional, where it is dependent on their behaviour, character and achievements. Conditional recognition might be reflected in expressions of approval or status, envy or prestige, or in terms of payments of money (Taylor 1992). Alasdair MacIntyre calls these 'external goods' (MacIntyre 1981). These are distinguished from 'internal goods', which are the satisfactions, achievements and skills that might be gained through involvement in a 'practice', be it a kind of work or sport or art. Roughly speaking, other things being equal, practices tend to be satisfying partly in relation to their complexity, and their scope for the development of skills. Where we excel in such practices we may also gain external goods in recognition of our achievements. MacIntyre accepts that people need external goods but argues that internal goods can be gained and enjoyed even in the absence of related external goods.[20] However, external goods without corresponding internal goods are empty. We want not merely recognition but to have done things that deserve it, and if we get it without having done anything that warrants it then not only might we feel guilty (and perhaps that the recognition is insincere and patronizing) but we have missed out on the internal goods which they are supposed to acknowledge. Assurances from the Right that class does not exist because everyone is supposedly recognized as being of equal worth or value have this spurious character.

MacIntyre's definition of practices is rather restrictive and arguably elitist, but it could be stretched to a wider range of activities and indeed to relationships such as those of parenting, which also have their own internal goods, and for which 'good-enough' performance can bring recognition. In allowing for conditional as well as unconditional recognition, we can make a connection to the struggles of the social field as being both a competition for internal and external goods, and a struggle over the definition of internal goods, or more generally over what is worthy of esteem. While Bourdieu rightly emphasizes such struggles over definitions of goods, his concept of capitals conflates internal and external goods, and therefore obscures their different sources and normative structure (Bourdieu 1984; Sayer 1999, 2005). Life politics are not only about the struggle for power and esteem but over the nature of internal goods (just what is valuable and important?) and who should have access to them and hence to the distribution of external goods (praise, esteem, money) in response to those who achieve them. In practice, access to money is largely a function of power, and even where money is a reward or payment for the achievement of internal goods, it has to be remembered that access to the practices embodying those internal goods is highly unequal in morally arbitrary ways, particularly with respect to gender, class and 'race'. However, from a normative point of view, external goods should be deserved and hence related to qualities that people actually have, and as Bourdieu and Weber noted, one of the striking things about the powerful is that they usually try to present their dominance as legitimate and merited (in terms of achieved internal goods and other qualities) even though they might still be able to maintain their power without doing so.

In order to understand the struggles of the social field we therefore have to go beyond the matter of distribution and recognition to the question of recognition for what? What is (held to be) worthy of recognition and reward through distribution? They are not simply about power per se: the dominant would hardly be dominant if they were not able to monopolize the most valued goods, which gave them advantages over those who lacked them. Dominant values are not necessarily identical to the values of the dominant. Others may share them, and not necessarily because they have been conditioned into believing them, as a sociologically reductionist iconoclasm would suggest, but because they probably rightly judge them to be important for their well-being.

Here we can make a connection back to shame, for shame may be engendered by invidious comparison with others who have been done better than us in competition for goods which we value, such as educational achievements (Tomkins in Sedgwick and Frank 1995: 161). Within the educational systems of class societies, the shaming of those who fail is a structurally generated effect, as Bourdieu's extensive research on such systems demonstrates, even though it is felt as an individual failure (e.g. Bourdieu 1996). Those who believe that society is basically meritocratic are most vulnerable to shame.

Thus, one of the most important features of class inequalities is that they present people with unequal bases for respect, not just by being objects of *un*warranted respect or disdain, but as having unequal access to the practices and goods that allow them warranted respect or conditional recognition. Being able to participate in practices and such relationships and gain their internal goods if one so wishes is crucial for well-being, though access to them differs radically across the key social divisions of gender, class and 'race' and across others too. They also figure prominently in the kinds of things which bring external goods of conditional recognition. To get more equality of recognition we need not merely a different view of and way of behaving towards class others but more equality of access to the social bases of respect and self-respect, and being able to participate in such practices and relationships is crucial.

Incidentally, in this respect, class is significantly different from gender and 'race'. Whereas sexism and racism are primarily produced by 'identity-sensitive' behaviour and can hence be reduced by people changing their attitudes and behaviour towards others, class inequalities need a great deal more than an elimination of class contempt to erode, for they can be produced by identity-indifferent mechanisms of capitalism, such as the unintended effects of changes in consumer spending on workers: they need a redistribution of resources.[21] It is easy for the rich to 'recognize' their others as equal, but giving up their economic advantages is quite another matter. Thus, as Nancy Fraser argues, an appropriate slogan would be 'no recognition without redistribution' (Fraser and Naples 2004).

Conclusion

I have tried to further understanding of class by emphasizing the moral dimensions of how it is experienced. People are evaluative beings. We need to take the normative rationales implicit in the way people value each other seriously, as evaluations of themselves and others and of what enables flourishing or suffering, involving implicit ideas about the good, and not simply as social facts about their holders. These moral beliefs and standards are generally assumed by actors to be universally applicable. Such rationales may be flawed, as we saw in the case of the belief in a just world, and therefore they must be viewed critically, but they can also reveal much about people's situations. Here certain ideas from moral philosophy, including a broadly cognitivist view of emotions such as shame, and of recognition and internal and external goods, can help illuminate lay normativity, for they are based on attempts to understand this from the standpoint of actors rather than spectators, as matters of justification rather than external explanation. Recognition of others is partly conditional upon behaviour and achievements, and these depend on access to valued goods and practices. Class contempt and moral boundary drawing exacerbate the effects of class, but distributional inequalities in access to valued practices and goods in any case render equality of conditional recognition impossible.

Notes

1 This paper builds upon ideas introduced in Sayer (2005).
2 Feminist scholarship is a partial exception.
3 A 'positive' approach is of course not necessarily positivist.
4 For an insightful analysis of this modern shift from justification to external explanation and the alienation of social science from the actor's point of view, see Manent (1998).
5 Any object can be externally culturally *construed* in various ways, but this is different from being internally restructured by cultural constructions.
6 There are of course many qualifications to be made to this simple claim, particularly regarding the narrative character of emotions and the influence of significant events in early life on them (Nussbaum 2001).
7 This does not necessarily mean it is innate; it could still be a product of socialization.
8 It is interesting that we would have doubts about the moral character of someone who could not respond morally to everyday events without first deliberating on them.
9 This lay 'conception' of the good is likely to be much less examined than a philosophical conception of the good, and consists mainly of taken for granted cultural assumptions.
10 However, a careful inspection of Bourdieu's data shows that many of the relationships are quite weak.
11 Of course the distinction between aesthetics and ethics is sometimes fuzzy; for example, where modes of dress are seen as indicators of respect for others.
12 Though obviously fallible, moral imagination is a crucial pre-requisite for many kinds of social interaction, and it can include recognition of difference as well as similarity.
13 This does not mean that they are universally *held*. Thanks to a referee for pointing this out.
14 'Shame is the most reflexive of the affects in that the phenomenological distinction between the subject and object of shame is lost' (Tomkins, in Sedgewick and Frank 1995: 136).
15 This is less obvious than in the case of its opposite, pride, instances of which are often described as 'false'.
16 Following the work of Sandra Lee Bartky (1990) and Cheshire Calhoun (2003), I argue elsewhere that there are also more chronic forms of class-related shame that involve a feeling of inadequacy even in the absence of specific failures (Sayer 2005).

17 In this way, far from contradicting this kind of universalism, cultural variety actually presupposes it (Collier 2003).
18 This is borne out by Diane Reay's research on working- and middle-class mothers' experience of putting their children through school (Reay 1998) and also the experience of academics of working-class origin (Reay 1997).
19 Hayek used this argument to refuse calls for redistribution, arguing that inequalities might be unfortunate for some, but there was no injustice in this respect, since no-one need have acted unjustly to bring it about.
20 This was also Smith's view (Smith 1759).
21 I acknowledge that identity-sensitive mechanisms of class contempt, racism, sexism, etc., can also help reproduce class inequalities but these are contingent rather than necessary conditions of the reproduction of classes in capitalism, for class could exist even in their absence (see Sayer 2005, chapter 4).

References

Archer, M.S. (2000) *Being Human*, Cambridge: Cambridge University Press.
Barbalet, J.M. (2001) *Emotions, Social Theory and Social Structure*, Cambridge: Cambridge University Press.
Bartky, S.L. (1990) *Femininity and Domination: Studies in the Phenomenology of Class*, London: Routledge.
Bourdieu, P. (1984) *Distinction: a Social Critique of the Judgement of Taste*, London: Routledge.
Bourdieu, P. (1996) *The State Nobility: Elite Schools in the Field of Power*, Cambridge: Polity.
Bourdieu, P. (2000) *Pascalian Meditations*, Cambridge: Polity.
Calhoun, C. (2003) 'An apology for moral shame', *The Journal of Political Philosophy*, 11, 2: 1–20.
Collier, A. (2003) *In Defence of Objectivity*, London: Routledge.
Coole, D. (1986) 'Is class a difference that makes a difference?', *Radical Philosophy*, 77: 17–25.
Dean, K. (2003) *Capitalism and Citizenship: the Impossible Partnership*, London: Routledge.
Foucault, M. (1977) *Discipline and Punish*, Harmondsworth: Penguin.
Fraser, N. (1999) 'Social justice in the age of identity politics: redistribution, recognition and participation', in Ray, L.J. and Sayer, A. (eds) *Culture and Economy after the Cultural Turn*, London: Sage.
Fraser, N. and Naples, N. (2004) 'To interpret the world and change it: an interview with Nancy Fraser', *Signs: Journal of Women in Culture and Society*, 29, 4: 1102–1124.
Gilens, M. (1999) *Why Americans Hate Welfare: Race, Media and the Politics of Antipoverty Policy*, Chicago: Chicago University Press.
Hayek, F.A. (1960) *The Constitution of Liberty*, London: Routledge.
Helm, B.W. (2001) *Emotional Reason: Deliberation, Motivation and the Nation of Value*, Cambridge: Cambridge University Press.
Honneth, A. (1995) *The Struggle for Recognition: the Moral Grammar of Social Conflicts*, Cambridge: Polity.
Kefalas, M. (2003) *Working-Class Heroes: Protecting Home, Community and Nation in a Chicago Neighbourhood*, California: University of California Press.
Lamont, M. (1992) *Money, Morals and Manners: the Culture of the French and American Upper-middle Class*, Chicago: Chicago University Press.

Lamont, M. (2000) *The Dignity of Working Men: Morality and the Boundaries of Race, Class and Imagination*, New York: Russell Sage Foundation and Harvard University Press.

Lawler, S. (2000) *Mothering the Self: Mothers, Daughters, Subjects*, London: Routledge.

Lerner, M.J. (1980) *The Belief in a Just World: a Fundamental Delusion*, New York: Plenum Press.

MacIntyre, A. (1981) *After Virtue*, London Duckworth.

Macleod, J. (1995) *Ain't No Makin' It: Aspirations and Attainment in A Low Income Neighbourhood*, 2nd edn, Boulder, Co: Westview Press.

Manent, P. (1998) *The City of Man*, Princeton, NJ: Princeton University Press.

Nussbaum, M.C. (1986) *The Fragility of Goodness*, Cambridge: Cambridge University Press.

Nussbaum, M.C. (2000) *Women and Human Development: the Capabilities Approach*, Cambridge: Cambridge University Press.

Nussbaum, M.C. (2001) *Upheavals of Thought: the Intelligence of Emotions*, Cambridge: Cambridge University Press.

Probyn, E. (2004) 'Everyday shame', *Cultural Studies*, 18, 2/3: 328–349.

Rawls, J. (1971) *A Theory of Justice*, Oxford: Oxford University Press.

Reay, D. (1997) 'The double-bind of the "working class" feminist academic: the success of failure or the failure of success', in Mahoney, P. and Zmroczek, C. (eds) *Class Matters: Working-class Women's Perspectives on Social Class*, London: Taylor and Francis.

Reay, D. (1998) *Class Work: Mothers' Involvement in their Children's Primary Schooling*, London: University College London.

Savage, M., Bagnall, G. and Longhurst, B. (2001) 'Ordinary, ambivalent and defensive: class differentiation in the northwest of England', *Sociology*, 35: 875–892.

Sayer, A. (1999) 'Bourdieu, Smith and disinterested judgement', *The Sociological Review*, 47, 3: 403–431.

Sayer, A. (2002) '"What are you worth?": why class is an embarrassing subject', *Sociological Research Online*, 7, 3, www.socresonline.org.uk/7/3/sayer.html.

Sayer, A. (2005) *The Moral Significance of Class*, Cambridge: Cambridge University Press.

Scheff, T.J. (1990) *Microsociology: Discourse, Emotions and Social Structure*, Chicago: Chicago University Press.

Sedgewick, E.K. and Frank, A. (eds) (1995) *Shame and its Sisters: a Silvan Tomkins Reader*, Durham, NC: Duke University Press.

Skeggs, B. (1997) *Formations of Class and Gender: Becoming Respectable*, London: Sage.

Skeggs, B. (2004) *Class, Self, Culture*, London: Routledge.

Smith, A. (1759) [1984] *The Theory of Moral Sentiments*, Indianapolis: Liberty Fund.

Southerton, D.K. (2002) 'Boundaries of "us" and "them": class, mobility and identification in a new town', *Sociology*, 36, 1: 1171–1193.

Taylor, C. (1992) "The politics of recognition", in Gutman, A. (ed.) *Multi-culturalism: Examining the Politics of Recognition*, Princetown, NJ: Princetown University Press.

Williams, B. (1993) *Shame and Necessity*, Berkeley, CA: University of California Press.

Yar, M. (2001) 'Beyond Nancy Fraser's "perspectival dualism"', *Economy and Society*, 30, 3: 288–303.

7 Feminist appropriations of Bourdieu

The case of social capital

Christina Hughes and Loraine Blaxter

This chapter offers an account of the rise to prominence of the concept of 'social capital', its use in social policy and government agencies and the predominance within research and theory in this area of the work of Coleman (1988), Putnam (1995, 2000) and Fukuyama (1995). The extent of take up of these theorists, we note, is at the neglect of Bourdieu's more sociological and critical conceptualization. We detail the differences, and indeed similarities, between these various conceptualizations of social capital and illustrate the tendency to either marginalize or assimilate Bourdieu's work to dominant usage. We also point to a relative neglect of 'social capital' among those feminists who have engaged critically with Bourdieu. We believe this feminist neglect is a matter of regret not only because social capital is being taken up exponentially and globally by government and non-governmental agencies to tackle social justice issues related to poverty and social exclusion but also because, as we demonstrate, the unpaid physical and emotional work associated with the production of social capital is, most usually, women's work.

Nevertheless, whilst in this paper we do privilege a Bourdieusian approach to the analysis of social capital, our position follows Moi's (1999) injunction to take care in such appropriations. Thus, after setting out how social capital is being framed – and not framed – in policy discourses, we turn to the potential and problems that feminists have identified with a Bourdieusian approach. Our arguments will be that a Bourdieusian account of social capital offers the potential to link the material and cultural in ways that are now of central concern for the achievement of social justice. However, his framework is less useful for developing analyses of the realm of affect and ambivalence that mark women's engagement with the unpaid work that constitutes social capital. We draw, primarily, from research into gender and education to illustrate our points.

In the past decade, feminists have paid an increasing amount of attention to the contribution Bourdieu's social theory can make to pressing issues of feminist analysis.[1] As Adkins notes, this includes theories of social versus performative agency; the relationship of the women's movement to social change; and 'what might be termed a new feminist materialism which goes beyond Bourdieu's own social logics' (Adkins 2005: 3). In so doing, the Bourdieusian concepts of habitus, field and capital have been applied in, for example, feminist theorizing in education to explore a range of concerns that include: classed femininity (Skeggs 1997), gender identity (Millard 1997), status in higher education (Heward 1994), academic power (Luke 1998) and working-class masculinities (Reay 2002).

More recently, feminist scholars have begun to work with Bourdieu's social theory for the development of a key concept that is prominent in national and international policy and programmes: social capital. The importance of 'social capital' is evidenced by the World Bank having a 'social capital library' (www.worldbank.org/poverty/scapital/library). Social capital appears in Bourdieu's taxonomy of capitals although, as we have indicated and will go on to detail, his conceptualization is strikingly absent in the discursive frame of public policy and social programmes. Here, the dominant usage is built upon the methodological individualism and rational choice models developed in Coleman's (1988) conceptualization of social capital. These theoretical under-pinnings have been disseminated through the writings of Putnam (1995, 2000). Fukuyama's (1995) economic perspectives on trust have also been heavily referenced.

Whilst social capital has experienced a phenomenal trajectory in social policy writing, this does not appear to be the case within feminism. This is despite feminism's growing interest in Bourdieu's capitalistic analysis. For example, a citation search of the journal *Gender and Education* (Blaxter and Hughes 2003) has indicated that cultural capital was the most cited of Bourdieu's capitals and was central to seven out of ten articles that engaged in various forms of capital-istic analysis. Social capital was the specific focus of only one article across the whole sample of 332 articles (Riddell *et al.* 2001).[2] We should not be surprised at this neglect given the strength of the 'cultural turn' in recent feminist theory. However, to engage with 'social capital' is to engage with political programmes where there may seem to be a fit with a much older feminist practice of making connections, building social support, mutual aid and reciprocity (Blaxter and Hughes 2000). In addition, the policy imperatives associated with the develop-ment of social capital draw strongly on the physical and emotional labour that is profoundly women's work (ibid.) and an 'ethic of care' associated with feminin-ity (Hughes 2002). So, in practice, as Rankin (2002) notes, development agen-cies now routinely target microfinance services to women viewing them as central to the development of social capital relations.

This chapter is organized through one theme and three associated explora-tions. Our theme, following Lovell, Moi and more recently the contributors to the special issue of *The Sociological Review* (2005: 52, s2), focuses on the implications of Bourdieu's theory for the development of feminist knowledge and politics. At a general level, we consider the usefulness of feminist appropri-ations of a Bourdieusian account of social capital. Second, we examine empiri-cal research on social capital that takes a Bourdieusian conceptualization. Our aim is to explore the specificities of such an approach noting how social capital is inserted in the academic field. Here, we observe how dominant interpretations of social capital shape intellectual critique and engagement; we explore methodological concerns; and we draw attention to the potential of a Bourdieusian approach to social capital to bridge the material–cultural dichotomy that has been of much recent concern within feminism. Finally, we explore a range of critical concerns associated with appropriations of a Bourdieusian analysis of social capital. We believe these issues are highly important for feminists to contribute, at national and international policy levels, to debates and practices that are, ostensibly, concerned with social justice. They are important because, as Aldridge *et al.* (2002) have evidenced, there has been an 'exponential' growth of interest in social capital across diverse social policy areas and within economic development literatures. This growth has continued.

We begin with a discussion of the conceptualizations of social capital that have predominated the policy arenas through the work of Coleman, Putnam and Fukuyama, before turning more fully to a discussion of Bourdieu's theorization. These prefacing sections prepare the way for addressing the three concerns we have set out above.

Defining social capital: Coleman, Putnam and Fukuyama

> Current orthodoxies of social capital literature ... abstract society from economy and assume a universal and undifferentiated form for social capital, potentially available to all. The effect is to link outcomes to presence or absence of social capital, rather than to the unequal productiveness of different social capitals.
>
> (Gamarnikow and Green 1999: 7)

Gamarnikow and Green (1999) indicate that, as it is currently deployed, the concept of social capital is associated with three sources: Coleman's (1988) rational action theory and sociology of education, Putnam *et al.*'s (1993) study of Italian politics and Fukuyama's (1995) comparative study of national capitalisms. We begin by summarizing these three approaches. What they all share in common is the idea that the presence of social capital is key to prosperity, social cohesion and successful outcomes in education, employment, health, family and so forth. For example, Coleman's main concerns were to demonstrate how an individual's attainment of human capital, say in the levels of their examination and scholarly successes, were influenced by family and inter-family relations. By recognizing the significance of family and household, the explanatory framework that Coleman develops does take more account of the influences of temporality and social structures than is found in the explicit individualism of earlier work on human capital. Nevertheless, it is a muted development of an individualistic discourse.

Within Coleman's work there are two ways through which social capital is developed. These are through the development of trustworthiness and through generational investment in children that enhances their human capital (Gamarnikow and Green 1999). In this regard we would emphasize the element of time in Coleman's account. For example, when we consider the development of social capital between households, it is sustaining reciprocity, over time, that generates trust. In addition, according to Coleman, an important source of social capital is the amount of time that parents spend with their children and one another. Thus, Coleman offers an explanation of why parents rich in human capital themselves might not pass this advantage to their children. In this, and as we have indicated previously (Blaxter and Hughes 2000), our feminist analysis would point to an implicit critique in Coleman not only generally of mothers' engagement in paid work, given the euphemism 'parent' usually stands in for mother (Hughes *et al.* 1991), but of middle-class women specifically. It is they, after all, who are already 'rich' in various forms of capital. Thus, it is mothers who are being called to account for having limited contact with their children and with their (male) partners. The result, for Coleman, is a lack of necessary investment of time and energy in their children's potential human capital.

Despite Coleman's important recognition of the micro-relations that structure social capital, the essential functionalism in his perspective is replicated in those that follow him. The work of Putnam (1993) is salutary in this respect. Although Putnam builds on Coleman's work, his use of social capital is different. Rather than treating social capital as a resource that works to assist individuals, Putnam treats it as a property of collectivities, such as groups and regions. In addition, rather than focusing on reciprocal relations within and between households, the indicators of social capital in Putnam's work are found in social participation in clubs and associations. In Putnam's view civic action, through the work of clubs and associations, is a key source of regional wealth creation and good governance. His field of study originated in research on the institutional changes in Italy that had arisen from the introduction of decentralized regional government in 1970. Putnam argued that economic performance, and the performance of regional governments, was influenced by the form and intensity of networks of civic engagement. He argued, for example, that the North of Italy had prospered more than the South because of its history of vibrant horizontal networks that had fostered 'robust norms of reciprocity' (Putnam 1993: 173) and had facilitated communication. In contrast, the South of Italy, with a history of amoral familialism, fragmentation and distrust, and vertical social ties had been less economically prosperous. In this, we can see how Putnam's argument illustrates a functional conception of social capital and it is this that has been taken up in the public policy of new capitalism. In addition, through his linkage of social capital to forms of democracy and democratization, Putnam makes explicit the normativity in his conceptualization. As Gamarnikow and Green (1999: 9) put it: 'all communities have social networks, but not all of these networks are productive in terms of social capital'.

In turning to the work of Fukuyama (2001) we would note how he, importantly, draws attention to the social realm by indicating how understandings of economic life have to be located within the customs and mores of which it is part. Thus, Fukuyama defines social capital as:

> an instantiated informal norm that promotes co-operation between two or
> more individuals. The norms that constitute social capital can range from

the norm of reciprocity between two friends all the way up to complex and elaborately articulated doctrines like Christianity or Confucianism. They must be instantiated in an actual human relationship: the norm of reciprocity exists *in potentia* in my dealings with all people, but is actualised only in my dealings with *my* friends. By this definition, trust, networks, civil society, and the like, which have been associated with social capital, are all epiphenomenal, arising as a result of social capital but not constituting social capital itself.

(Fukyama 2001: 7, emphasis in original)

Fukuyama's (1995) proposition is that trust was the social virtue that explained prosperity. Whilst, therefore, Fukuyama is arguing that trust is not social capital but that it arises from social capital transactions, he does argue that trust is a useful measure of a society's social capital. In policy terms, as Aldridge *et al.* (2002) indicate (see also Office for National Statistics 2001), the measurement of trust through social surveys has become a key aspect of measuring social capital.

In tandem with this theoretical heritage, the conceptualization that has been taken up, and disseminated by government and inter-governmental agencies, locates social capital in community, rather than in class relations (Aldridge *et al.* 2002). Of course, within ruling hegemonic relations, there is always space for critique. For example, within the development policy arena, the take-up of Putnam's usage within the World Bank and the international development industry has been subject to a substantial critique (Harris 1997). This includes a reminder of the racial and sexual violence and discrimination that can co-exist within strong communities (Putzel 1997). Indeed, it is to a more critical view of social capital that we now turn while noting that Bourdieu shares with Coleman, Putnam and Fukuyama a gender-neutral account of social capital.

Bourdieu and social capital

There is little, at a descriptive level, to distinguish Bourdieu's definition of social capital from that of definitions more generally. However, whilst Bourdieu is acknowledged in UK government publications on social capital (Office for National Statistics 2001; Aldridge *et al.* 2002), his theoretical framework is notably absent in public and international policy arenas. This neglect of Bourdieu reflects the silence that surrounds any recognition of social antagonism in New Labour ideology and policy. Here, 'policy development and implementation increasingly proceeds as though the political representation of resentments is now quite outmoded, even if it is accepted that some residual inequalities of opportunity remain' (Ahier and Beck 2003: 327. See also Avis 2000; McRobbie 2000).

The aim of Bourdieu's work is to demonstrate how social advantage is historically based and maintained. In emphasizing the importance of a Bourdieusian approach to the study of social and health inequalities, Pevalin (2003) comments on how research examining the collective dimensions of social capital as a 'public good' associated with Putman and Coleman's conceptualization of social capital ignores issues of difference in access to that public good. In contrast to, say, Coleman, who tends to view social capital as an incontestable good, in Bourdieu's work social capital is a 'club good' and in consequence his work focuses on exclusionary practices that create and sustain inequalities. As a critical theorist, Bourdieu's work illustrates the lack of concern with conflict and oppression found, not only in contemporary policy debate, but also in dominant positivistic theories and in forms of ethnomethodology. Bourdieu's theoretical viewpoint is explicit. Like positivist social researchers, Bourdieu believes in social facts. Unlike positivists, for Bourdieu these facts are not neutral. They are brutal and concerned with inequality between social actors.

Further, Bourdieu's conceptualization of capital was not in terms of a descriptor of empirical positions as found in functionalist accounts. The concept of capital is used primarily as a metaphor to capture the differential interests, resources and benefits of groups in society (Skeggs 1997). These differential values given to groups in society means that capitals are not tradeable commodities in relations of equality. As Bourdieu (1986: 241) comments: 'all forms of capital are accumulated labour, take time to accumulate and have a capacity to produce and reproduce themselves so that in society people are not equal and everything is not equally possible or impossible'.

In this, Bourdieu distinguished between economic, cultural, social and symbolic capital and it is the interrelationship of these various capitals within relations of class that inequalities are reproduced. Indeed, it is this focus on relationality that marks one of the differences between Bourdieu's conceptualization and that of Coleman, Putnam and Fukuyama. For example, Bourdieu refers to social capital as a network of bonds and connections or social obligations. A focus on connections and social obligations is useful in understanding how clubs, particularly elite clubs, and families act as the main sites of accumulation and transmission of social capital. It is, however, the relational aspect of the various capitals that sustains or diminishes advantage in a given field. Thus, Bourdieu (1998: 70–71) comments as follows on how 'great' families maintain their dominance:

> One of the properties of dominant social factions is that they have particularly extensive families ('great' families are big families) that are strongly integrated because they are united not only by the affinity between habitus but also by the solidarity of interests, that is, both by capital and for capital, economic capital naturally, but also symbolic capital (the name) and perhaps above all social capital (which can be shown to be the condition and the effect of successful management of the capital collectively possessed by the members of the domestic unit).

This focus on how those with high levels of the various forms of capitals, and associated habitus, maintain their social position indicates how the conversion of social capital into other forms of capital is not accomplished within a neutral space. And it is this issue of spatial positioning that is significant for critical analysis. For example, Skeggs' (1997) research on young working-class women engaged in a further education course to become nursery nurses demonstrates how social mobility, promised by achieving educational qualifications, is restricted by issues of class and gender. Skeggs' research demonstrates the power relations extant within asymmetric, vertical ties.

It would be a danger, however, to imply a deterministic reading of Bourdieu through which, as Moi (1999: 269) puts it: 'amor fati – love your destiny – is an appropriate motto for every socially determined act'. However, in this regard there are different readings of Bourdieu. McCall (1992: 839) notes that determinism can be imputed through a 'first' reading of Bourdieu where 'occupational and educational status [act] as primary determinants of social class position within which gender differences operate as secondary determinants'. McCall offers a 'second' reading of Bourdieu which 'exposes how real principles of selection and exclusion are hidden behind nominal constructions of categories such as occupation and educational qualification' (ibid.: 842). Nonetheless, McCall is not suggesting that the first reading is wrong and the second reading is correct. Rather she is arguing that both readings confirm much feminist knowledge about the gendered relations of social domination. For example, the 'first' reading confirms recognized class divisions between groups of women. The second reading confirms the pervasiveness of gender that is consistently rendered invisible through attributions of its naturalness. Indeed, it is the interrelation between positions (first reading) and dispositions (second reading) that offers possibilities for understanding social change.

In this regard, we need to introduce two further concepts from Bourdieu's schema. These are habitus and field. Moi (1999: 269) notes that these terms are 'deeply interdependent'. In social fields agents confront one another. They are sites of competition and struggle for dominance. Associated with specific fields (such as the scientific, artistic, political, bureaucratic) are rules. Within social fields agents strategize with the aim, in Moi's terms:

> to become the instance which has the power to confer or withdraw *legitimacy* from other participants in the game …. Such a position of dominance is achieved by amassing the maximum amount of the specific kind of symbolic capital current in the field.
>
> (Moi 1999: 269–270, emphasis in original)

Each field generates its own habitus. Moi uses an educational analogy and compares habitus with the 'silent curriculum' through which norms and values are not explicitly learnt but are inculcated through the everyday of interaction. To think with 'habitus' is to recognize actions as neither externally determined nor acts of conscious choice. Lovell (2000: 12) summarizes habitus as: 'ways of doing and being which social subjects acquire during their socialization. Their habitus is not a matter of conscious learning, or of ideological imposition, but is acquired through practice'. This 'practical sense' enables one to be effective within a given social field. This means, as Lovell notes, that one unconsciously or 'naturally' 'knows how' to behave in a particular social field because its ways of doing and being are so deeply ingrained. As Adkins (2003: 23) also notes:

> [habitus] produces enduring (although not entirely fixed) orientations to action. But while the habitus structures and organizes action it is also generative. Specifically, the habitus is productive of individual and collective practices: practices which themselves are constitutive of the dispositions of the habitus.

In conceptualizing habitus, Bourdieu aimed to transcend binaries (determinism/ freedom; individual/society). Habitus 'is what makes it possible to produce an infinite number of practices that are relatively unpredictable (like the corresponding situations) but also limited in their diversity' (Bourdieu 1990: 54). An analytic attention to habitus and different forms of capital in a field may enable feminist agency to enact strategies for change. The unconscious commonsense, taken-for-granted aspects of habitus associated with a field may become conscious through the experience of disjuncture between disposition and position (McCall 1992). One example would be through those moments when one says 'This is *not* me' through which 'The ontological complicity between habitus and field breaks down: *fit* no longer explains the relationship between positions and dispositions' (McCall 1992: 850).

We turn, now, to research on social capital that, by and large, takes a Bourdieusian frame. The analysis that follows contains three elements. First, it indicates the hegemonic influence on intellectual debate that arises when an area of study is colonized by dominant interests and, in consequence, how researchers have to take account, in various ways, of this influence. In this respect, the widespread take-up of Coleman (1987, 1988), Fukuyama (1995, 2001) and Putnam (1993, 1995, 2000) has meant that researchers cannot ignore their contribution. Second, our analysis indicates how feminist research on social capital has been, so far, broadly qualitative. This methodological approach needs to be set against the widespread growth of attention governmental and non-governmental agencies have given to developing quantitative indicators of social capital. Third, our analysis demonstrates how a Bourdieusian approach to social capital requires researchers to consider its interrelationship with other capitals: economic, symbolic and cultural. This suggests that Bourdieu's social theory has the potential to build bridges between the material and the cultural in the ways that are of contemporary concern (see for example Fraser 1995; Fraser and Honneth 2003; Lawler 2005; McNay 2005; Young 1997).[3]

The academic field and social capital

This section looks at the academic field with attention to two aspects. One is concerned with the implications of 'the rules of the game' of academic research for feminist impact on public policy. The other explores the implications of a 'social capital' analysis for the higher education access movement in the UK. So far, we have argued that whilst on the one hand there has been an exponential interest in social capital within social policy and development fields, Bourdieu's social theory is strikingly absent. In addition, we have noted the relative neglect by feminists of this particular concept. Rather, it would appear that cultural capital has been the first capital of feminist choice. However, and in contrast to the broader social policy and development literature, when feminists do explore aspects of social capital, they are more likely to take a Bourdieusian approach (Blaxter and Hughes 2003).

In the fit between the concerns associated with 'social capital' and those of feminism a central difference emerges. This is that whilst social capitalists are infused with a concern to reduce inequality, 'there is little sense of its structural, rather than personal, origins' (Baron 2004: 10). In contrast, the attention paid to the perpetuation of privilege, and consequent structuring of class inequalities, has certainly been an important factor in feminist take-up of Bourdieu. For example, Liddle and Michielsens' (2000) Bourdieusian analysis of women's political representation demonstrates the structuring of class and gender in women's access to forms of public power. In the field of education, Bourdieu and Passeron (1977) have demonstrated how education is a significant place in the transmission of power and its reproduction in other social spheres. This is through the ways that education is an important site for the enactment of the symbolic violence that, say through ideas of meritocracy and egalitarianism, produces a belief in the legitimacy of prevailing power structures. Thus, Rankin (2002: 17) finds Bourdieu useful because his theorization 'clarifies the coercive and exploitative dimensions of social capital (as one of many goods in an "economics of practice"), and its role in maintaining social hierarchies'.

However, in seeking to influence intellectual debate in a particular area, we are mindful of Fraser's (1997: 81) warning 'that it is not possible to insulate special discourse arenas from the effects of societal inequality'. As we have shown, the rational choice and methodological individualism favoured by Coleman, Putnam and Fukuyama fits with the dominant policy discourse of the public arena. This gives critical scholars a choice. They can ignore these conceptualizations and circulate counter-discourses in 'subaltern counterpublic spheres'. They can take them up or they can adapt them for their own purposes. To ignore these conceptualizations risks, on the one hand, one's professional credibility through accusations of not knowing the central literature of a specific area of study. On the other hand, ignoring a dominant sphere of knowledge can render one marginal and ignored. Dominant perspectives, therefore, have to be addressed. For those who do use Bourdieu in their analyses of social capital, the consequence is twofold, though not necessarily in a mutually exclusive way. One response is to combine Bourdieu with Putnam, Fukuyama and Coleman by stressing that:

> While there are differences in theoretical grounding, definitions and usage of the concept social capital, there is consensus around basic elements that

relate to the norms and values people hold that both result in, and are the result of, collective ties and relationship.

(Thomson *et al.* 2003: 37)

The other response is to critique the theoretical adequacy of conceptualizations arising from Coleman, Putnam and Fukuyama. This is the approach of Morrow (1999, 2002), Rankin (2002), Edwards (2004) and Blaxter and Hughes (2000). In this way, Bourdieu serves as an antidote to, and enables researchers to illuminate, the normativity of such conceptualizations. However, the extent to which in the broader social policy arena this ghettoizes feminist and Bourdieusian accounts of social capital and reduces the potential impact of feminist knowledge on political programmes is a moot point. It is to issues of methodology that we now turn and where issues of potential marginalization of feminist knowledge remain.

Methodological concerns

McCall (1992) reminds us of the heritage of feminist methodological debate through which the god of objectivity was critiqued as being malestream. In this respect, she suggests that Bourdieu's use of the terms 'truth' and 'objectivity' may be a step too far for many feminist, and indeed postmodern, sensibilities. Nonetheless, Skeggs (2005: 20) notes that Bourdieu's social theory is useful because of the 'parallels between feminist approaches to epistemology and methodology, in which theoretical frameworks and political programmes are always embedded in social relations'.[4] In particular, a Bourdieusian methodology enables us to make sense of the micropolitics of power. This arises through a 'painstaking attentiveness to the particular case, a wish to take the concrete manifestations of human behaviour as the starting point of thought' (Moi 1999: 301). A Bourdieusian methodology is viewed as reflexive and as comprising a variety of tools and techniques of data collection.

However, McCall's reminder of feminist interventions should also alert us to another aspect of methodological history. This is the paradigm wars between qualitative and quantitative methodologies and through which the status binaries of 'hard'/'soft' were reified into forms of epistemological critique. We would be mistaken to believe that this particular 'debate' can now be relegated to the past. In their analysis of contemporary methodological concerns, Denzin and Lincoln point to a 'fractured future' in which, unless we are careful, we shall be returning to the days of a strong methodological, and status, divide between qualitative and quantitative approaches. Denzin and Lincoln reflect that:

methodologists will line up on two opposing sides of a great divide. Randomized field trials, touted as the 'gold standard' of scientific educational research, will occupy the time of one group of researchers while the pursuit of a socially and cultural responsive, communitarian, justice-oriented set of studies will consume the meaningful working moments of another.

(Denzin and Lincoln 2005: 1123)

It is with an eye on this terrain that we address our concerns about the development of a Bourdieusian methodology for the analysis of social capital and in particular feminist approaches to social capital. This is a methodological focus that is usually qualitative and concerned with the specific and the contextualized. One example is Yates (2001: 211) who comments that:

> We wanted to look at how *particular* schools interacted with *particular* biographies: and we wanted, by an intensive and qualitative study, to be open to how the students were constructing their world now; and to reflect on whether the themes we were bringing about mattered or about how 'disadvantage' or 'school effects' could be described, needed revision.

This emphasis on qualitative approaches stands in contrast to the wider social capital literature which is primarily quantitative in approach. In their review of methodological approaches to social capital, Silva and Edwards (2003) confirm our analysis (Blaxter and Hughes 2003) that most empirical work on social capital has been quantitative (see also van Deth 2003). For example, the public policy arena is highly concerned with the measurement of social capital through quantitative indicators. The UK Office for National Statistics has developed a survey matrix and social capital question bank to compare and contrast the wording of the questions from fifteen aspects of social capital (see www.statistics.gov.uk/socialcapital). Eighteen large surveys have been identified as including some measurement of social capital. Thus, concepts such as trust, reciprocity, social cohesion, neighbourhood and community involvement, social efficacy, perception of community level structures or characteristics, social interaction, social networks and social support are collected through questions in the following social surveys:

> British Crime Survey, British Election Study, British Household Panel Survey, British Social Attitudes Survey, Citizen Audit Questionaire, Communal Establishments Survey, English Longitudinal Study of Ageing, English House Condition Survey, General Household Survey, Health Education Monitoring Survey, Health and Lifestyles Survey, Health Survey for England, Home Office Citizenship Survey, National Adult Learning Survey, Scottish Household Survey, Survey of English Housing, Poverty and Social Exclusion Survey, UK Time Use Survey.

This data is potentially susceptible to a critical gender analysis. Silva and Edwards (2003: 3) link this dominant quantitative approach with the dominant theorization of this field by noting that:

> Coleman's and Putnam's conceptions of the mechanics of social capital are quite specific, even formulaic, and this makes them easily amenable to empirical investigation, particularly through surveys.

However, in seeking to appropriate a more Bourdieusian conceptualization, Silva and Edwards find that operationalizing Bourdieu empirically 'is quite a different matter, and a more complex one' (Silva and Edwards 2003: 4). This is because for Bourdieu theory and method should not be separated from the construction of the object but should be integral. Thus, in addition to selecting an appropriate methodology, researchers have to construct the objects of research for themselves or they are left with the already pre-constructed that arise from narrow frames of analysis.

In addressing their responses to this challenge in the *Families and Social Capital ESRC Research Group Programme of Work* (www.lsbu.ac.uk/families), Silva and Edwards note that the team begins with a broad definition of social capital and then moves on, in each specific project, to a more detailed focus. For example:

> the 'Provision and deployment of care through family, mutual aid and local state' project focuses on time use and levels of social capital, and has developed a conceptual framework of milieu and the networks and shared values/expectations derived from them to guide investigation.
>
> (Silva and Edwards 2003: 9; see also Gray 2003)

Given the predominance in public policy to seeking out measures of social capital, there is a question of how those with interests in micro-analyses of power gain legitimacy for their research approaches. For example, noting that there is now a broader definition of what constitutes scientific research in the twenty-first century than when Bourdieu began his empirical research, Silva and Edwards indicate that their approach has been one of using multiple methods. Of course, this was something with which Bourdieu's research group engaged. However, and perhaps with a recognition of that 'hard'/'soft' status binary of quantitative and qualitative research science, they also add the caution that: 'this does not mean that anything goes in producing good research. Methods and procedures need to be well established, within defined criteria, and the choices made need to be constructed with reference to the original theoretical assumptions' (2003: 14). Such cautions remind us of the continuing need for both tactical and strategic feminist engagement in the scientific field as well as the ever prevalent dangers of misrecognition of feminist research and methodology.

Bridging the material and the cultural

The third area of our analysis relates to the concerns within feminism of the shift to a cultural analysis at the expense of a focus on the material realm. Thus, whilst:

> On the one hand, statistical evidence ... shows that inequalities between social groups have been increasing .... At the same time interest in material inequalities as a topic for social scientific analysis has been steadily

diminishing, especially those forms of inequality ... which were formerly explained in terms of relationships of class and capitalism.

(Bradley 2000: 476)

This characteristic of the scientific field mirrors the field of politics. In seeking to bridge the material and the cultural opposition, Fraser (1995) uses the concepts of recognition and redistribution. The politics of recognition is the term Fraser uses for the contemporary predominant focus on identity and cultural expression. This includes demands to valorize groups in society who are devalued and despised on the basis of, for example, their sexuality, ethnicity, religion and sex. The politics of redistribution is concerned with priorities on inequalities of material wealth. She comments that: 'Increasingly ... identity-based claims tend to predominate, as prospects for redistribution appear to recede. The result is a complex political field with little programmatic coherence' (Fraser 1995: 70). Thus, Fraser highlights how redistribution and recognition demands may undermine each other. For example, the aim of programmes such as affirmative action is to write-out or obliterate any issues of cultural differentiation. This is the pursuit of sameness. On the other hand, those who argue for a revalidation of aspects of identity, such as Gay Pride or those feminists who extol the virtues of motherhood, are emphasizing and make more obvious cultural differentiation.

Fraser sees her task as developing 'a *critical* theory of recognition, one which identifies and defends only those versions of the cultural politics of difference than can be coherently combined with the social politics of equality' (Fraser 1995: 69). This is because of the interrelationship between economic and cultural inequalities. For example, the low value placed on womanhood is reflected in wage levels, career opportunities, educational pathways, sexual exploitation, domestic violence and so forth. To do this, Fraser argues that it is necessary to conceptualize cultural recognition and social equality in ways that support rather than undermine one another.

In this respect, our analysis suggests that social capital analyses worked within a Bourdieusian frame make important connections between the material and the cultural. We are not alone in seeing the potential of Bourdieu in this way. For example, in her analysis of habitus, power and resistance, Lawler (2005: 113) reflects that: 'Bourdieu's attempt to cut through antinomies such as self/other, structure/agency and, in Nancy Fraser's (2001) terms, recognition/redistribution gives us a method for considering the ways in which inequalities can circulate culturally, as well as materially'. Similarly, McNay (2005: 188) works through the concept of experience within a Bourdieusian frame to argue that this offers: 'a possible way in which the impasse between material and cultural styles of analysis may begin to be overcome'.

Because of the emphasis on relationality between capitals in Bourdieu's social theory, it appears that those researchers who are using a Bourdieusian conceptualization of social capital are almost required to focus on its interrelationship with other forms of capital, and particularly cultural capital. This is not the case in the broader public policy literature that separates social capital as a measurable variable from other forms of capital production. For example, Morrow (1999) indicates that Putnam's concept of social capital is not broad enough to incorporate the very wide range of factors that impinge on young people's well being. In this respect, she notes that there is a danger that the material/economic/political are overlooked as the 'social' is reified and separated from other forms of 'capital'. One way in which such links are made is through extending the list of different forms of social capital (for example bridging, linking and bonding). However, Morrow suggests that adding more and different forms of social capital to the equation will not bridge the gap between the social and the economic in Putnam's theories. Morrow (2002: 58) comments:

> Social capital is thus useful as a tool or heuristic device for exploring social processes and practices around young people's experiences of their environments, and in doing so, it has highlighted young people's 'social resources' (or lack of them). The implication of this is that 'social capital' (singular or plural) needs to be conceptualised in relation to the other forms of capital that underpin it or are related to it. The relationship between the different forms of capital to each other, and to wider economic and political structures, and the attention to processes rather than outcomes, are missing from the current debates about social capital that follow Putnam's definition.

Edwards (2004: 6) similarly draws attention to the interrelationship between social and other forms of capital when she comments that Bourdieu sees the type and content of social capital 'as inevitably shaped by the material, cultural and symbolic status of the individual and family concerned'. Indeed, as Yates (2001: 216) comments, the relationship between the material and the cultural is precisely what a relational focus taken to capital brings:

> One important feature of class in its traditional and also Bourdieuian sense is that it is a *relational* concept, not just a descriptive one. Schooling effects and *social* outcomes are created not just because young people have more or less of the goods required (materially, and in terms of known-how), but because the schooling and the social world is operating in terms of a mode which produces and reproduces the unstated things that matter.

This relationality can be seen in the ways in which Bourdieu's work has demonstrated how individuals rich in economic, social and political capital are able to overcome a lack of educational capital. As Moi (1999: 276) comments: 'When it comes to measuring social success in later life ... Bourdieu chillingly demonstrates how a certain lack of educational capital can be compensated for by the possession of other forms of capital'. Tellingly, particularly at a time in the UK when higher education institutions are in the process of being consolidated into the status divisions of 'research' and 'teaching', Bourdieu offers another insight of particular relevance to the 'widening access' movement for 'non-traditional' students. For those lacking in the culturally, economically or politically useful social relations associated with social capital, attendance at a non-prestigious school or university will be of little benefit. This is because: 'if capital is what it takes to produce more capital, an agent lacking in social capital at the outset will not benefit greatly from a relatively non-prestigious ("low-capital") education' (Moi 1999: 276). Whilst working-class access continues to be high on the policy agenda, the Bourdieusian message is that there is little benefit for working-class students attending low ranking universities in terms of future higher social and economic returns.

Appropriating Bourdieu: some critical concerns

Our analysis of a Bourdieusian approach to social capital indicates both dilemmas and potentialities. We turn, now, more broadly to a range of critical concerns surrounding an appropriation of Bourdieu. We first address the language of capitals. Currently, there is a trend to capitalize a growing range of social phenomena, yet Silva and Edwards (2003: 11) argue that:

> The use of the term 'capital' gives primacy to the economic or political effects or outcomes of family and social relationships, rather than social justice, and in a way that imposes a functionalist economic rationality on social life. At the same time, however, it moves towards causative explanations that take attention away from the economy to families and culture as the focus of policy intervention.

Whilst Silva and Edwards indicate that Bourdieu's theories may be less subject to these double effects than that of Coleman and Putnam, they add nonetheless that: 'his work still retains elements of economic rationality' (ibid.). We would make a number of points here that are concerned, first, with Bourdieu's own position on this matter and, second, how feminist social theorization of Bourdieu is moving towards a critique of his lack of attention to the realm of the affect. In terms of the former point, the retention of rationality in Bourdieu's analysis of social behaviour does not necessarily impute rational choice to actors in a field (Bourdieu 1998). As we have noted, Bourdieu uses 'capital' primarily as a metaphor for distributions in social space. Indeed, as Sayer (2005: 40) comments: Bourdieu 'vehemently rejects the rationalist, utilitarian reading ... actors are not rational, self-interested decision-makers making investments, but, rather, their habitus attunes them to the game'. Moreover, because Bourdieu argues that in the last analysis economic capital underpins other forms of capital, he specifically wants distribution of wealth to be kept in the frame in order to retain attention on inequality.

In terms of our latter point, we would suggest that in Bourdieu's work 'rationality' is not always and only economic (and the rationality of action is in the eye of the beholder). Rationality, in terms of a reasoned response arising from ongoing reflection, can also be ascribed to the sphere of the affect.[5] Thus, Sayer further comments: 'Actors also tend to invest emotionally in certain things not merely for the rewards but because they come to see them as valuable in themselves, sometimes regardless of any benefit to themselves' (ibid.). In a critique of Bourdieu, Skeggs (2005: 29) notes that his social theory ignores 'Values such as altruism, integrity, loyalty and investment in others [thus] the use values that we have in everyday life are of minimal value to Bourdieu's analysis' (see also Skeggs 2004). Skeggs' important point here is that some activities are not undertaken in the spirit of 'investment', rather they are expressive of values (see also Sayer 2005). A researcher may analyse the unpaid physical and emotional work of women in the activities of everyday life as expressive of habitus and productive or destructive of forms of capital. Indeed, as Reay (2000, 2005) has argued in respect of emotional capital, forms of affective investment in others do not necessarily bring reward but they can certainly be viewed as costs.

These points are important in terms of an analysis of how research on social capital is proceeding in the social policy arena. Here, as we have also noted, the social capital literature draws on a range of other concepts, such as trust, networks, civic engagement and community. These concepts can be found in older feminist literatures but the dominant policy discourse has rendered them capitalized. Similarly, the unpaid physical and emotional labour of women in developing and maintaining family and community relationships means that women act as central producers of the social capital associated with those social groups who are priority objects of social policy. What are the implications of this for feminist scholarship and politics? These terms, and associated activities, we would argue, require renewed feminist attention before they are finally bound together, without distinction, under the 'capital' label. We would argue that renewed attention needs to ask who 'invests' and who 'profits' in transactions when relationships are described using a capital metaphor and what dimensions of social practice are neglected and what is put into the foreground.

Notwithstanding, the seductive language of capitals is of concern. Such languages appeal to particular groups in society and we should ask whether, when we hear the word 'capital', we envisage it as a Bourdieusian metaphor through which it speaks of social inequalities and privilege or as Siles (2002: 1) suggests as an economic determinism:

> social capital, when defined as sympathy, has many important capital-like properties including transformation capacity, durability, flexibility, substitutability, opportunities for decay (maintenance), reliability, ability to create other capital forms, and investment (disinvestment) opportunities.

In this respect, and following Lankshear *et al.* (1997: 97), social capital is a contemporary key word that has 'positive connotations across multiple Discourse communities'. In effect, therefore, such language brings together diverse groups whose aims and political objectives may similarly be diverse but for whom, without critical interrogation of the key concepts and underlying theorization being used, believe that they have similar goals. Thus, we share Silva and Edward's concern to raise this privileging of economic rationality as it remains the case that if, as we have demonstrated, critical accounts of social capital remain marginalized in the public policy literature, their sphere of influence will be similarly so.

We also need to consider issues related to agency as they are central to a consideration of social change. Morrow (1999, 2002) asks how social capital, predominantly theorized and conceptualized from studies of adult lives, can be applied to children. Morrow (2002: 40) notes that, in much existing work on social capital: 'children and young people are constructed as the passive recipients of culture whose agency is denied'. Thus, '[T]here is no acknowledgement of how children actively generate, draw upon, or negotiate their own "social capital" or even provide active support for parents' (ibid.). As Morrow further notes, due to the simple fact of 'being young' children carry negative symbolic capital. This issue of agency connects with Lovell's critique of Bourdieu's view of women primarily as capital bearing objects rather than as also capital accumulating subjects. Thus, Lovell asks: 'How may the existence of women as objects – as repositories of capital for someone else – be curtailing or enabling in terms of their simultaneous existence as capital accumulating subjects?' (Lovell 2000: 22). Women's 'kinship work' (di Leonardo 1987) would seem to be an area of potential social capital accumulation: under what circumstances and in what forms do women gain from this? Similarly, Morrow (1999: 757) reflects in respect of children that:

> We can move forward, I suggest, by coupling Bourdieu's original formulation of social capital as in relation with other forms of capital and as rooted in the practices of everyday life, with a view of children as having agency (albeit constrained): thus linking micro-social and macro-social structural factors. This usage of social capital contrasts with the static and circular models of social capital developed by Coleman and Putnam, and sees 'social capital' as a tool or heuristic device for exploring processes and practices that are related to the acquisition of other forms of capital.

Finally, because it is social class that is predominant in Bourdieu's work, it could be that other social divisions are relegated into a second, or ancillary, position (Lovell 2000). There is, therefore, a need to be wary of ignoring gender effects with respect to social capital but at the same time the pendulum cannot swing to the point where gender is reified above other social divisions. Thus, there is a need to retain a focus on the gendered nature of the work of social capital (re)production whilst at the same time taking account of other key social divisions. For example, Moi (1999) argues that we could see gender as a social field equivalent to Bourdieu's analysis of class but she also comments that the relationship between class and gender still remains problematic. Lovell's (2005: 52) analysis of women as a social class extends these concerns further by indicating the centrality of the 'sharp sexual division of labour in human reproduction'. For Lovell:

If women constitute a class, it is a class differentiated not only along the lines of 'race', socio-economic class, sexuality – the three 'differences' that are most commonly recognized – but also differentiated by those who become, willy nilly or by choice, the mothers of children and those that do not.

(Ibid.)

These concerns resonate with the findings of research on social capital where gender appears to cut across class and other social divisions yet at the same time such social divisions cannot be discounted in both their effects and meanings. For example, Riddell *et al.*'s (2001) research on social capital confirms a much earlier analysis by di Leonardo (1987: 447–448) who noted that the gendered 'kin work' of maintaining family contacts and relationships 'is not an ethnic or racial phenomenon, neither is it linked only to one social class'. Riddell *et al.* indicate, therefore, that although disability cuts across class lines, stereotypical gender relations remain:

For both women and men, the advantages of middle class social and eco- nomic capital are overridden by the negative category of learning dif- ficulties. In relation to gender, men with learning difficulties are more likely to receive post-school training, but in inappropriate areas of the labour market. Their domestic needs are also likely to be attended to by others, but in the absence of employment, they find themselves without any valued social role. Women with learning difficulties are also likely to be excluded from the labour market, but are more likely to be involved in reciprocal, albeit limited, social relationships.

(Riddell *et al.* 2001: 57)

Similarly, Reay (2000) notes how anxiety in respect of children's educational success cuts across divisions of class and 'race'. And, in respect of class, Morrow (1999: 761) comments on how: 'We need to be wary of reading Bour- dieu as implying that cultural capital and related social capital is something that middle classes possess in abundance'. Thus, whilst the 'kin work' of social capital remains women's work, analysis has to consider how other social divi- sions cross-cut not only women's access to resources and support but must also be attuned to the relativity of 'historical and cultural contexts, and to positions occupied within "the social field"' (Lovell 2000: 22).

Conclusion

This chapter has detailed the rise of a particular conceptualization of social capital. It is one that is based on the methodological individualism of economet- ric analysis while carrying a social face. Confirming our own analysis of the influence of the social capital idea, Gilchrist (2003, personal communication) comments:

Major international institutions such as the World Bank and European Union are currently investigating the value of social capital and devising programmes to promote and strengthen it, for example, through public health, housing, active citizenship or regeneration programmes. The British government is likewise interested in the links between social capital and improvements in 'community capacity' and 'social inclusion'.

Nonetheless, we would argue, as Uguris (2000: 49) does for community, that social capital, like empowerment, partnership and participation are concepts that 'homogenize and naturalize' and assume 'common interests and goals'. In this respect, the prominence given to the formulations of Coleman, Putnam and Fukuyama, rather than that of Bourdieu, has protected power in social relationships and social systems from renewed scrutiny. Linked to public policy, this sustains the marginalized, poor or the socially excluded as *objects* of social research and of development interventions. As Baron (2004: 15) comments:

As formulated by the Cabinet Office Strategy Unit and by the ONS Question Bank, social capital is based on the implicit claim by government to be the moral voice of a unitary community which has the right and capacity to define good, deficient and bad forms of spontaneous social life. In part this reproduces the thirty year old policy discourse of deeming people, particularly young people, in structurally impoverished areas as being socially, culturally and psychologically pathological. In part this represents an extension of this thirty year old discourse further into the realms of personal life and spontaneous social networks, opening these up for more intrusive surveillance and intervention through new 'soft policing' methods.

In contrast, and turning to a Bourdieusian analysis, Skeggs (2005) notes how feminists have found three aspects of Bourdieu's social theory highly useful. These are in terms of the ways that a Bourdieusian social theory offers opportunities for linkage across, for example, agency and structure; gives feminists a metaphoric capitalistic concept that facilitates analyses between different types of value and social mobility; and, through his attention to reflexivity, provides a bridge between feminist methodological concerns and masculine dominated research agendas.

In this paper, we have been concerned with the use of a Bourdieusian framework for the analysis of social capital. We have indicated that this has the potential to link the material and the cultural in ways that are now vital for future feminist enquiry and social justice concerns. In this regard, we believe it is a matter of regret that the attention given to cultural capital has yet to be given to social capital within the feminist literature. As McNay (2005: 176) reflects on the problem of cultural models: 'they are essentially ahistorical because they disconnect questions of identity recognition from the context of access to economic resources and other types of social capital'.

Nevertheless, we have also raised a range of potential concerns about the use of Bourdieu in social policy research on social capital. Thus, whilst a Bourdieusian framework clearly serves as an antidote to the methodological individualism of the exponentially disseminated theories of Putnam, Coleman and Fukuyama, there remains much work to do to extend his take-up beyond the (possibly) already converted. In addition, more general analyses of Bourdieu have highlighted a number of areas through which Bourdieu is less helpful. This includes issues of affect and ambivalence (Skeggs, 2004, 2005; Sayer 2005). Thus, given that, via their unpaid physical and *emotional* labour in the family and community, women are the main (re)producers of social capital, such a gap remains particularly concerning. In this respect, we would echo Moi's (1999: 265) concerns that Bourdieusian social theory will not serve us better unless we undertake 'a critical assessment ... with a view to taking it over and using it for feminist purposes' (Moi 1999: 265). In this paper, we have been concerned with an initial exploration of this through a review of feminist theoretical assessments of Bourdieu and the use of a Bourdieusian framework for the consideration of 'social capital'.

Notes

1 See, for example, Moi (1999), Lovell (2000), Skeggs (1997); and the special issue of *Sociological Review*, 2005, 52, s2.
2 This lack of attention to the specifics of social capital is also evident in the special issue of *Sociological Review*. This may, of course, be a reflection of the divisions between theory and policy extant, not only within feminism, but in intellectual debate more broadly.
3 Whilst our concern in this chapter is to specifically focus on the work of Nancy Fraser, Baron (2004) has drawn attention to how New Labour's approach to social capital moves, albeit slightly, in the direction of Iris Marion Young's (2000) account of deliberative democracy. Nonetheless, he further notes that: 'These modest moves towards a deliberative democracy of social capital are overshadowed by the consequences of marrying a partial reading of the concept onto an aggregative democratic model and an unquestioning commitment to capitalist markets and rational choice economics'.
4 The connections between Bourdieu's methodological approach and feminist concerns have also been raised by Lovell (2000). Lovell notes that Bourdieu's 'reflexive sociology' has a certain affinity with feminist traditions of reflexivity in research and his sociology of intellectual life may be made to resonate with long-standing concerns over 'academic feminism' (Lovell 2000: 26). For Lovell this means that Bourdieu shares with feminists a need to address how 'feminist theory and feminist politics are themselves "practices" in Bourdieu's (and feminism's) terms. They demand considerable "investments" of the self, of social, and cultural capital' (ibid.). As Lovell points out, a Bourdieusian analysis would lend itself to exploring the competition between feminists in the 'ghettoized' field of feminist theory and how feminist theory establishes its own forms of symbolic violence that reproduces class and 'race' hierarchies.
5 Noting Archer's (2003) work on the 'internal conversation', Sayer (2005) reminds us of the importance of lay normativity. Sayer's concerns are to illustrate how neglecting the terrain of values and affect from analyses of discourse and socialization effectively removes an important aspect of sense-making and thus leads to incomplete analyses (see also Bottero 2004; Clegg 2006; Hughes, 2007). In this respect, Sayer critiques Bourdieu for ignoring 'a mundane but crucial aspect of our lives: our "internal conversation"'.

References

Adkins, L. (2003) 'Reflexivity: freedom or habit of gender?' *Theory, Culture and Society*, 20, 6: 21–42.

Adkins, L. (2005) 'Introduction: feminism, Bourdieu and after', *Sociological Review*, 52, 2: 3–18.

Ahier, J. and Beck, J. (2003) 'Education and the politics of envy', *British Journal of Educational Studies*, 51, 4: 320–343.

Aldridge, S. and Halpern, D. with Fitzpatrick, S. (2002) *Social Capital: a Discussion paper*, London: Cabinet Office Performance and Innovation Unit.

Archer, A. (2003) *Structure, Agency and the Internal Conversation*, Cambridge: Cambridge University Press.

Avis, J. (2000) 'Policy Talk: reflexive modernization and the construction of teaching and learning within post-compulsory education and lifelong learning in England', *Journal of Educational Policy*, 15, 2: 185–199.

Baron, S. (2004) 'Social capital in British politics and policy making', in J. Franklin (ed.) *Politics, Trust and Networks: Social Capital in Critical Perspective*, London: South Bank University.

Blaxter, L. and Hughes, C. (2000) 'Social capital: a critique', in J. Thompson (ed.) *Stretching the Academy: the Politics and Practice of Widening Participation in Higher Education*, Leicester: NIACE.

Blaxter, L. and Hughes, C. (2003) 'Revisiting feminist appropriations of Bourdieu: the case of social capital', *Fourth International Conference of Gender and Education*, University of Sheffield, April 2003.

Bottero, W. (2004) 'Class identities and the identity of class', *Sociology*, 38, 5: 985–1003

Bourdieu, P. (1986) 'The forms of capital', in J. Richardson (ed.) *Handbook of Theory and Research for the Sociology of Education*, New York: Greenwood Press.

Bourdieu, P. (1990) *The Logic of Practice*, Cambridge: Polity.

Bourdieu, P. (1998) *Practical Reason*, Cambridge: Polity.

Bourdieu, P. and Passeron, J. (1977) *Reproduction in Education and Society*, London: Sage.

Bradley, H. (2000) 'Social Inequalities: coming to terms with complexity', in G. Browning, A. Halcli and F. Webster (eds) *Understanding Contemporary Society: Theories of the Present*, London: Sage.

Clegg, S. (2006) 'The problem of agency in feminism: a critical realist approach', *Gender and Education*, 18, 3: 309–324.

Coleman, J. (1987) 'Norms as social capital', in G. Radnitzky and P. Bernholz (eds) *Economic Imperialism: the Economic Method Applied Outside the Field of Economics*, New York: Paragon.

Coleman, J. (1988) 'Social capital in the creation of human capital', *American Journal of Sociology*, 94: 945–1558.

Denzin, N. and Lincoln, Y. (2005) *The Sage Handbook of Qualitative Research*, 3rd edn, Thousand Oaks, CA: Sage.

Di Leonardo, M. (1987) 'The female world of cards and holidays: women, families, and the work of kinship', *Signs: Journal of Women in Culture and Society*, 12, 3: 440–453.

Edwards, R. (2004) 'Present and absent in troubling ways: families and social capital debates', *Sociological Review*, 52, 1: 1–21.

Fraser, N. (1995) 'From redistribution to recognition: dilemmas in justice in a "post-socialist" age', *New Left Review*, 212: 68–93.

Fraser, N. (1997) *Justice Interruptus: Critical Reflections on the "Postsocialist" Condition*, New York: Routledge.

Fraser, N. (2001) 'Recognition without ethics?', *Theory, Culture and Society*, 18, 2–3: 21–42.

Fraser, N. and Honneth, A. (2003) *Redistribution or Recognition? A Political–Philosophical Exchange*, London: Verso

Fukuyama, F. (1995) *Trust: the Social Virtues and the Creation of Prosperity*, London: Penguin.

Fukuyama, F. (2001) 'Social capital, civil society and development', *Third World Quarterly*, 22, 1: 7–20.

Gamarnikow, E. and Green, A. (1999) 'The third way and social capital: education action zones and a new agenda for education, parents and community?', *International Studies in Sociology of Education*, 9, 1: 3–22.

Gray, A. (2003) *Towards a Conceptual Framework for Studying Time and Social Capital*, Families and Social Capital ESRC Research Group Working Paper No 3, London: South Bank University.

Harris, J. (1997) 'Missing link or analytically missing: the concept of social capital', *Journal of International Development Policy Arena*, 9, 7: 919–971.

Heward, C. (1994) 'Academic snakes and merit ladders: reconceptualising the "glass ceiling", *Gender and Education*, 6, 3: 249–262.

Hughes, C. (2002) *Women's Contemporary Lives: Within and Beyond the Mirror*, London: Routledge.

Hughes, C. (2007) 'The equality of social envies', *Sociology*, 41, 2: 347–363.

Hughes, C., Burgess, R, and Moxon, S. (1991) 'Parents are welcome: head teachers' and matrons' perspectives on parental participation in the early years', *International Journal of Qualitative Studies in Education*, 4, 2: 95–107.

Lankshear, C. with Gee, J. Knobel, M. and Searle, C. (1997) *Changing Literacies*, Buckingham: Open University Press.

Lawler, S. (2005) 'Rules of engagement: habitus, power and resistance', *Sociological Review*, 52, 2: 110–128.

Liddle, J. and Michielsens, E. (2000) 'Gender, class and political power in Britain: narratives of entitlement', in S. Rai (ed.) *International Perspectives on Gender and Democratisation*, London: Macmillan.

Lovell, T. (2000) 'Thinking feminism with and against Bourdieu', *Feminist Theory*, 1, 1: 11–32.

Lovell, T. (2005) 'Bourdieu, class and gender: "The return of the living dead"?' *Sociological Review*, 52, 2: 37–56.

Luke, C. (1998) 'Cultural politics and women in Singapore higher education management', *Gender and Education*, 10, 3: 245–264.

McCall, L. (1992) 'Does gender fit? Bourdieu, feminism and conceptions of social order', *Theory and Society*, 21: 837–867.

McNay, L. (2005) 'Agency and experience: gender as lived relation', *Sociological Review*, 52, 2: 175–190.

McRobbie, A. (2000) 'Feminism and the third way', *Feminist Review*, 64, (Spring): 97–112.

Millard, E. (1997) 'Differently literate: gender identity and the construction of the developing reader', *Gender and Education*, 9, 1: 31–48.

Moi, T. (1999) *What is a Woman?* Oxford: Oxford UP.

Morrow, V. (1999) 'Conceptualising social capital in relation to the well-being of children and young people: a critical review', *The Sociological Review*, 47, 4: 744–765.

Morrow, V. (2002) 'Young people's explanations and experiences of social exclusion: retrieving Bourdieu's concept of social capital', *International Journal of Sociology and Social Policy*, 21, 4/5/6: 37–63.

Office for National Statistics (2001) *Social Capital*, http://www.statistics.gov.uk/social-capital (accessed 2 April 2003).

Pevalin, D. (2003) 'More to social capital than Putnam', *The British Journal of Psychiatry*, 182: 172–173.

Putnam, R. (1993) *Making Democracy Work: Civic Traditions in Modern Italy*, Princeton: Princeton University Press.

Putnam, R. (1995) 'Bowling alone: America's declining social capital', *Journal of Democracy*, 6, 1: 65–78.

Putnam, R. (2000) *Bowling Alone: The Collapse and Revival of American Community*, New York: Simon and Schuster.

Putzel, J. (1997) 'Accounting for the dark side of social capital: reading Robert Putnam on democracy', *Journal of International Development Policy Arena*, 9, 7: 939–947.

Rankin, K. (2002) 'Social capital, microfinance, and the politics of development', *Feminist Economics*, 8, 1: 1–24.

Reay, D. (2000) 'A useful extension of Bourdieu's conceptual framework? Emotional capital as a way of understanding mothers' involvement in their children's education?' *Sociological Review*, 48, 4: 568–585.

Reay, D. (2002) 'Shaun's story: troubling discourses of white working class masculinities', *Gender and Education*, 14, 3: 221–234.

Reay, D. (2005) 'Gendering Bourdieu's concepts of capitals? Emotional capital, women and social class', *Sociological Review*, 52, 2: 57–74.

Riddell, S., Baron, S. and Wilson, A. (2001) 'The significance of the learning society for women and men with learning difficulties', *Gender and Education*, 13, 1: 57–74.

Sayer, A. (2005) *The Moral Significance of Class*, Cambridge: Cambridge University Press.

Siles, M. (2002) 'Is social capital really capital?' *Review of Social Economy*, 60, 1: 1–22.

Silva, E. and Edwards, R. (2003) *Operationalising Bourdieu on capitals: a Discussion on 'the Construction of the Object'*, ESRC Research Methods Programme, Working Paper No 7, Manchester: University of Manchester, www.ccsr.ac.uk/methods/publications/documents/WP7_000.pdf (accessed 3 March 2006).

Skeggs, B. (1997) *Formations of Class and Gender*, London, Sage.

Skeggs, B. (2004) *Class, Self, Culture*, London: Routledge.

Skeggs, B. (2005) 'Context and background: Pierre Bourdieu's analysis of class, gender and sexuality', *Sociological Review*, 52, 2: 19–33.

Thomson, R., Henderson, S. and Holland, J. (2003) 'Making the most of what you've got? Resources, values and inequalities in young women's transitions to adulthood', *Educational Review*, 55, 1: 33–46.

Uguris, T. (2000) 'Gender, ethnicity and "the community"', in A. Suki, K. Coates and W. Wangui (eds) *Global Feminist Politics: Identities in a Changing World*, London: Routledge.

van Deth, J. (2003) 'Measuring social capital: orthodoxies and continuing controversies', *International Journal of Social Research Methodology*, 6, 1: 79–92.

Yates, L. (2001) 'Subjectivity, social change and the reform problematic', *International Journal of Inclusive Education*, 5, 2/3: 209–223.

Young, I.M. (1997) 'Unruly categories: a critique of Nancy Fraser's dual systems theory', *New Left Review*, 222: 147–160.

Young, I.M. (2000) *Inclusion and Democracy*, Oxford: Oxford University Press.

8 'NQOC'[1]

Social identity and representation in British politics

Joanna Liddle and Elisabeth Michielsens

Introduction

'Political equality matters'

(Anne Phillips 1999: 125)

In a context in which the concept of 'the political' has become ubiquitous, Anne Phillips has expressed concern that what is specific to politics in the narrower sense is sometimes lost from sight.

It is now fully in the frame in Nancy Fraser's integrated theory of justice (Fraser 1995, 1998), with the explicit inclusion of 'representation' alongside recognition and redistribution, within the broad frame of 'participatory parity', her most general definition of justice (Fraser 2005). Our paper is based on empirical research on representational institutions in a specific context, with a focus on inequalities of class and gender, and was developed drawing (critically) on the conceptual framework of Pierre Bourdieu. As a preliminary to our analysis, however, it may be helpful to locate it in relation to Fraser's broader and more general discussion.

Fraser's main concerns in her recent work are first, with representational justice within deliberative democracy, but second and most important, with the 'who' of representation, in 'which' frame. With an eye upon the context of an increasingly global capitalist system, she asks questions that go beyond what she terms the 'Keynesian-Westphalian' political frame of modern welfare capitalism, with its focus on the territorial nation-state, to the problems of representational justice in a world where economic systems and political communities no longer share the same boundaries. Political communities may wrongly exclude some who have claims to representation within it, and increasing numbers of people may be excluded from membership in any political community and so from Hannah Arendt's 'right to have rights' (Arendt 1973).

Our concerns in this paper are with misrepresentation within one of the most important of the formal arenas of deliberative democracy in the UK, the political system of party and of power within the national legislative assembly. With the addition of 'representation' to Fraser's model, and the recognition of 'the political' as a conceptually distinct dimension of justice in addition to 'the economic' and 'the cultural', these forums gain a specific place within the model even as national assemblies and institutions may appear to recede in significance with the switch of focus to the global frame. Political obstacles to parity 'arise from the political constitution of society, as opposed to the [related] class structure or status order' (Fraser 2005: 76). The obstacles to political parity in relationship to class and status are the central focus of this paper. However the research on which the paper is based does not take Fraser's concerns over representation to her 'second level' of 'the political', that of boundary-setting in the 'post-Westphalian' world of global capitalism: it is limited to her first level of '*ordinary-political* misrepresentation ... the familiar terrain of political science' (ibid.: 76). We hope to show that these issues still matter, are unresolved, and are deeply embedded along the lines of social injustice and inequality. We would hold they continue to matter in the politics of representation in the broader post-Westphalian frame, although we shall not be developing this contention here. On the one hand, the death of the nation-state has been somewhat exaggerated in some of the literature on globalisation; on the other hand, the processes of exclusion, misrecognition, maldistribution, and misrepresentation remain significant within emerging trans-national forums, both hegemonic and counter-hegemonic.

Our paper focuses on political elites. The research subject, 'Kevin', whose responses are under analysis here, has all of what Bourdieu terms 'the lucidity of the excluded'. However, he hardly ranks among 'the excluded'. Members of the ruling party who have made progress within government hierarchies are *power-holders*, to whatever marginalised *categories* of the social world they belong, along the various lines of social disadvantage. The paper focuses on the processes that are revealed by our interview with one of Bourdieu's 'oblats miraculés' – the 'lucky' few who gain entry to high status positions of power against the grain of habitus and position in social space – in order to illuminate normal processes of exclusion and resulting under-representation of the large sectors of the population of which they are *representative*. This paper is based on research into obstacles to parity of political representation and strategies for overcoming them. It focuses on the constraints and conditions which research subjects, identified in terms of class and gender, have had to negotiate in their political trajectories; the extent of their awareness of the constraints and conditions along the lines of disadvantage; and the effects and outcomes in terms of both parity of participation and the pathways along which participation took place.

We draw on Bourdieu's conceptual framework for our analysis of these constraints, conditions, and processes. Unlike Bourdieu *et al.*'s research respondents in *The Weight of the World* (1999), ours are serious 'contenders', movers and shakers in the exclusive 'game' of political power. Nonetheless, the 'deficits' of class and gender have cut deep into the *form* that their participation took, and the *trajectories* of their careers. Even at this level then, among those who made it through the eye of the needle and gained access to the power to represent and influence policy, full parity of participation remains elusive. The skewed social composition of parliamentary membership cannot but have a bearing on the representational injustice suffered along lines of social disadvantage among the rank and file members of the political community.

Our particular focus here is with inequalities of access to participation in party politics and political processes along the lines of class and gender: an aspect of participatory parity that is addressed in some of the literature as 'the problem of social bias'.[2] 'Social bias' in parliamentary representation, and how to diversify candidate selection and election to reflect the demographic structure of the population, has remained a topical issue since the Labour party introduced all-women shortlists (AWS) for the 1997 election. No other party has yet adopted positive discrimination strategies on gender, and no party has adopted strategies to deal with other significant social divisions in society.[3] But since the Labour government introduced permissive legislation on positive gender discrimination for the 2005 general election, it is arguably the Conservatives, as the second largest party, that need to deal with the question of social bias if the House of Commons is to become more diverse and representative of the population. The impact of class divisions may be seen as a different kind of social bias, inasmuch as the two major parties have, historically, explicitly represented divergent class interests; but given that both parties have claimed in the last decade or two to be broadening their appeal to a wider class base in line with changes to the class structure of British society, the under-representation of people from working-class origins in parliament in both major parties is also an important part of the problem of social bias.

The Conservative party is ideologically opposed to positive discrimination strategies because of its belief in the virtue of meritocratic individual competition and the ability of selection panels to choose the best candidate (Norris and Lovenduski 1995). But it is apparent that strategies of exhortation or even affirmative action (for example, women-only training), as distinct from positive discrimination (such as quota systems) have failed to produce results. Our aim in this paper is not to propose or support a particular strategy for achieving diversity in political representation. It is to attempt to explain why it is so difficult to achieve change. We would like to suggest that the widely held understanding of the problem of social bias in political representation, particularly the view that a more diverse parliament can be produced solely by institutional measures such as the reform of selection procedures, both misunderstands and significantly underestimates the nature of the problem.

Understanding the process of political selection: supply and demand

In 1995, Pippa Norris and Joni Lovenduski published a major study of political recruitment, providing the 'first full account of legislative recruitment in Britain for 25 years' (1995: 1). This research constitutes an impressive and detailed examination of the power relations of gender, 'race', and class in the operation of British parliamentary selection and election based on the 1992–7 parliament. The study shows that 'the typical candidate in all parties tends to be a well-educated, professional white male', as a result of which the 'traditional composition of parliament' is 'overwhelmingly middle class, male and white' (ibid.: 87).

The authors seek to explain the social bias in the composition of parliament using an economistic model based on the concepts of 'supply' and 'demand'. Supply-side explanations 'suggest that the outcome of the selection process reflects the supply of applicants *wishing* to pursue a political career' whereas demand-side explanations suggest that 'selectors *choose* candidates depending on their perceptions of the applicants' abilities, qualifications and experience' (ibid.: 15, 14, emphasis added). Their analysis shows that the *class* and *education* bias of parliament is the product of *supply* rather than demand (ibid.: 113, 115). *Gender* varies by party: *supply* is more important for women in the Conservative party, while *demand* is more important for women in the Labour party (ibid.: 116–18). This means, in Norris and Lovenduski's terms, that Conservative women do not 'wish' to pursue a political career and therefore do not stand, whereas Labour women do 'wish' to stand, but fail to be 'chosen' by the selectors.

The three major reasons given by party members for not applying were lack of time and energy, lack of experience, and anticipated failure, only the first two of which distinguish marginalised groups from others (ibid.: 172). Norris and Lovenduski therefore conclude that marginal groups did not anticipate failure and discrimination, rather 'they saw themselves as *unqualified for the job*' (ibid.: 170–1, emphasis added). Overall, and particularly in the case of the Conservative party, they argue that 'on balance, supply-side factors are the most persuasive explanation for ... social bias' (ibid.: 247). Although Norris and Lovenduski do acknowledge that supply and demand factors interact (ibid.: 108), they rarely consider this interaction in their analysis. Lovenduski's later study of the 1997 election adopted a less polarised conceptualisation of supply and demand by acknowledging that the lack of positive measures to signal a demand for women in the Conservative party may have adversely affected supply (1997: 712). It was Sarah Childs, however, who subsequently demonstrated the importance of demand in producing supply in her study of women's representation in the Labour party after the introduction of AWS, arguing that 'the earlier emphasis placed upon supply-side explanations' should be tempered (2004: 33, 39).

In addition to the effect of demand on supply, however, a polarised conceptualisation of supply and demand fails to recognise that supply also affects demand. The lack of 'non-traditional' candidates and the predominance of 'traditional' candidates may actually contribute to the production of political identity as gendered, classed, and 'raced' in particular ways, thus helping to construct political 'entitlement' among social categories constituting the 'traditional MP', and constructing political 'illegitimacy' among social categories constitutive of the 'non-traditional MP'. Childs does address this issue, referring to a woman Labour MP who still does not feel 'legitimate' despite her election to parliament, thus acknowledging the importance of symbolic representation in challenging the 'identification of politics ... with men' (2004: 59). But she offers no theory to help explain 'the link between the identity of the representative and the representative's attitudes and behaviour', other than recognising 'different women representatives operating in different gendered environments' (ibid.: 69, 196). The need for a more socially-based gendered analysis of political representation is now acknowledged (Lovenduski 1998; Puwar 2004; Mackay 2004). We would add that the gendering (and classing and 'racing') of the 'political field' itself must also be considered (Moi 1999): a field that, Bourdieu argues, was traditionally reserved for the expression of the masculine 'libido dominandi' or 'desire to dominate' (2001: 80).

We would like to suggest that what is needed to understand political representation and social identity, particularly how and why certain social categories see themselves as 'unqualified', is a theory that does not polarise subjectivity and social structure in the way that 'supply' and 'demand' are polarised in the economistic approach. To this end, we propose to use concepts from the work of Bourdieu (1984, 1990a, 2001).[4] Building on our earlier examination of how entitlements to power are generated in relation to particular political identities (Liddle and Michielsens 2000a, 2000b), and taking as the starting point Norris and Lovenduski's (1995) supply-side explanation that women, working-class and less-educated party members see themselves as 'unqualified' for the job of political representative, the questions we are interested in are: why do certain social categories see themselves as differentially qualified for public office? How do members of different social groups develop a sense of entitlement in themselves and get that entitlement recognised by others as legitimate? In other words, how do they come to see themselves as 'qualified for the job', and how do they convince others that they are qualified? We will look at these questions in relation to masculinity and working-class identity.

Generating entitlement to political power: habitus, field, institutions

Bourdieu understands the relationship between subjectivity and society through the concepts of the habitus and the field. The habitus is a system of dispositions acquired experientially through childhood socialisation and shaped by the social circumstances of its production (Bourdieu 1984: 101, 1990b: 123). It therefore differs by class, gender, and ethnic positioning (Bourdieu 1977: 72–95; Thompson 1980: 12; Moi 1991; Lovell 2000: 11–32). It is through the dispositions of the habitus that people perceive, categorise, understand, evaluate, and act upon the social fields to which they belong (Bourdieu 1990a: 61), as well as make decisions about whether and on what terms they wish to enter other fields, or feel themselves to be disqualified from entering. Relational social fields *map the differential distribution* of economic, social, cultural, and symbolic capital, the form which different types of capital take when they are recognised as legitimate (Bourdieu 1984: 114). The value of the various capitals in the social field is assessed by the extent to which they can be converted into symbolic capital (ibid.: 291). As Bourdieu points out, the capitals held by those who are 'unequally armed in the fight to impose their truth' (Bourdieu 1987: 11) are not valued or acknowledged as legitimate (Bourdieu in Wacquant 1989: 39); for example, the naturalisation of female occupational skills as mere 'nimble fingers' (Elson and Pearson 1981) disallows recognition of women as skilled workers. The 'general social field'[5] refers to a set of positions in social space defined through the social relations of the field, structured by the distribution of capitals, and producing relations of power in which we may include those of class, gender, and 'race' (Moi 1999: 288). Bourdieu shares a common sociological thesis of differentiation and specialisation of social systems over historical time, with the emergence of relatively autonomous fields – the economic, political, cultural, intellectual and so on. Each specialised field has, Bourdieu claims, its 'price of entry', specific 'rules of the game' or nomos, distribution of capital, and 'stakes of struggle'.[6]

The specialised field of politics has not been subjected by Bourdieu to in-depth analysis. His comments on it are sketchy. He identifies its characteristics as verbal combat, where politicians 'form and transform their visions of the world and thereby the world itself ... [where] words are actions and the symbolic character of power is at stake' (Thompson 1991: 26–7). Politicians are engaged in 'a labour of representation', seeking to 'construct and impose a particular view of the social world' and mobilising those on whom their power depends; what is at stake is 'the representation of the forces engaged in the struggle and their chances of success' (Bourdieu 1991: 134). Politicians are '"professionals of representation" in every sense of the term' (ibid.: 243). Politics is the field that is least autonomous from economic interests (Bourdieu 1991: 173; Lash 1990: 244), and the verbal combat of politicians is ordered, not by a disinterested search for truth and falsity through argument and refutation, as in the case of the intellectual or scientific fields, but by the logic of 'friend or foe' (Lash 1990: 244 quoting Bourdieu 1986), by 'denunciation and slander, "sloganisation" and falsification of the adversary's thought' (Bourdieu 1988: 9).

People may participate in the political field through the franchise, and may enter or aspire to compete in the field through membership of political parties and through standing for election (Bourdieu 1991; Wacquant 2005). But the political field is increasingly professionalised, and is distinctive in the need for politicians to 'appeal to groups or forces which lie *outside* the field' (unlike the fields of science and art) (Thompson 1991: 28). The stakes of the political game are the 'legitimate division of the social world and, thereby, of the mobilization of groups', and the 'use of objectified instruments of power' such as the law, police or public finances (Bourdieu 1991: 181). The professionals must be able to manipulate ideas and groups at the same time, 'producing ideas capable of producing groups by manipulating ideas to gain the support of a group' (ibid.: 182).

This is an uncompromisingly bleak view of the political field. It is also informed by stereotypical understandings of 'masculinity' in which people armed with such a habitus would feel most at home and at ease: like 'fish in water'. These may include women as well as men, as Margaret Thatcher among others obliges us to recognise. But whatever their habitus, it is not surprising that women confront particular problems when they enter such a field. In terms of the common feminist distinction between sex and gender, it is primarily their sex that makes them 'legitimate targets' of misrecognition or symbolic violence, even though this abuse may be expressed in terms of stereotypes of *gender* so that women MPs are either faulted for being 'not feminine enough' and therefore not 'real women', or 'too feminine' and therefore unsuited for politics (Sreberny-Mohammadi and Ross 1996; McDougall 1998).

Habitus is developed through practice – through learning to do rather than to know, in specific contexts. The basic lineaments of an individual's habitus are laid down in early life, therefore, within that specific part of the 'general social field' into which s/he is born. The 'capitals' that accrue through familiarity – in the family, neighbourhood, at a particular place and time – are then carried forward in the processes of secondary socialisation in the education system, where they may be discounted, devalued, or augmented. Some of the capitals accumulated are recognised and honoured in a relatively seamless manner from birth, through education, and into careers in specialised fields such as the political field – our concern here. At every stage, individuals who have accumulated capital that carries legitimacy will find themselves able to pay 'the price of entry'. Such individuals may become highly skilled, but without having a great deal of insight into the conditions of their own easy passage onwards and upwards. The 'capital holdings' that eased their passage may remain at the level of 'doxa' – taken for granted and misrecognised as natural gifts.

Although Bourdieu has been criticised for determinism (Archer 1983, 1993; Adkins 2003; Skeggs 2004a), and while it is true that structure and agency are sometimes collapsed in his work, his approach has been defended by Lois McNay on the grounds that he also provides a framework for avoiding determinism, through the concept of the habitus as *generative* in its construction of meaning imposed onto the field; through the concepts of strategy, position-taking, and trajectory where there is rarely only one route through the *space of possibles* (Bourdieu 1993); and through the concept of *temporality*, producing changes to the habitus and field over time and permitting 'dynamism and mutability' (McNay 2000: 38–40). Beverley Skeggs, despite her criticisms, believes Bourdieu's approach offers explanatory power that is not otherwise available in the sense of linking objective structures to subjective experiences and constructing a metaphoric model of social space (2004a: 21). McNay's assessment of his contribution is that:

> it is through developing mediating concepts, in this case agency, that the determining force of economic and cultural relations upon daily life can be made visible and, in this way, the issue of identity can be connected to that of social structure.
>
> (McNay 2004: 175)

Moi's view is that 'the close, concrete relationship between subjectivity, institutions and social field ... constitutes the original and powerful intellectual contribution of Bourdieu's sociology of culture to contemporary thought' (1999: 310). It is for these reasons that Bourdieu's work, in particular his linking of subjectivity, institutions, and field, provides such a valuable framework for analysing the questions in this paper.

Using these concepts, we have argued elsewhere (Liddle and Michielsens 2000b) that the entitlement to power is acquired early in political life by 'traditional' political elites, and is both embedded in the habitus of those belonging to dominant social categories, and is imbricated in those categories as constituent aspects in the perceptions of others. In other words, the practice of power generates a sense of entitlement to power, and recognition of that entitlement by others. Through the conversion of concrete forms of capital into symbolic power, and mediated by the structures of the political field, entitlements are attached to dominant social categories such as masculinity, whiteness, a middle-class position, and educationally qualified status. In contrast, power deficits are attached to femininity, ethnic-minority status, working-class origins, and uneducated status. Thus, feeling qualified and being recognised by others as qualified are part of the same process of identity construction through which entitlements are enacted, embodied, institutionalised, and legitimated, or alternatively undermined, restricted, delegitimated, and withheld. As Bourdieu says: 'Objective limits become a sense of limits, a practical anticipation of objective limits acquired by experience of objective limits, a "sense of one's place" [as limited]' (1984: 471). So we may posit that 'feeling unqualified' and experiencing doubts about one's right to exercise power within the political field derives from objective limits, a 'sense of one's place' as limited, whereas 'feeling qualified' and experiencing a sense of one's right to exercise political power derives from objective opportunities and entitlements, a 'sense of one's place' as unlimited.

Within this framework, we propose that a person's 'entitlement' to political power can be understood as having two interlinked components. One is the person's belief, embedded in the habitus, in his or her own right to exercise power: we refer to this as a 'sense of right'. The second is recognition by others of a person's legitimacy to exercise power: we use the concept of 'authority' to refer to the recognised, legitimate exercise of power, conferred by the institutions and capitals of the field. We use the concept of 'entitlement' as a general term to cover both one's own sense of right and other people's recognition of the right to exercise power. Thus, the sense of right is transformed into an authority recognised by others through the conversion of economic, social, and cultural capitals in the field into symbolic capital or symbolic power.

Excavating social identity in British politics

The analysis in this paper is based on quantitative and qualitative data from a study of British MPs in the 1992–7 parliament which we conducted between 1995 and 1997. The survey and interviews were undertaken as part of the Comparative Leadership Study, an international study of gender and public power examining 27 industrialised countries (Vianello and Moore 2000).[7] For the British study we conducted extended interviews with ten male and 11 female MPs, matched as far as possible for party, position, and age, in which we explored their family, class, educational, and organisational backgrounds and experiences in relation to how they achieved their positions of power and their strategies for success.

Questions about how and why 'non-traditional' categories of people enter particular fields of power cannot readily be answered through quantitative analysis alone, although statistical comparisons are invaluable in elucidating overall patterns of demographic representation and change. But to understand how and why changes occur, detailed qualitative analysis of the concrete empirical processes affecting the construction of classed and gendered power in specific institutional contexts is vital (Crompton 1993: 128). Biographical narrative accounts as a method of research and analysis can reveal a great deal about both masculine and feminine subjectivities (Beynon 2002; Stanley and Morgan 1993; Stanley and Wise 1983). What the analysis of respondent narratives does is to allow access to aspects of the field of power, the habitus, and some of the intermediate structures and processes as they impinge upon the strategies and trajectories of the actors within the political system.

We have chosen to focus mainly on a qualitative analysis of interview material because it can illuminate some of the processes and links involved in the production of political entitlement in relation to a specific social category in the context of a particular political system. Interviews represent a way of accessing all three levels of habitus, institution, and field as they map onto the individual trajectory and experiences of the agent. In this paper we attempt to elucidate the entitlement to power of a working-class male MP belonging to the Conservative (then ruling) party. In order to understand how he saw his political career, constructed his right to power and accounted for his political trajectory, we analyse his interview in terms of the capitals and deficits in the field of power, his narratives of entitlement and his strategies for dealing with the opportunities and obstacles in the 'space of possibles'. We will compare this 'non-traditional' MP on key points with a 'traditional' MP. A detailed analysis of the 'traditional' MP's interview has already been published in a sustained gender comparison with a female MP (Liddle and Michielsens 2000b). In what follows, we will first set out some of the main characteristics of the British political system. We will then summarise the main features of the 'traditional' MP's narrative as a counterpoint for the analysis of the working-class male MP, and will insert quotes from the 'traditional' MP for comparative purposes during the analysis of the 'non-traditional' MP. We will then present an analytical comparison of the construction of class and masculinity in the two cases.[8] We shall argue that working-class subjectivities are constituted as power deficits in the field of Conservative parliamentary politics, and will show how a white, working-class male MP constructs his entitlement to power on the basis of specific forms of capital which do convert into respect and recognition. The names of the MPs have been changed.

Class and masculinity in British politics

The key features of the national political institutions in the UK are the 'First Past The Post' (FPTP) rather than proportional electoral system in the lower house (the House of Commons), bicamerality where the upper house (House of Lords) is subordinate to the Commons, a parliamentary system of representation and a mixed system of government whereby government members may be chosen by the Prime Minister from either house, but in practice are predominantly made up of members of the elected House of Commons rather than the non-elected Lords[9] (see Sansonetti 2000: 278–9 for international comparisons). FPTP tends to favour larger parties and dominant social categories. In the UK, unlike in federal systems such as the US, there is a 'single ladder' into positions of power in national politics, the first rung of which is to be selected as a parliamentary candidate for a local constituency (Norris and Lovenduski 1995: 2). Approximately three-quarters of parliamentary seats are 'safe' with margins of more than 10 per cent. With the system of FPTP, this means that the party 'selectorate' rather than the constituency electorate chooses the majority of MPs and therefore the composition of those who will exercise political power. So a national politician has to compete in relation to three audiences: the constituency party; the electorate; and if successful, the parliamentary party.

The changing allegiances to political parties over the last half century reflect changes in economic growth, declining deferentialism, and increasing social mobility in the decades after the Second World War, featuring changes not only in modes of traditional working-class Conservatism, but also more recent manifestations of 'champagne socialism'. This has been matched by an increasing 'populism' in British politics, at least in terms of appeals by 'professional' politicians to the electorate and rank-and-file party workers, in an effort to reduce the distance between them and to counter the erosion of public trust in 'professional' politics. For examples, we may look to how Conservative party leaders from Edward Heath onwards have been able to capitalise on their status as 'men (sic) of the people' (not forgetting Margaret Thatcher), by virtue of their 'ordinary' social backgrounds. The lowly social origins of the last three Conservative Prime Ministers[10] would traditionally have been counted as deficits, although both Heath and Thatcher were able to acquire the cultural capital of an Oxbridge degree via their success at grammar school. John Major failed even to acquire educational capital, leaving grammar school with 'O' levels. Thus it may be that the cultural and social capitals that win political recognition at national level are changing.

One of the religious metaphors that Bourdieu uses of himself and others who followed a trajectory from obscure class origins to a position of (intellectual) recognition through the educational system is that of the 'oblat miraculé' (Bourdieu 2000: 34). The miraculous 'oblate', originally an apprentice of the monastic life, is here defined as the 'pupil of humble origins who "gives everything" and owes everything to the educational system' (ibid.: 35). Bourdieu claims that political parties, like churches, 'often appoint oblates to lead them' (Bourdieu

1991: 195). He develops the metaphor through the idea of the miraculous exceptions who gain entry to the field against the grain of their class habitus and who are 'bedazzled' by the institution that gives them entry to a new, more powerful world. In the same context, Bourdieu talks about the 'space of possibles' (2000: 34) which acceptance into the elite educational institutions opens up. In the political field too, educational capital is one of the means by which deficits in family capitals may be compensated for. In relation to the British educational system, Archer draws attention to differences between the centralised structure in France after the reforms of the Napoleonic code, and the decentralised British structure that allows for variability (Archer 1983, 1993), and therefore creates room for a more open 'space of possibles' and more opportunities for the 'miraculous oblates'.

Despite the variability and potentially greater openness in the British education system, however, Norris and Lovenduski show that in the field of politics 'the typical candidate in all parties tends to be a well-educated, professional white male' and as a result 'the traditional composition of parliament' is still 'overwhelmingly middle-class, male and white' (1995: 87). In the 1992–7 parliament, middle-class candidates made up 99 per cent of the Conservative and 92 per cent of the Labour party. Males constituted 85 per cent of candidates in the Conservatives and 74 per cent in the Labour party. And candidates were 67 per cent graduates in the Conservative party and 72 per cent in the Labour party (ibid.: 88). As Moi (1999) points out, the distinctions in entitlement based on gender, class, and 'race' become embedded not only as dispositions in the habitus, but also become attributes of the practices instituted in the field itself. For example, masculinity is not just an attribute of masculine habitus that is taken into the armed forces, but the military itself is a powerful arena in which the embodied cultural capital of masculinity can be invested and legitimated because it 'fits', and is recognised by, the nomos or rules of the field. The military field, like the political field, is gendered masculine as a field of power. Entitlement and legitimacy are embedded in both the habitus and the field.[11]

Charles Smythe: the 'traditional' MP

Charles Smythe is a classic example of a 'traditional' Conservative MP whose social identity represents the gendered, classed, and 'raced' demography of the British parliament: white, professional, middle class, educated at public school, and Oxbridge. Our previous analysis (Liddle and Michielsens 2000b: 131–6) showed that he saw himself and was seen by others as having a 'natural' entitlement which needed no explanation. Charles Smythe constructed his political career as 'normal', not as 'successful', because it was what the men of his family 'naturally' did. When asked to account for how he got into politics, the important decision points and the major hindrances and facilitators along the way, he was completely unable to do so. He had no insight into the process of his decision-making, he had 'no strategies', and encountered 'no obstacles'. Getting on the approved list of the party 'wasn't difficult'. It was by 'luck' that he was chosen in the first seat to which he applied, a safe seat which was likely to assure him a parliamentary career for as long as he wanted it. It was, in his view, simply a 'natural' and 'normal' career trajectory, not particularly noteworthy in terms of either personal success or structural power. Charles' effortless and unconscious authority and entitlement to power can be understood as doxic. It is embedded in practice and instantly recognised as legitimate by others through his political habitus, but he was quite unable to articulate the process by which his entitlement was constructed or acquired. We concluded from this analysis that the process through which this middle-class professionally-educated white man held entitlements to power was revealed through its absence in the narrative of his political trajectory.

Kevin Briggs MP: 'NQOC'

The acronym 'NQOC' stands for 'Not quite our class'. It was told to one of us by a man who had been to a public school where it was in common usage.[12] The acronym has particular resonance for Kevin Briggs in some parts of the political field, although, as we shall see, not all. Mr Briggs is what used to be thought of as a contradiction in terms: a Conservative MP from a working-class background. He is in no sense a 'natural' MP like Charles Smythe, nor did he follow the 'traditional path of attending public school and Oxford or Cambridge' (Norris and Lovenduski 1995: 10). Notwithstanding the phenomenon of working-class Conservatism, working-class representation among Conservative MPs has never been more than 4 per cent, and has never exceeded 1 per cent since the 1951 election (Norris and Lovenduski 1995: 97).

Capital accounting in the field

Kevin began his parliamentary career in 1983 at the age of 31. He retained his seat in two further elections, and reached the level of Parliamentary Private Secretary (PPS). In-between gaining his degree and winning his first seat, he worked for ten years in various professional jobs. His father was a skilled manual worker who reached the level of foreman, while his mother did a range of different jobs before marriage, including dinner lady and dressmaker. His parents were from a 'very, very, poor background', they 'didn't have a terribly good education' although they wanted their two children to be educated, and the family lived in a council house in a 'rank Labour area'. He was brought up in a practising Catholic family with strong religious values, which he still holds. The family showed no interest in politics, although Kevin himself knew he wanted to be an MP from childhood, taking part in mock school elections and joining his local Conservative association at 16. The contrast with Charles, who attended a major public school, whose father was in the foreign service, and whose social milieu constituted the political elite, could not be more marked.

Kevin Briggs inherited little recognised cultural or social capital, and even less economic capital, from his family. Without Charles Smythe's politically active family, cosmopolitan relatives or access to and knowledge of political and international elites, he had no sense of belonging in politically influential networks, and no 'naturally absorbed' understanding of what it meant to exercise political power. He attended a Catholic grammar school followed by a College of Technology, which provided some accredited cultural capital that allowed him to enter professional occupations but without significant convertibility into symbolic value in the political field. Nevertheless, when asked who shaped his ideas and expectations in relation to his political life, he has no doubt that it began with his entry into state schooling:

> I owe everything to my infant school. At the age of five, the teacher called my mother to say 'Do you realise that your son has got severe learning difficulties?' I had a very bad stutter. My sister used to have to interpret for me. For three years I went to speech therapy. That's why I'm not a Cockney, which is really what I should be. So it was 'How now brown cow' and all of that. It had a huge influence on me. I owe those teachers so much, they were very dedicated teachers.

Here we see Kevin's first 'lucky break' in the 'field of possibles': a chance intervention by the educational system that changed his life. This intervention brought about the reconstitution of his 'inherited linguistic competence (Bourdieu 1984: 65) from one that would have instantly signalled his inferior class position to one which disguised it. He began to develop and delight in his newly acquired communication skills, taking part in school shows, acting, learning to project his voice and develop arguments, and all of this new competence and knowledge supported and encouraged by his parents who had never had the opportunity to acquire it. Kevin acquired the legitimate cultural capital of speaking without an identifiable working-class accent,[13] and began to talk and perform like the middle classes, marking the first step on the road to social mobility. What is visible here is the beginning of the verbal competences of the political habitus (Bourdieu 1991: 176), something he held in common with Charles, who identified 'listening and talking' as the key activities for the exercise of political power.

But Kevin Briggs had another sort of cultural capital that was not shared with Charles: a form of capital that did not receive recognition as legitimate among the political elite, but which constituted a specific localised form of knowledge about a class and community that came to have particular purchase in the socially-mobile context of post-war Britain and the changing allegiances to political parties that went along with it:

> My mother came from a very, very poor background, one of 11 children, my father's family had no money …. If you are 'hungry' in life, I don't mean literally, and nothing has come easily for you, then you achieve things.

What Kevin achieved was an escape from his 'historical positioning' (Skeggs 1997: 12), along with the desire to change things, to represent the people of his class and community not as a Labour politician, by whom he felt they had been let down, but as a Conservative. This gave him a unique set of credentials and cultural knowledge which was not easily matched by 'traditional' middle-class Conservatives applying to marginal seats in working-class parliamentary constituencies.

In the early stages, being a working-class Conservative in a working-class Labour area, 'it meant that Conservatives were few on the ground, so I quickly rose up through the ranks' of the local party, suggesting that here his background was an asset. Joining the party at 16, he became ward chairman 'in no time at all', stood twice for the local council, once for the county council, and was accepted as Conservative parliamentary candidate in 1979, all without electoral success. But he received much support and encouragement from the local, rather beleaguered Conservative party, who told him when he moved to another area ' "Oh you are marvellous Kevin, don't leave us, if you go away the organisation is going to collapse" '. Of course, he says, this did not happen, but 'it's nice to hear people say that actually you can do things', revealing the need of the 'self-made man' for validation of his political abilities, rather than his entitlement to political power constituting a natural and self-evident part of his habitus as was the case with Charles.

On moving in 1981 to a nearby 'new town' to which many of his family and neighbours had moved, and which also constituted itself as a socially mobile working-class community, his electoral success took off. He was elected to the local council 'immediately', became vice-chair of one of the important committees, and was selected as the Conservative parliamentary candidate for a nearby Labour constituency in 1982, winning the seat 'unexpectedly' in 1983. He thought it would be 'third time lucky, but it wasn't, it was second time lucky': his second 'lucky break' in the 'space of possibles' of the political field.

How he sees his political career

In order to understand how Kevin sees his political career, we first need to understand why he identified with Conservative rather than Labour policies:

> It's simple. Everything was Labour, the council, the GLC, the government. They were very good at describing the problems, but they had no solutions. I saw the area I loved deteriorating – roads, streets, education, social services. At the age of 11 I couldn't articulate what socialism and capitalism were about, but I wanted to oppose those who were running things. I took them all on. I challenged the sitting Labour MP who had been here for 32 years. I can see him standing there saying '*You, you* come to *my* palace at Westminster?!'

The roots of Kevin's Conservatism lay in a conservative Catholic upbringing,

Labour complacency, and the desire for social mobility as part of the newly-educated former working class who rejected second-class status and aspired to a middle-class lifestyle. This historically specific upward mobility created both a vision of opportunity and a mistrust of its reality. As a result, Kevin does not see politics in any sense as a 'career' in the way the 'traditional MP' did. In response to a question about how much he felt in control of his career, Charles, for example, explained that 'Politics is as natural to me as going into medicine, which is another sort of family trade'. Kevin, however, challenged the terms of the question:

> I do not believe anyone has a career in politics – here today and gone tomorrow. If anyone sits down and thinks, this is what I'm going to do and eventually I'm going to become a Minister – it is ridiculous. Many good intentions but all sorts of things get in the way …. I'm one of only 300 or so Conservative Members of Parliament, you've got a tiny, tiny chance of ever getting here.

So his election was far from 'natural', 'normal', or 'ordinary', which is how Charles constituted his political trajectory. Kevin's trajectory 'took an extra-ordinary turn'. It was 'a dream come true'. And although he is pleased with his rise to PPS, he is still intensely ambitious for more power.

Strategies

Kevin's political progress is conceived, not as a natural progression like Charles Smythe's, but as a conscious decision, strategically planned but within a 'restricted market', and with limited expectation of success. His strategy is punctuated by self-doubt and framed by self-imposed limitations. The first con-scious strategy was to get recognition for his political abilities in the local party and in local government. The second was to undertake a national apprenticeship by applying to unwinnable seats, one of the recognised ways of moving up the ladder to a safe or less marginal seat. To get on the approved list 'wasn't easy' he says (in contrast to Charles' experience that it 'wasn't difficult'). In a stark example of Kevin's self-doubt and his unfamiliarity with the 'rules of the game', he was quite unable to assess his own or his competitors' performance:

> You have to be sort of screened by Central Office, they may say 'All right' and then you go away for a weekend, where you are watched and you are broken down into groups of eight and you go through a number of tests. Now I didn't think I had passed my weekend. It turned out I was the only one who had passed the weekend, but I was very surprised because I was with people who I thought were far cleverer than I was, much grander jobs than I had. But I was the one who actually got through that weekend. So whether it is self-deprecation, in which probably I don't indulge so much now, I don't know.

His third strategy was 'communication', building on his long-appreciated acquisition of and pleasure in his verbal skills: 'If you are able to relate to people, communicate your message, then that's a key to success. I think I've been able to do that'. Here we can see the development of a crucial part of the political habitus: what Bourdieu refers to as the skills of 'particular language and political rhetoric', including the 'popular orator' for relations with the non-professionals, and the 'debater' for relations with the professionals (Bourdieu 1991: 176). But at this point, despite Kevin's longstanding ambition, he applied only to Labour-held seats in his own region of the country, thus restricting his chances of gaining a seat both geographically and electorally. This was a doxic act, a strategy 'not based on conscious calculation but rather result[ing] from unconscious dispositions towards practice' (Bourdieu 1993: 17–18). Our evidence for this judgement is that Kevin never mentioned limiting himself to local constituencies despite being pressed to identify his success strategies and to explain how he had succeeded in entering parliament. This is one of the few places where Kevin aligns with Charles in doxic practice, except that Charles could not articulate any strategies whatsoever.

The seat that was offered to Kevin and that he accepted in 1983 was not even on the list of marginals. He did not expect to win, and the party was taking no risk in selecting him. Kevin's feeling of entitlement combined with his self-deprecation did not permit him to take advantage of the accepted Conservative party culture of 'carpet-bagging', but framed his 'sense of place' as limited to working-class constituencies in the London area – a strategy reminiscent of the working-class artists in Bourdieu's *The Rules of Art* (1996) who chose regional rather than cosmopolitan locales and marginal rather than mainstream genres in which to compete.

The local committee had not intended to choose him, they had settled on a 'number one male tennis player'. Kevin's view of why he was chosen is that: 'I was young, I was engaged to be married, I think it was the right image for them'. His embodiment of heterosexual respectability and his commitment to marriage and family values helped his candidature, as did his youthful energy and promise to 'take the battle onto the streets'. Although Kevin's class background and image failed to fit the party in the way the tennis player's did, what Kevin did fit was the constituency. He was 'one of us' among the voters. The 'grassroots' were his own roots, in contrast to the social origins of the party hierarchy. Kevin's cultural and social capital had more value and convertibility *in that particular social and regional locality* than that of a 'traditional' Conservative candidate, in that Kevin's capitals of local identity, working-class origins, and achieved social mobility were recognised as legitimate by those specific voters in that particular sector of the political field. We suggest that this is why Kevin limited himself to constituencies in which he 'belonged' and felt a strong sense of community connection, a self-imposed limitation based on the restricted cultural and social capitals to which he had access. And we suggest that this cultural and demographic 'match' in social identity between candidate and constituents is what the selection meeting recognised when they changed their minds about their choice of candidate.

Hindrances

When asked about the barriers to his political career, Kevin lists class snobbery, the wrong education, and a lack of the right social contacts: a clear reference to the deficits in his economic, cultural, and social capitals.

JL: What do you think were the most important factors that hindered your career in politics?

KB: Well, I'm sure there are some people in the House of Commons who think, 'Oh, fancy someone like that being a Member of Parliament, what is this place coming to?'

JL: What does 'someone like that' mean?

KB: There is still a little bit of snobbishness. Some people are still a bit patronising. And that may have been a barrier for me to get on.

JL: How do you deal with that?

KB: I try not to let it show (laughs), but it annoys me. You do become very hard actually. As time goes on, you become hardened to all that ... I think it's extraordinary that really, if I had been clever enough to go to Oxford or Cambridge and then come out with a first class degree and known the right people, then I might be in a different position to the one I'm in .... My course might have been a little bit different if I had been to, gone to – (pause) –

JL: In what way?

KB: Well, if I had been to one of the best universities, I might have met the right sort of people and that might have helped me with the party network here.

In this last response, Kevin is clearing referring to social capital. This exchange compares with Charles' simple answer when asked what obstacles he had to overcome in his political career:

CS: I haven't .... You don't have to overcome things.

JL: But how *did* you overcome obstacles?

CS: I didn't have to.

Despite his Conservative politics, Kevin clearly sees his class background as inhibiting his promotion and acceptance in the parliamentary party. He understands the social and cultural capital deficits he has brought with him into parliament as the root of the symbolic violence enacted against him by his colleagues. He consoles himself for his failure to rise above PPS by constituting himself as an effective constituency MP, for it is only in his local constituency that his particular working-class capitals have symbolic value: 'I have not wasted my time as an MP, we made a difference to the lives of thousands of people .... That's why I've been elected to this constituency on three occasions'.

But Kevin certainly feels he has been hindered from fulfilling his potential. These hindrances are not related to family life, despite his having five children;

quite the reverse, he sees his job as MP as 'short-changing' his wife and family. But Kevin's hindrances derive from not being recognised in the party: 'You have to recognise your limitations. I'm not saying what mine are, I'm not that self-deprecating. But there are a number of things I think I could do well, but I haven't been given the opportunity'.

These symbolic forms of violence have had their effect. Although he does not 'indulge in self-deprecation' so much now, his belief in his own political judgement and authority have developed only slowly, and he still feels a sense of betrayal and exclusion. But his exclusion is what has prompted his reflexivity – Bourdieu's 'lucidity of the excluded' (cited in McNay 2000: 69) – allowing him to reflect and make a conscious decision to change his approach: 'You learn with situations really. Over the years I made many mistakes in trusting people whom I never should have trusted, and as you make more and more mistakes, you know, all of that really has an effect on you. It has changed my style'.

Narrative of entitlement: how he sees his right to represent

Kevin's narrative of entitlement is strongly centred on 'being a local'. To 'be a local' in the Labour-held towns in which he lived and stood for election meant being proud of his working-class background and heritage, having experienced the hardships and deprivations associated with it. It meant being in touch with the aspirations of his own community at that particular time, their desire for respectability, their wish to own their own houses. Kevin had a passionate message to communicate to the working-class community from which he had emerged, which was that Labour complacency had resulted in the deterioration of the community infrastructure, but that, like him, the community could improve its conditions if they abandoned Labour orthodoxy and turned instead to Margaret Thatcher who 'changed this country and changed the world. I mean it is all there to see. She has changed the other political parties'. He attributes his success to Thatcher, and he compares himself and his background directly with the subsequent Prime Minister, John Major, compensating for his misrecognition in the parliamentary party by acknowledging the recognition from his party leader:

> I've got no chip on my shoulder about being – I mean the Prime Minister always says he comes from a working-class background, he wants the society to be at ease with themselves. I couldn't care less about the class system. I decided, being working class, living in a little terrace house, that I was every bit as good as the next person.

But where did this sense of right come from, this belief that he was as good as the next person? It rested not only on a class-based, upwardly-aspiring local identity, but also on a specific ethnic and national identity in which a working-class Londoner could see himself as having more entitlement than foreigners, even if he had less entitlement than those with a 'natural' right to rule the country. It came from a conscious national identity sustained by a belief in the superiority of British political institutions:

> As a youngster I was attentive to what Enoch Powell seemed to represent. I am not talking about immigration now but in terms of patriotism. He seemed to be a very patriotic figure. I'm thinking about the Common Market which I felt very strongly about because I voted no in the 1975 referendum. I thought that we lost a lot of our sovereignty .... We are the mother of all parliaments, our democratic process is envied throughout the world. The way our politicians are selected is envied by everyone frankly.

His sense of right also comes from a belief that only women can care for children, while men are biologically and morally incapable of doing so, thus claiming priority, though not exclusivity, for men to engage in the public world of politics:

> Women are totally different to men. I don't believe in the equality of the sexes. I actually think that women are superior to men and that can be demonstrated by the fact that they live longer and that they are able to have babies and they take stress and strain much more easily than men ... I mean, I'm only saying this as a man: I think it's preferable if women look after their babies. I think we are totally different and men are nowhere near as good as women are with babies. Presumably God made us this way or men would have the babies. I don't quite see how we overcome that, I mean we are physically different and the things that flow from a woman having a baby are different, so that means that the amount of time and the amount of dependence has to be different for women and men. But because women live longer and take the strain better, it really doesn't matter when they get here. I've got no problem if women outnumber us in this place as long as they're good.

This 'different but superior' approach presumably helps to resolve the contradiction of his inspiration, Margaret Thatcher, being a woman ('she had to be not only as good as any man, but so much better'). And despite his man-made view ('I'm only saying this as a man') that 'it's preferable if women look after their babies', when asked why there are so few women in parliament, his answer is not to attribute it to the sexual division of labour but to blame the women in his party: 'It's very easy, on the Conservative side, it's because women predominate on the selection committees and they don't pick women'. Norris and Lovenduski have shown that this explanation is a myth (1995). And against all the evidence, Kevin claims that: 'In the Conservative party at the moment, if you are a woman you've got a far better chance of becoming a Minister than if you are a man'.

When asked if he thinks there is a difference in leadership style between men and women, he is defensive and patronising:

> Mm, I've got to be careful what I say. Oh there is a difference of style. Women I think do use by and large their femininity, all of that guile. I am not saying they burst into tears if they don't get their own way, but I think yes, they do.

But equally, it may be said that Kevin uses a stereotypical form of masculinity to get what he wants. When asked about his own leadership style, it is clear he is directive if not authoritarian:

> I am not a consensus politician. I don't believe in having big committees and everyone droning on endlessly giving their point of view. You need a bossy dominant person to chair the committees and try to pull things together. I'm not talking about dictatorship, but I think you need someone to have some sort of vision and structure to pull things together or you don't get decisions taken at all.

And he admits that his wife finds he has 'become more and more bombastic'. This is no effortless, 'doxic' form of authority such as is held by the 'traditional MP'. Charles' response to the question on leadership and how he gets other people to do what he wants lacks any sense that this might be problematic: 'The simplest way to get anybody to do anything is to ask them', suggesting that he has rarely encountered resistance to his leadership and does not have to engage in manipulation or coercion to get people to follow his lead. But Kevin's approach is a conscious and strategic kind of male dominance behaviour, suggesting that he encounters resistance to his leadership and retreats into authoritarianism to get his way. (And of course Margaret Thatcher, without the doxic authority of masculinity, exhibited all these authoritarian and bombastic qualities.)

This is also the strategy Kevin adopts with the opposition party:

> I give my opposition no platform, no quarter at all. I can give – not as good as I get – but better than I get. That might sound a bit pompous, but that's how it is. So I take them on, I wipe the floor with them. We've been successful as a result of that. If you are cowed by the opposition, then you don't get on.

Here we can indeed see the politician's habitus as delineated by Bourdieu, where debating skills are deployed in verbal combat with the professional foe (Bourdieu 1991: 176, 196; Thompson 1991: 27), not in the interests of 'truth' but according to the logic of 'denunciation' (Bourdieu 1988: 9). Kevin's bombastic style may be described as stereotypically masculine, and yet Charles's is very different while hardly meriting the 'feminine' label. Bourdieu's characterisation of 'the political field' is most clearly recognisable on the floor of the debating chamber, but this is not the only venue of significance in 'the political field'.

Nevertheless, although it is true that 'masculinity is not a single pattern'

(Connell 1995: 205), it is also true that 'public politics on almost any definition is men's politics' (ibid.: 204), the dominant culture of which has been described as 'macho, adversarial' (Brown 1996: 33), 'aggressive and confrontational' (Childs 2004: 181), and reproducing an 'old boys' club' (ibid.: 184). Kevin is not an 'old boy', but he has had no difficulty adopting the combative habitus in his approach to politics, scorning the 'feminine' style of negotiation and compromise used in consensus politics. However, 'public' is surely the key term here. 'Foes' in the form of the 'opposition party' may be publicly trounced, but this does not work too well with 'friends' and those whose support has to be won. Kevin clearly recognises his failings in this particular skill of the political field, a skill whose mastery has enabled Charles to forge alliances and generate compliance with his wishes.

Kevin sees being an MP as a position of great power, acknowledging his entry to the political elite, and is still 'bedazzled' (Bourdieu 2000: 34) by his membership in a way Charles could never be. Charles is one of those who say MPs have no power, but Kevin disagrees:

> I've got enormous power as an MP. All my colleagues who say they've got no power at all, it's rubbish! I've got lots of power and I love it. But it's exercising it well …. There are a limited number of MPs, and MPs make the laws which affect everyone …. I mean during your lifetime there aren't that many people who are MPs, so of course it must be an elite.

Despite his elite membership, however, the limits of Kevin's reflexivity are delineated by his lack of awareness of the process of political management through strategies such as social construction and normalisation that Charles used to such effect. Where Charles talked about political influence in terms of 'presenting something in an attractive way or trying to make it appear to be natural', Kevin's only conscious strategy of political influence is 'bombast' and 'domination', suggesting that he bears no 'natural authority' in the parliamentary party, and that he is himself excluded from much of the knowledge of how to get people to do what you want that circulates among the political elite. As he says, 'I have seen others getting influenced … I have been thinking "Oh my God, how the hell did they do that? I'd better get in on the act!"'

Kevin's construction of a narrative of entitlement to political power centres on a socially mobile working-class London identity, patriotic white English national identity and dominant heterosexual masculinity, forms of class, gender, sexual, ethnic, and regional identities from which he can draw symbolic capital in relation to unspecified 'others', whether they be women, foreigners, homosexuals, or indeed 'carpet-baggers'. His sense of being qualified for the job is built upon and bolstered by these 'other' identities. But his narrative presents him with an unseen contradiction. He believes that the British model of parliamentary democracy has allowed 'someone like him' to join the political elite: 'I personally think it's great the way the British way of life enables people to come forward to become Members of Parliament. Anyone can become a Member of

Parliament. I am anyone and I am a Member of Parliament'. But despite his doxic practice, Kevin does not recognise that 'someone like him' is unlikely to become a Conservative MP outside the restricted currency market of a working-class constituency in his specific local community, because his economic, cultural, and social capitals produce symbolic capital deficits in the party nationally and in parliament as a whole. Kevin's self-limiting practice paid dividends. He played the game with skill, and the habitus he developed was well adapted to this particular corner of his chosen field. But he never went 'carpet-bagging' because his capitals were not convertible into symbolic power in other parts of the country, not even in working-class areas. His sense of right to represent others derives from the sites of his subjective respectability, but it is a restricted entitlement that is recognised and legitimated only by his own community. His symbolic capital deficits do not give him the right to represent other communities in terms of social class or geographical region. His self-imposed limits show that, doxically, he knows this. And in case he should attempt to stray outside these limits, the knowledge is enforced by the misrecognition and symbolic violence that he encounters from his parliamentary colleagues.

Kevin's perspective of the improbability and insecurity of a political 'career' is framed by his capital deficits, his consequent 'non-traditional' route into parliament, and his application to and acceptance in 'un-winnable' seats. In stark contrast to Charles Smythe, the 'traditional' MP, politics for Kevin is 'extraordinary' not 'normal and natural' because of its absence in Kevin's cultural family history, nor can it be seen as a 'career' because of the unpredictability of standing in seats held by the opposition. Kevin's understanding of his political trajectory as *out of* the ordinary reflects not an inability to account for his entry into national politics, but the uncertainty, ambiguity, peripherality, and boundedness of Kevin's position as a contestant in the political field, the contradictions of his habitus, and the limitations of his doxic political strategy.

Constructing class and masculinity

Charles and Kevin both began their political careers in earnest in 1979. But the two MPs' views of the process of political selection could not be more different. Charles encountered no obstacles and is unaware of the privileges conferred by his capitals, whereas Kevin faced innumerable hindrances, and identifies them without hesitation as capital deficits. Charles does not experience being an MP as a position of privileged or unusual power and displays a natural embodied authority, and a direct, effortless approach to leadership; whereas Kevin is highly conscious that he has entered an 'elite', 'loves' his power, and exerts his authority through a bombastic and dominating leadership style. Charles had no strategies, or none he could articulate, but Kevin's strategies entailed explicitly broadening the social boundaries of his political activities through unsuccessful apprenticeships at local and national level, and developing his skills of communication. Charles conveys a feeling of belonging in the political field, but in Kevin's interview there is a sense of both inclusion and exclusion. Charles' narrative never explicitly articulates political entitlement, it simply assumes it, but Kevin's reveals a struggle between his ideological belief that he has every right to be an MP, and a persistent questioning of this right that gnaws at his legitimacy.

Both Charles' and Kevin's sense of right derives from their habitus, but in Charles' case his habitus presents an embodied natural authority and a 'doxic' entitlement of which he is completely unconscious and which he cannot articulate. Kevin's habitus is ambiguous, he can identify and articulate the sources of his entitlement but he also expresses their contradictory and fluctuating nature. Kevin is conscious of having to construct for others a convincing narrative of his entitlement, whereas Charles carries his legitimacy to hold political power in his 'bearing, accent, attitudes, aptitudes and ways of being' (Wacquant 1993: 31–2). This embodied entitlement is recognised as legitimate by others in local, national, and international contexts, among voters, constituency party and parliamentary colleagues, giving Charles unlimited opportunities, a 'sense of his place' as unlimited and an unquestioned and unquestionable *feeling* of entitlement. Charles' symbolic power derives from who he is: a white middle-class man from a privileged background educated in the best institutions in the world.

Kevin Briggs' habitus is constituted by the conservative beliefs of his religious upbringing and education, including his views on the family and on the natural God-given roles of male and female, and by his identity as a white working-class Londoner brought up in poor circumstances and inadequate housing. A key process, etched in his memory, in the development of his sense of right to aspire above his 'historical positioning', derives from the recognition and resolution of his early educational needs. This intervention made such a strong impression on his young mind because it reconstituted his habitus, enabling him to expand his cultural performance from the confines of the family to the wider location of the school ('my sister used to translate'), and subsequently across the class ('I'm not a Cockney, which is … what I should be'). It is important because of the complex disposition it produced in relation to his place in society. The 'objective limits' of Kevin's working-class childhood produced his sense of place as 'restricted', but the reconstitution of his cultural competence and the opening up of the 'space of possibles' produced a sense of entitlement to cultural and social mobility. This ambiguity in Kevin's entitlement to power can still be seen in the persistent expression of self-doubt, in conjunction with an unfulfilled ambition. It is reproduced in the political field where he is both 'recognised' and 'misrecognised' in different sites of struggle. Kevin's legitimacy, like Charles', derives from who he is: a patriotic, white Englishman, a socially mobile, working-class Londoner and a masculine, dominating heterosexual. But Kevin's *illegitimacy* also derives from who he is: for he is 'NQOC'. Kevin's symbolic value *changes* depending on the audience, on the field or the particular fraction of the field, on who it is that gives or withholds respect, reproducing and reinforcing within him an ambiguous, contradictory, and fluctuating subjectivity and feeling of entitlement.

Conclusion

In this paper we have considered the issues raised in empirical studies such as that of Norris and Lovenduski concerning 'social bias' in political representation, with particular reference to class as well as to gender. We identified the limited ability of the 'supply/demand' model to answer the question of why certain social categories see themselves as differently qualified for public office, and how, against the grain, some members of these categories managed to develop a sense of entitlement and to get this sense recognised by others as legitimate. We drew upon Bourdieu's categories of habitus, field, and 'capitals' to frame an explanation in terms of which we have analysed Charles' and Kevin's narratives. We registered the criticisms mounted by Archer, and those that circulate in the (critical) feminist take-up of Bourdieu, namely his neglect of 'reflexivity' in favour of habitual action, and the consequent narrowness of his scope for admitting any significant role for human agency. And we have located the research and the analysis within the terms of Fraser's model of justice, particularly in the light of her addition of 'representation' to stand alongside recognition and redistribution. They are now of equal standing, under the broad umbrella of 'participatory parity', in her integrated theory of justice.

In the case of the two MPs, Charles and Kevin, we were able to conclude, using Bourdieu's categories, that social identity is constructed through the differential distribution of capitals in the social fields of its production, mediated by the strategies and trajectory of the agent in relation to the 'space of possibles' within the specific institutions of the political field. Entitlements are imbricated in specific social identities and are embedded in both the general social field and in particular specialised fields of power, including the political field. As Moi points out (1999: 309–10): 'only a field can grant symbolic capital' and 'the field-specific competition generates its own specific habitus in agents competing for field-specific symbolic capital'. The institutions of the political field are gendered and classed as masculine and middle-class, providing legitimacy to middle-class male politicians, but this does not mean that all professional politicians are constituted by these dominant social identities, since the 'space of possibles' allows opportunities for non-traditional contenders, including Bourdieu's 'oblats miraculés', to gain entry to political institutions, particularly through the educational system. But the habitus of those with 'traditional' identities and that of politicians of 'miraculous' provenance are differentiated with respect to their sense of entitlement. This is evidenced by the 'fractured' habitus of the 'oblat miraculé' in contrast to the less conflicted, more insouciant habitus of the 'traditional' occupant of the field of power. Thus, we concur with McNay and Skeggs that Bourdieu's framework lacks a concept of 'multiple subjectivity' (McNay 2000: 56, 72) and that he 'underestimates the ambiguities and dissonances' in how agents occupy positions in the field (ibid.: 54), particularly in relation to those 'whose positions are not legitimated by dominant symbolic relations' (Skeggs 2004b: 86).

The field too must be seen as 'fractured' in terms of sensitivity to differential types of habitus, as evidenced by the differential symbolic value attached to the oblate's capitals in different sectors of the political field, producing capital deficits in the parliamentary party but symbolic power in the constituency; and the field must be seen as fractured not only in social space but also temporally, where changes are witnessed to the value of symbolic capital in the political field over time, as well as at different stages of a politician's trajectory.

So although outcomes, *pace* Archer, are not predetermined, and the space of possibles allows for changes in fields and in habitus, the oblats miraculés are still miraculous *exceptions*, and the reproduction of dominant identities in powerful positions is still predominant in political institutions. The example of the 2006 leadership election in the Conservative party reinforces this point. The final stage of the competition was between two candidates, David Cameron and David Davis, who may be seen as examples of the 'traditional' Conservative MP and the 'oblate' respectively. Davis is the son of a single mother, brought up in a council house, who became company director of a large corporation through the educational route of grammar school and a first-rate but not elite university. In his appeals to national party members who would decide the vote, he made no attempt to conceal his 'illegitimate' background; on the contrary, he drew attention to it as a way of signalling his break with the 'traditional' values and policies of the party which were understood to be inimical to the general population, who saw them as old-fashioned and out of date. Davis was initially in the lead in his bid for the highest position in the party, and clearly reckoned on his 'non-traditional' background being read as an asset in the party nationally. Cameron went to Eton and Oxford, was a member of a number of exclusive clubs (including one that excluded women), and his father was a stockbroker. His claim to 'populism' was based on his relative youth. But Cameron came from behind to win the election. Despite the opportunities available in the field for the miraculous oblate, it appears that the symbolic capital attached to elite educational institutions and wealthy middle-class origins does not yet represent a power deficit in the field of Conservative party membership.

So to answer the questions posed at the start, we would argue that the reason people from different social categories see themselves as differentially qualified for public office is that subjectivity, habitus, and feelings of entitlement are closely related to the social relations expressed through differential capital holdings within the general social field of society and the specialised social field of politics, as well as the social practices generated by the limits and opportunities – the 'universe of possible options' (Bourdieu 1993: 32) – of the fields. 'Legitimate' contestants carry with them the symbolic power derived from the capitals attached to class and gender (and other) positionings in the general and specialised social fields. The 'image or reputation for competence, respectability and honourability' (Bourdieu 1984: 291) into which those capitals have been converted is deeply imbricated in the habitus and the entire 'way of being' (Wacquant 1993: 32). Their sense of entitlement is doxic. 'Oblates' develop a sense of right in themselves in a more fractured way, drawing on the subjective sites of their respectability and taking recognition from specific sectors of the field that produce symbolic power. Their sense of right is recognised by others through the conscious, often skilled, deployment of those capitals which *are* convertible into an image of respectability. Oblates challenge their status as unqualified by focusing the contest on social fields where their capitals are legitimate, although this can mean confining the contest within the boundaries of the restricted capital markets that provide such recognition (Bourdieu 1984: 95). The working-class male drew on his masculinity and ethnicity, and turned his limited class capitals to advantage by restricting his contest to the social and geographical sites of struggle in which his class capitals brought respect.

Thus, we would argue that the process of political recruitment reproduces to a significant, though not fully-determining extent (because of the fractured nature of the field), the social relations of power within the field of politics, in which differential symbolic values are attached to specific (gender, sexual, class, ethnic, national and regional) social identities. We would suggest, therefore, that Norris and Lovenduski's (1995) 'supply' and 'demand' are better seen as different aspects of the same complex processes through which entitlements to power are generated in the institutions of the political field. Within this framework, 'supply' may be understood as the generation of the 'sense of right' to represent others, while 'demand' may be understood as the authority recognised by others to be a political representative. But both the sense of right and the authority to hold political power are produced by the interconnected practices and processes linking habitus, field, and institutions together.

This analysis has implications for the goal of participatory parity, the defining characteristic of justice for Fraser. It may be unrealistic to hope to create a representational body whose social composition exactly matches social divisions, and were this to be achieved there would be no guarantee that the views of the populations it morphs would actually be represented, yet the existing deep disparities between the two are too disproportionate not to cause concern from the point of view of social justice. There is little doubt that the remedies for injustices of representation will depend on the transformation of the deliberative democratic public sphere outside the formal system of political representation, in addition to changes in that system itself. A politics of recognition must target the deep recesses of habitus, bringing unthinking symbolic violence into the light of day. At the level of redistribution, while some have objected to Bourdieu's 'capitals' as too economistic, it is a metaphor that suggests very powerfully that there are problems of unjust distribution across them all – economic, cultural, educational, political, and social.

In terms of strategy, we would argue that social bias cannot be eliminated from the process of political selection through exhortation, training for 'illegitimate' social groups, or the reform of selection procedures alone, because the assessments that are made of a person's 'competence, respectability and honourability' are deeply imbricated in the very social identity of that person – the social categories to which they belong, their subjectivity, and the images portrayed by these social categories. Candidates are not always judged solely on the basis of their individual political skills; they are also judged on the symbolic value of the economic, social, and cultural capitals they bring to the political field. These capitals are not distributed randomly across social categories. They reflect the concrete and symbolic power which those social categories hold in the field, and are attached to specific forms of social identity, such as masculinity, whiteness, and middle-classness. Social identity *signals* to a considerable though not exclusive extent the distribution of capitals in society.

The Conservative party has reviewed its assessment procedures in relation to gender bias, by bringing in an occupational psychologist to draw up an MP's job description, design practical tests and exercises to reveal candidates' competencies, and train selectors to make objective judgements (Childs 2004: 209–10). But as Childs points out: 'the expectation that women will be, as a consequence, selected has not been fulfilled' (ibid.: 210). Why not? Why do strategies that require anything less than compulsion fail to produce results?[14] We would suggest that job descriptions and assessor training, while necessary and welcome, will not resolve the problem of social bias, because decisions are taken, not only on the basis of objective competencies, but also on the basis of the symbolic value of gender, class, sexual, ethnic, national, and regional identities. The most intractable problem is not the failure of assessors to be objective (although this may also be an issue), but the differential distribution of capitals among specific social identities in the field. And it is only through the social *practice* of more and more non-traditional candidates, including 'oblates', entering the field, challenging the patterns of capital distribution, and enacting political authority through recognition by constituencies of people who form a conscious 'social and collective group' (Lovell 2003: 10), that changes in the symbolic value of these political actors can be achieved.

What are the implications, then, with regard to Fraser's frame of representation, recognition, and redistribution under the broad head of 'participatory parity'? The processes that circumscribed the terms of Kevin's participation and success were used, not to make the case that 'non-traditional' MPs suffer the injustice of misrecognition (Bourdieu's 'symbolic violence'), which indeed they do, but rather to explain why the social groups from which they are drawn are so poorly represented in the forums of the political field. We therefore conclude that transformational remedies must continue to be sought at the institutional level itself, *pace* Archer, but that it is equally clear that institutional reform alone will do little to advance the cause of representational justice. Transformational remedies of both 'recognition' and 'redistribution' (the redistribution of all Bourdieu's capitals, not just the economic) will also and at the same time be necessary. The politics of recognition, focusing on the injustices of the status order, must also address the challenges of the 'unsaid' and the 'less than conscious' as they are embedded in the habitus, and this will certainly involve strategies that foster the greater degrees of awareness and reflexivity that are essential to effective human agency, individual and collective.

Notes

1 'Not quite our class.'

2 'Social bias' is the term used by Pippa Norris and Joni Lovenduski (1995). We would prefer the term 'demographic imbalance', but in the context of engaging with their approach to political recruitment, we will deploy their term to avoid confusion.

3 But note that David Cameron has proposed 50 per cent female representation on the national 'approved list' of candidates.

4 It must be acknowledged that Bourdieu too draws heavily on economic metaphors in his sociology of domination. Where Norris and Lovenduski use the language of supply and demand, Bourdieu identifies types of 'capital' which may be 'accumulated', 'traded', and which may have 'profits' etc. This language fuels accusations of economic determinism (Honneth 1986) and has occasioned reservations among some feminists who have engaged with his sociology (Hughes and Blaxter, this volume; Siles 2002; Skeggs 2004c; Silva and Edwards 2003). However, our understanding of Bourdieu's concept of capitals is that they are rooted in the social relations of the field, thus providing a more socially-based, rather than purely economically-based theorisation.

5 'General' social field is Moi's (1999) terminology, taken from Beate Krais (1993), in Moi's critique of Bourdieu's under-theorisation of what he terms the 'whole' social field (Moi 1999: 288–9).

6 Again, the economic metaphor is striking.

7 The Comparative Leadership Study consisted of a survey of men and women in positions of power in business and politics, followed in some countries by interviews. The total sample size consisted of nearly 1,500 respondents. Since positions of top leadership are filled overwhelmingly by men, random sampling is inappropriate for making gender comparisons, and so a purposive sample of respondents was chosen for the survey, selecting women in top leadership positions at four specified levels and matching the male sample to the female (see Vianello and Moore 2000, chapter 2 for details).

8 Norris and Lovenduski (1995) point out that because there were so few ethnic minority MPs in the 1992–7 parliament, it was difficult to draw conclusions about 'race' from the statistical analysis. Although we requested interviews from some of the ethnic minority MPs, none of them agreed to take part in the research. This should not be regarded as unusual, since it was extremely difficult to get research access to any of the female MPs, of whom there were only 60, because their small number meant that they were in constant demand as respondents. However, the concept of ethnicity does not refer exclusively to ethnic minorities (Ware 1992). In the following analysis we refer to ethnicity through the concept of whiteness.

9 The system whereby people gain access to the Lords is currently in transition.

10 Edward Heath's father was a carpenter, his mother a maid. Margaret Thatcher's father was a grocer and alderman. John Major's father was a travelling showman.

11 Once 'masculine' fields are opened up to women, no doubt they are likely to attract women whose habitus is not a stereotypical 'feminine' one. But as we have argued, it is their sex rather than a feminine habitus that provokes the symbolic violence they encounter (and in the case of the military, this may extend to physical violence). One response that sometimes buys off some of this symbolic violence is to 'become one of the boys', as Julia Wheelwright (1989) describes it in her study of the history of women in the militia. This would be an example of the nomos of the field in terms of its preferred habitus, bringing those that do not 'fit' into alignment with it. However, the hope of feminists who want to see more women in such fields is that the field itself would be transformed as a result. It may be that a critical number of women are needed if the reverse effect, in which habitus reforms or transforms the field, is to be possible. But the Labour party's introduction of a quota system through AWS in

1993, which doubled the proportion of women Labour MPs at the 1997 election, still left female representation at only 18 per cent.

12 What is significant about the term is its formulation as a private code such that those who do not belong are unaware of their categorisation.

13 None of the 'miraculous' Conservative leaders from less than 'traditional' backgrounds retained this particular marker of class.

14 Of course, strategies that involve compulsion may produce other problems. See the *Guardian* report, 8 May 2006, p.4:

> The Welsh secretary, Peter Hain, apologised to voters in the South Wales seat of Blaenau Gwent yesterday for imposing an all-women shortlist on them in the last general election. The row lead to Labour losing its safest Welsh constituency by more than 9,000 votes to an independent, Peter Law, who had split from Labour over the issue'.

References

Adkins, Lisa (2003) 'Reflexivity: freedom or habit of gender?', *Theory, Culture and Society* 20, 6: 21–42.

Archer, Margaret (1983) 'Process without system', *Archives Europeenes de Sociologie* XXIV, 1: 196–221.

Archer, Margaret (1993) 'Bourdieu's theory of cultural reproduction: French or universal?', *French Cultural Studies* iv: 225–40.

Arendt, Hannah (1973) *The Origins of Totalitarianism*, New York: Harcourt Brace.

Beynon, John (2002) *Masculinities and Culture*, Buckingham: Open University Press.

Bourdieu, Pierre (1977) *Outline of a Theory of Practice*, Cambridge: Cambridge University Press.

Bourdieu, Pierre (1984) *Distinction*, London: Routledge

Bourdieu, Pierre (1986) 'La force du droit: éléments pour une sociologie du champ juridique', *Actes de la Recherche en Sciences Sociales* 64: 3–19.

Bourdieu, Pierre (1987) 'What makes a social class? On the theoretical and practical existence of groups', *Berkeley Journal of Sociology: A Critical Review* XXXII: 1–17.

Bourdieu, Pierre (1988) *Acts of Resistance*, Cambridge: Polity.

Bourdieu, Pierre (1990a) 'La domination masculine', *Actes de la Recherche en Sciences Sociales* 84: 2–31.

Bourdieu, Pierre (1990b) *In Other Words*, Cambridge: Polity.

Bourdieu, Pierre (1991) *Language and Symbolic Power*, Cambridge: Polity.

Bourdieu, Pierre (1993) *The Field of Cultural Production*, Cambridge: Polity.

Bourdieu, Pierre (1996) *The Rules of Art*, Cambridge: Polity.

Bourdieu, Pierre (2000) *Pascalian Meditations*, Cambridge: Polity.

Bourdieu, Pierre (2001) *Masculine Domination*, Cambridge: Polity.

Bourdieu, Pierre *et al.* (1999) *The Weight of the World*, Cambridge: Polity.

Brown, Alice (1996) 'Women and politics in Scotland', in Lovenduski, Joni and Norris, Pippa (eds) *Women in Politics*, Oxford: Oxford University Press.

Childs, Sarah (2004) *New Labour's Women MPs*, London: Routledge.

Connell, Robert (1995) *Masculinities*, Cambridge: Polity.

Crompton, Rosemary (1993) *Class and Stratification*, Cambridge: Polity.

Elson, Diane and Pearson, Ruth (1981) 'Nimble fingers make cheap workers: an analysis of women's employment in third world export manufacturing', *Feminist Review* 7: 87–107.

Fraser, Nancy (1995) 'From redistribution to recognition? Dilemmas of justice in a "post-socialist" age', *New Left Review* 212: 68–93.

Fraser, Nancy (1998) 'Heterosexism, misrecognition and capitalism: a response to Judith Butler', *New Left Review* 228: 140–9.

Fraser, Nancy (2005) 'Reframing justice in a globalizing world', *New Left Review* 36, November, December: 69–88, reprinted in this collection.

Honneth, A. (1986) 'The fragmented world of symbolic forms', *Theory, Culture and Society* 3, 3: 55–66.

Krais, Beate (1993) 'Gender and symbolic violence: female suppression in the light of Pierre Bourdieu's Theory of Social Practice', in Calhoun, Craig, LiPouma, Edward and Postone, Moishe (eds) *Bourdieu: Critical Perspectives*, Chicago: University of Chicago Press, 156–77.

Lash, Scott (1990) *Sociology of Postmodernism*, London: Routledge.

Liddle, Joanna and Michielsens, Elisabeth (2000a) 'Women and public power: class does make a difference', *International Review of Sociology* 10, 2: 207–22.

Liddle, Joanna and Michielsens, Elisabeth (2000b) 'Gender, class and political power in Britain: narratives of entitlement', in Rai, Shirin (ed.) *International Perspectives on Gender and Democratisation*, Basingstoke: Macmillan.

Lovell, Terry (2000) 'Thinking feminism with and against Bourdieu', *Feminist Theory* 1: 11–32.

Lovell, Terry (2003) 'Resisting with authority', *Theory, Culture and Society* 20, 1: 1–17.

Lovenduski, Joni (1997) 'Gender politics: a breakthrough for women', *Parliamentary Affairs* 50, 4: 708–19.

Lovenduski, Joni (1998) 'Gendering research in political science', *Annual Review of Political Science* 1: 333–56.

McDougall, Linda (1998) *Westminster Women*, London: Vintage.

Mackay, Fiona (2004) 'Gender and political representation in the UK', *British Journal of Politics and International Relations* 6, 1: 99–120.

McNay, Lois (2000) *Gender and Agency: Reconfiguring the Subject in Feminist and Social Theory*, Cambridge: Polity.

McNay, Lois (2004) 'Agency and experience: gender as a lived relation', in Adkins, Lisa and Skeggs, Beverley (eds) *Feminism after Bourdieu*, Oxford: Blackwell.

Moi, Toril (1991) 'Appropriating Bourdieu', in Moi, Toril (1999) *What is a Woman?* Oxford: Oxford University Press.

Moi, Toril (1999) *What is a Woman?*, Oxford: Oxford University Press.

Norris, Pippa and Lovenduski, Joni (1995) *Political Recruitment*, Cambridge: Cambridge University Press.

Phillips, Anne (1999) *Which Equalities Matter?*, Cambridge: Polity.

Puwar, Nirmal (2004) 'Thinking about making a difference', *The British Journal of Politics and International Relations* 6, 1: 65–80.

Sansonetti, Sylvia (2000) 'Appendix: data about countries', in Vianello, Mino and Moore, Gwen (eds) *Gendering Elites*, Basingstoke: Macmillan.

Siles, M. (2002) 'Is social capital really capital?', *Review of Social Economy* 60, 1: 1–22.

Silva, E. and Edwards, R. (2003) 'Operationalising Bourdieu on Capitals: a discussion on 'the construction of the object'', ESRC Research Methods Programme, working Paper No 7, Manchester: University of Manchester. (www.ccsr.ac.uk/methods/publications/documents/WP7_000.pdf).

Skeggs, Beverley (1997) *Formations of Class and Gender*, London: Sage.

Skeggs, Beverley (2004a) 'Context and background: Pierre Bourdieu's analysis of class, gender and sexuality', in Adkins, Lisa and Skeggs, Beverley (eds) *Feminism after Bourdieu*, Oxford: Blackwell.

Skeggs, Beverley (2004b) 'Exchange, value and affect: Bourdieu and "the self"', in Adkins, Lisa and Skeggs, Beverley (eds) *Feminism after Bourdieu*, Oxford: Blackwell.

Skeggs, Beverley (2004c) 'Context and background: Pierre Bourdieu's analysis of class, gender and sexuality', *Sociological Review* 52, 2: 19–33.

Sreberny-Mohammadi, Annabelle and Ross, Karen (1996) 'Women MPs and the media: representing the body politic', in Lovenduski, Joni and Norris, Pippa (eds) *Women in Politics*, Oxford: Oxford University Press.

Stanley, Liz and Morgan, David (1993) 'Editorial introduction', *Sociology* 27, 1: 1–14.

Stanley, Liz and Wise, Sue (1983) *Breaking Out: Feminist Consciousness and Feminist Research*, London: Routledge and Kegan Paul.

Thompson, Edward P. (1980) *The Making of the English Working Class*, Harmondsworth: Penguin.

Thompson, John (1991) 'Editor's introduction', in Bourdieu, Pierre *Language and Symbolic Power*, Cambridge: Polity.

Vianello, Mino and Moore, Gwen (eds) (2000) *Gendering Elites*, Basingstoke: Macmillan.

Wacquant, Loic (1989) 'Towards a reflexive sociology: a workshop with Pierre Bourdieu', *Sociological Theory* 7: 26–53.

Wacquant, Loic (1993) 'From ruling class to field of power: an interview with Pierre Bourdieu on *La Noblesse d'Etat*', *Theory, Culture and Society* 10: 19–44.

Wacquant, Loic (ed.) (2005) *Pierre Bourdieu and Democratic Politics*, Cambridge: Polity.

Ware, Vron (1992) *Beyond the Pale: White Women, Racism and History*, London: Verso.

Wheelwright, Julia (1989) *Amazons and Military Maids*, London: Pandora.

9 (Mis)recognition, social inequality and social justice

A critical social policy perspective

Ruth Lister

Introduction

Nancy Fraser's work has been described as 'a model for politically engaged scholarship' (Fraser and Naples 2004: 1103). It is not surprising, therefore, that she is one of the contemporary political and social theorists whose writings have had a particular influence on critical social policy. While this chapter will touch on some of the theoretical debates raised by Fraser's work (discussed in greater depth elsewhere in this volume), its main purpose is to draw out some of its implications for social policy and social politics. It takes as its methodological motto that advocated by Fraser in *Feminist Contentions*: 'an impure, eclectic, neopragmatic approach' (Fraser 1995: 158).

The chapter is divided into two main parts. The first both engages with some of Fraser's writing on feminist welfare politics and questions the silence around disabled women and disability politics in her work. This also provides a link to the second part of the paper, which focuses on recognition and redistribution. This, in turn, first discusses the value and practical implications of a politics of recognition for the politics of poverty. It then, following Fraser (2005), considers how in a globalizing world the question of the 'who' of justice becomes as important as the more traditional question of the 'what' of justice. It does so in rather different terms to Fraser herself by posing the question: in a breathtakingly unequal globalizing condition, *who* do we recognize and *to whom* are we prepared to redistribute? It poses this question in relation to the treatment of asylum-seekers, an issue which requires more affluent societies to confront the demands of global justice on their own doorstep.

Feminist and disability politics

Fraser's writings represent an important contribution to politically engaged academic feminism, particularly in relation to the question of the relationship between employment and unpaid care work, which is discussed here. Significant also are her writings on need and (inter)dependence, which are referred to here in the context of disability politics, a social movement that Fraser typically ignores.

Beyond equality and difference

Fraser (1997) has characterized second-wave American feminism in terms of three phases, the first of which, 'gender difference', was dominated by the still unresolved 'equality vs difference' debate. The tension between equality and difference has long been at the heart of feminist debates about how to re-gender citizenship on terms more favourable to and inclusive of women (Lister 1997). In terms of current feminist politics in the UK – and some other European countries – it has taken on a new momentum in the face of the espousal by governments of what Fraser calls the 'universal breadwinner' and Jane Lewis 'the adult worker' model, in place of the old, discredited, 'male breadwinner' model (Fraser 1997; Lewis 2001). Paid work has been elevated to *the* primary citizenship obligation for all those capable of it.

The policy debate may not necessarily be couched explicitly in terms of feminist ideals in a supposedly 'post-feminist' era in which big 'F' feminism is seen as having little resonance in mainstream politics (Hewitt *et al.* 2004; Lister 2005). Nevertheless, policy debates around, for instance, the extent to which lone mothers should be expected to be part of the paid labour force and the changing role of fathers reflect more fundamental questions raised by many feminist welfare theorists in relation to the equality vs difference dilemma.

The debate about lone mothers and paid work illustrates how the equality vs difference dilemma is played out in different ways in different national, and sometimes local, contexts. Duncan and Edwards have suggested the notion of 'gendered moral rationalities' to describe 'collective and social understandings about what is the proper relationship between motherhood and paid work' (1999: 3). Dominant gendered moral rationalities vary between countries and also between social and ethnic groups within countries. In the US, where female labour market participation, in line with the equality model, is the norm, there has been remarkably little mainstream opposition to the harsh intensification of the paid work obligations imposed on lone mothers (Orloff 2002). The Netherlands, in contrast, provides an example of how a policy that goes against the grain of dominant gendered moral rationalities has been largely unsuccessful in its attempt to require lone mothers of school-age children to enter the labour market (Knijn and van Wel 2001).

The UK is one of very few OECD countries that impose no work obligations on lone parents (although it is moving in that direction with the introduction of obligatory, increasingly frequent, work-focused interviews). The fierce resistance to any such obligation reflects both dominant gendered moral rationalities (at least in relation to young children) and the barriers created by an inadequate social infrastructure and inflexible employment practices.

The task of 're-gendering' citizenship requires us to move beyond both the ostensibly gender-neutral equality model of citizenship, which offers women equal opportunities with men on men's terms, and the gender-differentiated model, which acknowledges women's particular concerns and contribution but runs the danger of trapping them within a second-class form of citizenship. Our

aim instead should be a gender-inclusive model. Such a model would reconstruct both equality and difference within the framework of diversity – what
Fraser terms 'multiple intersecting differences' (1997: 180). In the social welfare
sphere, this reconstruction would take as a touchstone the creation of the conditions that facilitate the meeting of human need and the exercise of caring
responsibilities in such a way as to ensure that all individuals can develop and
flourish as citizens. Difference could thus be incorporated into strategies for
gender equity without reference to potentially essentialist notions of women's
qualities and nature (Lister 1997).

In policy terms, the key lever lies in shifting the gendered distribution of
labour and time in both the public and private spheres. A key element of the
policy context is the 'care gap' that has opened up with the demise of the male
breadwinner model. As Lewis has observed, care work still needs to be done.
The question is by whom and 'on what terms' (Lewis 2001: 61). Fraser's answer
is the 'universal caregiver' model, which reflects what many feminists are
arguing for today as a practical resolution of the equality vs difference dilemma.
At the heart of this model is the unashamedly normative and utopian aim 'to
induce men to become more like most women are now, namely, people who do
primary carework' (Fraser 1997: 60). Indeed, even Gøsta Esping-Andersen has
begun to engage with these debates and concluded (without reference to most
feminist work in the area) that 'true gender equality will not come about unless,
somehow, men can be made to embrace a more feminine life course'
(2002: 95).[1]

The critical policy question is 'how can men be so induced?' The Nordic
countries, in their different ways, have gone furthest in attempting to engage
men in care work. Their main policy instruments have been: paid parental leave
with at least a month earmarked for fathers; working time policies; and public
education programmes. In the UK, even though New Labour has begun to talk
about the importance of men's role as active fathers – and not just breadwinners
– they have balked at introducing the kind of policies that would enable and
encourage men to *be* more active fathers. The introduction of two weeks' statu-
tory paternity pay and the promise of limited, additional paternity leave are
unlikely 'to induce men to become more like most women are now'. Without
adequate payment for parental leave, and a portion reserved for fathers, insofar
as parental leave is taken, it will be taken by women, thereby cementing rather
than challenging the traditional gendered division of labour.

It is very much the universal breadwinner not the universal caregiver model
that underpins current policy. How that model operates and its implications for
care in different societies depend in part on the adequacy of the infrastructure of
services and financial support for parents. Likewise, a genuinely progressive
universal caregiver model would have to be combined with an adequate social
infrastructure.

An important merit of the universal caregiver model is that it values both paid
work *and* caring work. In this way it can be supported both by those who place
greater emphasis on women's equality through paid work and those who place

greater emphasis on care as an important responsibility of and resource for citizenship, rather than simply viewing it as a barrier to equality in paid work. It avoids the potential trap of further locking women into the care-giving role, which is the danger of the 'caregiver parity' model of supporting informal care work, described and rejected by Fraser (1997).

Fraser sketches ideal (from a feminist viewpoint) versions of the universal breadwinner and caregiver parity models. Both, she suggests, are utopian but 'neither is utopian enough', for neither 'can actually make good on its promise of gender equity – even under very favourable conditions' (1997: 59). She ends her essay with her own utopian vision of the universal caregiver model: 'a social world in which citizens' lives integrate wage earning, caregiving, community activism, political participation, and involvement in the associational life of civil society – while also leaving time for some fun' (1997: 62). This points to how time is a crucial resource, which is part of the politics of redistribution, and to how we need time just to be as well as to do (Lister 2002).

However, if the universal caregiver model is to move beyond the utopian, as Kevin Olson has argued, it will require cultural as well as structural change. This, in turn, he contends, 'depends importantly on the cultural agency of women':

> the critical, cognitive, and discursive abilities to act as an agent in defining the terms through which oneself and one's society are understood. As such, it is the gauge of a person's capacity to alter gender norms and similarly constructed aspects of a social life.
>
> (Olson 2002: 407, 396)

'Multiple intersecting differences' – where is disability?

The notion of cultural agency takes us back to contemporary feminism, which, in some of its forms, can be understood as a struggle for cultural agency. Fraser has identified, as a third phase of contemporary US feminism, 'multiple intersecting differences'. The shift to this phase, she suggests, seemed 'to invite a turning outward' from a preoccupation with gender alone to focus on 'crosscutting axes of difference and subordination …. Not only gender but also "race", ethnicity, nationality, sexuality, and class would now require feminist theorization' (1997: 180). What is surprising both here and elsewhere in Fraser's work is the absence of any mention of disability as an axis of difference and subordination.

It is surprising for two main reasons. First, because disabled feminists' critique of traditional feminism has been important in the shift from a uni-focal to a multi-focal feminist lens, even if disability is still all too often out of focus. In the UK, Jenny Morris has written that disabled feminists 'feel betrayed and excluded by feminist analysis and activism' (1996: 5). In the US, Anita Silvers is critical of those feminists who would substitute an ethic of care for an ethic of equality, on the grounds that an ethic of care invites the marginalization of those 'consigned to the position of dependence' and 'an even more oppressive paternalism' (1997: 33). She also explores one of Fraser's themes – the equality vs difference dilemma – but from a disability perspective.

This leads in to the second, even more surprising, reason, which is that disability politics has exemplified so many of the themes in Fraser's work. Indeed, when teaching social policy theory I use it to illustrate both her earlier work on the politics of needs interpretation and her later work on redistribution–recognition. Just like the women's movement, the disabled people's movement has been instrumental in the establishment of the political status of needs, which were not previously recognized as such – most notably the need for public and private spaces to be accessible. The movement's demands provide a clear example of the clash between 'oppositional needs discourses' and 'expert needs discourses' (Fraser 1987), as disabled people have struggled against the professionals' medical model of disability, which had previously defined their needs in narrow medical terms.

As Mike Oliver, a leading disability activist and academic, has written: it is 'rights to appropriate welfare services to meet their own self-defined needs that disabled people are demanding, not to have their needs defined and met by others'. Indeed, he notes, there has been a challenge to the whole notion of needs-based welfare, with its implications of paternalistic professional gate-keeping to rationed resources, in favour of 'welfare services based upon the idea of citizenship' (1996: 74, 75). In other words, disability politics is in part about the translation of 'justified needs claims into social rights' (Fraser 1987: 183).

Disability politics also provides a perfect example of the two-dimensional social justice claims, which Fraser analyses in relation to class, 'race', gender and sexuality. As Tom Shakespeare writes: 'the social movement of disabled people is about the politics of recognition, as well as the politics of redistribution. Disabled people suffer socio-economic injustices, such as marginalisation and deprivation, as well as cultural injustices, such as non-recognition and disrespect' (2005: 164). Like other social movements, the disabled people's movement wrestles with the difficulties of integrating the two: in this instance 'a barriers approach, that seeks to dissolve differences and promote inclusion; and a minority group approach, which seeks a better deal for disabled people and celebrates disabled identity' (ibid.).

The embodied nature of the misrecognition of disabled people is underlined by Edwards and Imrie, who apply Bourdieu's conception of 'the body as a bearer of value in society' and his notion of habitus to disability theory (Edwards and Imrie 2003: 240). Their qualitative research 'shows that disabled people's lives are intimately connected to different "valuations" of corporeal forms, and to systems of signification and representation which underpin them' (ibid.: 241). Their 'bodies are subjected to the values of a society that renders them "less than valuable" and inferior to those considered to be the embodiment of "normality" ... disabled people's experiences reinforce their marginality and inferior status in society' (ibid.: 252; see also Meekosha 1998). Their marginality is further reinforced by economic exclusion and a high risk of poverty. Policies to promote social justice for disabled people therefore have to address both material inequalities and cultural misrecognition (Goodlad and Riddell 2005; Witcher 2005).

Dependency

Another issue taken up by disability theorists is that of dependency. The classic essay by Fraser and Linda Gordon traces the historical roots and ideological underpinnings of the concept of dependency – the 'single most crucial term' in US welfare reform debates (Fraser and Gordon 1994: 4). Unfortunately, it is among the discursive imports from the US that has had particular resonance in welfare politics in the UK under both the Conservatives and New Labour – though it has not carried the same racialized connotations.

Fraser and Gordon's essay sketches the beginnings of 'an alternative semantics premised on the inescapable fact of human *inter*dependence' (Fraser and Gordon 1994: 6). This involves, they argue, both challenging the false dichotomy between dependence and independence and the revaluation of the devalued side of that dichotomy – the rehabilitation of 'dependency as a normal, even valuable, human quality' (ibid.: 23). They recognize, though, that this needs to be done cautiously, given that 'dependence' on welfare can reduce self-esteem and autonomy. A less ideologically charged term such as 'reliance' might, however, be more appropriate in this context.

The emphasis on human *inter*dependence is important and it reflects one of the key arguments of feminist care ethicists. However, women's economic independence has always been a central tenet of the feminism of many women of my generation and the case for social and employment policies that promote women's economic independence has been an important strand in British feminism and in feminist social policy (Lister 2002, 2005). We must not forget that, as Fraser and Gordon themselves acknowledge, dependency can represent 'a social relation of subordination' (1994: 21) and that, as Fraser (1997) argues elsewhere, exploitable forms of dependency are inimical to gender equity. The unequal power relationship that underpins the economic dependence of some women on men means that the interdependence of which it is a part is skewed in men's favour. It is not surprising, therefore, that the other element of the equation – men's dependence on women for care and servicing, which facilitates their own independence as workers and citizens – is conveniently obscured. It is important that our arguments for recognition of human *inter*dependence are not used to obscure or even to justify economic dependence in the private, domestic sphere, which, even though much less prevalent today, still exists for some women. The principle of financial independence in income maintenance policy remains important (Bennett 2005).

Fraser and Gordon distinguish between 'socially necessary' and 'surplus' dependence. The former represents the need for care, which is 'an inescapable feature of the human condition'; the latter, in contrast, 'is rooted in unjust and potentially remediable social institutions'. The goal, they argue, is to eliminate the 'surplus' dependency, which currently adheres to the care giving involved in the 'socially necessary' dependency (Fraser and Gordon 1994: 24). Again, what is missing is the perspective of care-receivers, in particular disabled people who have also engaged in the debate around dependency. Others, though, have drawn on Fraser's work to explore 'the emancipatory potential of the concept of inter-dependence' so as 'to create a "discourses bridge" between feminist and disability perspectives' (Watson *et al.* 2004: 340, 345).

Disability theorists such as Jenny Morris (1993) argue that insofar as disabled people are physically dependent it is the result of disabling physical and socio-economic environments ('surplus' dependency perhaps) rather than of their impairments as such. Moreover, disabled people's reliance on others for help with the tasks of daily living is confused with dependence whereas, according to the independent living movement, independence stems from the ability to control the assistance required. The dependence that results from the lack of such control is, it is argued, corrosive of disabled people's rights as citizens.

Other disability theorists, such as Tom Shakespeare and Anita Silvers (1997), are thus concerned not to displace independence as a goal for disabled people. Shakespeare argues that the 'crucial move here is not just to recognize that everyone has needs, but to break the link between physical and social dependency .... The independent living model argues that independence consists in being able to make choices and exert control over one's life' (2000: 62). He points to the importance of direct payment and independent living schemes, which give disabled people control over the care they need, in achieving this. However, he does concede that the direct payments model may not suit everyone and that 'there can be too much stress on independence and autonomy within disability rights discourse' (ibid.: 63).

In a paper for the UK Disability Rights Commission, Morris (2005: 7) re-articulates independence as 'self-determination': the ability to make decisions for oneself. She identifies self-determination along with participation and recognition of disabled people's contribution to economic and social life as key principles of disabled people's citizenship. She argues that the common assumption that disabled people are 'in need of "care" ... undermines other people's ability to see us as autonomous people'. This in turn creates 'an attitudinal barrier' to citizenship participation (Morris 2005: 25).

Redistribution and recognition

Morris's conceptualization of disabled people's citizenship could be read as an expression of what Fraser terms 'participatory parity' in her more recent work on recognition–redistribution, which is the focus of the second part of this chapter. Participatory parity is a norm of justice, which 'requires social arrangements that permit all (adult) members of society to interact with one another as peers' (2003: 36).[2] In line with my pragmatic methodological motto and following Fraser in her original *New Left Review* article, I will treat the principles of redistribution and recognition, which underpin participatory parity, as a heuristic device in order to analyse the politics of poverty and, more briefly, global justice and asylum.

Poverty

Poverty stands at the extreme redistribution end of the recognition–redistribution 'conceptual spectrum' (Fraser 1999: 29). In her initial exposition, Fraser mentioned economic marginalization and deprivation as examples of 'socioeconomic injustice', although her analysis at this end of the conceptual spectrum has tended to focus on the wider working class. She observes, rightly, that 'the last thing [the proletariat] needs is recognition of its difference' (1997: 18).

Diana Coole has discussed in more detail the inappropriateness of a discourse of difference in relation to what she calls the 'underclass' – a term best avoided because of the pejorative connotations it has acquired. She writes that this group 'has no identity to be wielded with pride for which respect is demanded' and that 'a celebration or fostering of difference becomes simply nonsensical' (1996: 21, 22). Indeed, she goes further and argues that: 'respect for those on lower echelons is patronizing' (ibid.: 22).

On the face of it, this does not look very promising for the application of a politics of recognition to claims for justice among those living in poverty. However, a shift in emphasis in Fraser's more recent elaboration of her thesis helps point to its relevance, even though she herself does not apply it to poverty. First, she contests a 'widespread misunderstanding', which equates a politics of recognition with identity politics. As she points out, this 'forecloses the recognition dimensions of class struggles' and 'reduces what is actually a plurality of different kinds of recognition claims ... to a single type, namely, claims for the affirmation of difference' (1999: 27). The appropriate form of the recognition claim, she argues, depends on the nature of the misrecognition: 'in cases where misrecognition involves denying ... common humanity ..., the remedy is universalist recognition' (1999: 38). What people in poverty want is the universalist recognition of their common humanity and citizenship and of the equal worth that flows from that.

Second, *contra* Axel Honneth, Fraser insists on the need to break with the standard 'identity' model of recognition, under which 'what requires recognition is group-specific cultural identity. Misrecognition consists in the depreciation of such identity by the dominant culture and the consequent damage to group members' sense of self' (2001: 23). Instead she proposes a 'status model' under which recognition is treated as a question of 'social status'. 'What requires recognition is not group-specific identity but rather the status of group members as full partners in social interaction' – or 'participatory parity' (ibid.: 24, 27). Again, this is a much more helpful formulation of recognition politics from the perspective of people in poverty.

However, Fraser's position on the psychological effects of misrecognition can be interpreted as failing to give sufficient weight to their significance. In her exchange with Honneth she explains that, while the status model 'accepts that misrecognition can have the sort of ethical-psychological effects' described by himself and Charles Taylor (1992), 'the wrongness of misrecognition does not *depend* on the presence of such effects' (2003: 32, emphasis added). I have no quarrel with that position. However, elsewhere she contends that: 'when mis-recognition is identified with internal distortions in the structure of self-consciousness of the oppressed, it is but a short step to blaming the victim', thereby she argues, seeming 'to add insult to injury' (2001: 27). What is at issue here is a question of emphasis: whether in (rightly) challenging Honneth's argu-ment that social injustice is contingent on psychic harm, Fraser goes too far at times in down-playing the significance of such harm.

Evidence to support the case for acknowledgement of the importance of the psychological dimension of misrecognition can be found in some academic writ-ings about poverty and in the narratives of people with experience of poverty themselves. One piece, which combines the two, is an article in a special edition of *Sociology* on 'class, culture and identity' by Vivyan C. Adair who describes herself as a 'poverty-class scholar' (2005: 817). Her description of her experience of poverty as a child powerfully evokes the psychological scars of misrecognition and their embodiment, for 'poverty was written onto and into our beings as children at the level of private and public thought and body' (2005: 822). She records that:

> our dirty and tattered clothing; posture that clearly reflected guilt, shame and lack of a sense of entitlement; scars and bodily disease; and sheer hunger, marked us as Others among our more fortunate working-class neighbors and colleagues .... Other students and even our working-class teachers read us as 'trailer trash', as unworthy, laughable and dangerous .... We were paraded in front of these working class students shamed and humiliated in our ragged and ill-fitting hand-me-downs, our very bodies sig-naling our Otherness while representing and testing the limits of working-class identity and 'deservedness'.
>
> (Adair 2005: 823)

As Richard Wilkinson observes in his analysis of the psycho-social links between poverty and ill health: 'second-rate goods seem to tell people you are a second-rate person. To believe otherwise is to fundamentally misunderstand the pain of relative poverty or low social status' (2005: 71).

In an in-depth study of Australian poverty, the author, Mark Peel, reflects on the multi-dimensional understandings of justice held by the people to whom he spoke:

> Their justice was distributive and procedural and intimately connected with dignity and self-determination. Justice was about being respected, trusted and listened to because what you had to say was important. If social justice is a response to poverty, they argued, it must be a response to poverty's psy-chological and emotional wounds, not just its financial consequences.
>
> (Peel 2003: 167)

The following quotations from two people with experience of poverty underline the depth of such wounds. The first, Moraene Roberts, was speaking at a

National Poverty Hearing organized by Church Action on Poverty: 'The worst blow of all', she said, 'is the contempt of your fellow citizens. I and many families live in that contempt' (Russell 1996: 4). The second, an anonymous participant in a UK Coalition against Poverty workshop, described what the loss of self-esteem associated with misrecognition feels like:

> You're like an onion and gradually every skin is peeled off you and there's nothing left. All your self esteem and how you feel about yourself is gone – you're left feeling like nothing and then your family feels like that.
>
> (UKCAP 1997: 12)

To acknowledge the psychological pain that these two people are expressing as a result of misrecognition is not, in my view, 'to add insult to injury'. Similarly, if we look at poverty from the perspective of children, we see how lack of participatory parity and the psychological impact of poverty are intertwined. Tess Ridge analyses the impact of poverty on children in terms of the ability to 'fit in' and 'join in'. She observes that:

> inner worries, fears of social difference and stigma, and the impact of poverty on self-esteem, confidence and personal security may all exact a high price for children who are in the formative process of developing their self and social identities.
>
> (2002: 85)

Of course, if our starting point were simply to say that people in poverty have low self-esteem, as if this were somehow innate, then yes it would be to add insult to injury. But, if we analyse such psychological effects as the result of the Othering of 'the poor' by the 'non-poor', as articulated by Adair above, then we can understand these effects in terms of misrecognition (Lister 2004). They also represent a strong motivating force behind a politics of recognition among people in poverty, even though such psychological factors also act as a barrier to their participatory parity.

An example of how recognition involves an inter-connection between self-esteem and participatory parity was provided in a *Guardian* article about a young carers' project. It quoted a development worker with the project:

> the project gives young carers a voice they've never had. If you haven't got recognition, then you can't influence the delivery of services. The confidence and self-esteem of our young people have grown as their skills have been recognised.
>
> (11 December 2002)

Reframing the politics of poverty as a politics of recognition as well as redistribution has implications for how people in poverty are represented and treated at all levels of society. This includes the language and images that make up popular discourses of poverty (Lister 2004). As a parent living on benefit has put it: 'we hear how the media, and some politicians, speak about us and it hurts' (APPGP 1999: 11).

The psychological impact of misrecognition can be integrated into the status model of recognition without falling into the identity model's trap of making it a *sine qua non* of misrecognition. Attention to it does not necessarily detract from what Fraser describes as 'the essential slogan': 'no recognition without redistribution' (Fraser and Naples 2004: 1122). Rather, it can reinforce the case for redistribution through higher wages and benefits. This is exemplified by Wilkinson's (2005) analysis of the kind of psychosocial processes involved in misrecognition, which, he argues, demonstrate that material inequality does matter.

Low pay and benefits

Low pay and benefits provide an example of a more concrete policy issue of central importance to the politics of poverty, which illustrates Fraser's conclusion that in practice 'overcoming injustice in virtually every case requires both redistribution and recognition', involving a 'perspectival dualism' (1999: 33, 45).

The issue of low wages and its gendered character is touched on by Fraser herself in a chapter in Ray and Sayer's *Culture and Economy after the Cultural Turn*. She observes that 'what presents itself as "the economy" is always already permeated with cultural interpretations and norms' such as those which govern the differential value placed on 'men's and 'women's' jobs and which distinguish between 'working' and 'caregiving'. 'Virtually any claim for redistribution' will, she argues, 'have some recognition effects' (1999: 44, 46). Indeed, Majid Yar goes further and contends that: 'redistributive claims, *as moral claims upon others invoking the terms of justice and injustice*, irredeemably have the character of recognition claims' for they invoke '*normative* concepts which are based upon specific self-understandings about what kinds of beings we are, what our worth is, and what kind of treatment we properly deserve' (1999: 294, 295, emphasis in original).

His claim is the basis of a theoretical dispute with Fraser, which will not be developed here. The point rather is to underline how demands for raising low wages, even though quintessentially material, frequently represent recognition as well as redistribution claims. When Bill Morris, former general secretary of the Transport and General Workers Union, announced his retirement, he said 'respect' had been the byword of his leadership: 'I have always campaigned for our members to be treated with dignity and respect in their work' (*Independent*, 13 February 2003). Dignity has also been invoked by low paid workers campaigning for a 'living wage'.

Reflecting on her experience of living on low pay for Lent, the British journalist Polly Toynbee observes that: 'what a person is paid signifies their worth and it is of primary emotional and social importance' (2002a: 35).

> Low pay is low status … Just as pay is a cause for boasting among the fat cats, it is equally a source of daily humiliation for the low paid, seeing how little one hour of their hard work is valued at. [Tax] credits do nothing to improve that brutal fact.
>
> (Ibid.: 14)

Toynbee is one of few public commentators who has persistently raised the issue of 'what is a worker worth and who decides?' (Toynbee 2002b). This is a question that Barbara Wootton posed half a century earlier in her classic book *The Social Foundation of Wage Policy*. Like Toynbee, she observed the issues of status and prestige involved in pay and she drew attention to the unjustifiable spread of wages. It was, in part, the equivalence between her own earnings in the 1930s and those of the elephant that gave children rides at Whipsnade Zoo that led Wootton 'to fundamental reflections about the social and economic forces which determine the valuations which our society sets upon different kinds of work' (1955: 9).

One small example: the Government's childcare strategy could be undermined by the lack of an adequate supply of childcare workers, as it has acknowledged.[3] Nursery nurses earn little more than half the average wage and less than road sweepers (*Guardian*, 4 February 2003). In a series of studies, childcare workers 'said repeatedly that low pay encouraged society to afford low value to the work, which in turn affected recruitment and retention' (Cameron *et al.* 2002: 578). The lack of financial recognition for work that is so vital to children's development is experienced as demoralizing (Owen 2003; Scott *et al.* 2003). As many feminist commentators have observed, lack of recognition of the value of paid care work in the public sphere of the market and public sectors is linked closely to its association with the unpaid care work done, mainly by women, in the private domestic sphere.

This also has wider ramifications for social security policy, where the issue of benefit adequacy too can be interpreted from the perspective of recognition as well as redistribution. As with low wages, the level of social security benefits is in part a question of the recognition of human dignity, which is at the heart of a human rights conceptualization of poverty (Lister 2004). Back in 1992, the European Commission recommended that member states 'recognize the basic right of a person to sufficient resources and social assistance to live in a manner compatible with human dignity' (cited in Veit-Wilson 1998: 86).

Participation

Another relevant policy example concerns the growing demands among people with experience of poverty for a say in decision-making that affects their lives. How to remove the barriers to such participation was the key question addressed by an independent Commission on Poverty, Participation and Power in which I participated and half of whose members had direct experience of poverty. Our report took as its starting point the observation that:

too often people experiencing poverty are not treated with respect, either in general or by the people they come into contact with most ... The lack of respect for people living in poverty was one of the clearest and most heart-felt messages which came across to us as a Commission.

(Commission on Poverty, Participation and Power 2000: 3)

This lack of respect was identified as the main barrier to participation in decision-making and the ultimate disrespect was seen as 'being involved in phoney participation, by people who don't listen, when things don't change' (ibid.: 18).

Richard Sennett's book, *Respect*, starts with the observation that lack of respect, though less aggressive than 'outright insult, can take an equally wound-ing form'. Recognition is not extended to another person: 'he or she is not *seen* – as a full human being whose presence matters' (Sennett 2003: 3, emphasis in original). Far from being 'patronizing', as claimed by Coole (1996), respect is a vital indicator of recognition for many people in poverty. At the National Poverty Hearing mentioned earlier, one of the most common refrains was the desire to be treated with greater respect. As Millicent Simms, a young black woman, put it: 'I just feel very angry sometimes that people are ignorant to the fact that we are humans as well and we do need to be respected' (Russell 1996: 10).

For many people living in poverty, respect is closely linked to being listened to or 'voice'. According to Anne Phillips, this is typical of recognition struggles, which 'are and have been very much struggles for political voice' (2003: 265). People in poverty's struggle for political voice is about recognition of and respect for the expertise borne of experience and recognition of the unequal power relations which govern their lives. To quote Moraene Roberts again at the Poverty Hearing: 'No one asks our views .... We are the real experts of our own hopes and aspirations ... We can contribute if you are prepared to give up a little power to allow us to participate as partners in our own future' (Russell 1996: 4).

We have here a plea for the participatory parity that Fraser writes about at a more theoretical level. Fraser identifies 'at least two conditions' necessary for its achievement: the 'objective condition' of a distribution of material resources such as to ensure 'independence and "voice"' and the 'intersubjective condition' of 'institutionalized patterns of cultural value [which] express equal respect ... and ensure equal opportunity for achieving social esteem' (2003: 36). These are reflected in the more practical list of barriers to participation identified by the Commission on Poverty, Participation and Power (2000).

There is also a third possible condition, which, until recently, Fraser always relegated to a footnote. This refers to more explicitly political obstacles associ-ated with the injustice of '"political marginalization" or "exclusion"', the remedy for which is 'democratization' (Fraser 2003: 68). Opening up decision-making and politics generally to marginalized groups such as those in poverty will require change at the political level and more open and democratic decision-making procedures.

Although one of the questions Fraser poses with regard to the political dimension of justice is: 'do the community's decision rules accord equal voice in public deliberations and fair representations in public decision-making to all members?' (2005: 75), she develops this dimension in a rather different direction. For her it opens up the wider question of 'the politics of framing in a globalizing world'; this concerns the 'boundary-setting aspect of the political' as between members and non-members of territorial states (2005: 80).

The global context and asylum-seekers

As Fraser observes, the politics of framing opens up 'the question of the "who"': 'who is included in, and who excluded from, the circle of those entitled to a just distribution and reciprocal recognition?' (2005: 80, 75). Her analysis of the post-Westphalian re-framing of justice is scrutinized in Chapter 2. The aim here is simply to draw out some implications for critical social policy that are either implicit or absent in Fraser's own account. These concern the three inter-related issues of: global poverty; the perceived tension between solidarity and diversity in advanced welfare states; and forced migration, in particular the politics of asylum.

The issue of global poverty can be articulated at a more theoretical level in terms of the debate around cosmopolitan or global vs bounded citizenship (see, for instance, Hutchings and Dannreuther 1999) and the related but different question of the validity of notions of global or transnational justice (Jones 1999; O'Neill 2000; White 2003). What are the obligations of the richer towards the poorer parts of a globalizing, economically and ecologically interdependent and unequal world? Where are the boundaries of social justice to be drawn? A clear answer is provided by the Institute for Public Policy Research as part of a wider project on social justice:

> Today an exclusively national interpretation of social justice is neither morally defensible nor politically nor intellectually tenable. It is not morally defensible because the extent of poverty and human suffering across the world demands a comprehensive moral response. There is now a growing body of political philosophy that addresses 'global justice' and that considers the responsibilities of citizens and governments in developed countries towards poorer parts of the world or towards people in other countries whose human rights are abused. It is not politically or intellectually tenable because global interdependence and interconnectedness are reducing the distinction between domestic and international policy and increasing the number of issues that require a genuinely global response.
>
> (Mepham 2005: 133)

At a practical level this raises issues of aid, trade and debt policies, as articulated by the Make Poverty History campaign, as well as wider questions of global governance and democratic arenas, touched on by Fraser (2005; see also Barry and Pogge 2005). More fraught in terms of contemporary welfare politics is what has been described as 'the progressive dilemma' between solidarity and diversity. It was expressed by Alan Wolfe and Jytte Klausen in the following terms:

> A sense of solidarity creates a readiness to share with strangers, which in turn underpins a thriving welfare state. But it's easier to feel solidarity with those who broadly share your values and way of life. Modern progressives committed to diversity often fail to acknowledge this. They employ an over-abstract and unrealistic notion of affinity, implying that we ought to have the same feelings of generosity or solidarity towards a refugee from the other side of the world as we do towards our next door neighbour.
>
> (2000: 28)

The assumption that it is abstract or unrealistic to have feelings of solidarity towards a refugee or those who do not share the same values and way of life is premised on a particular understanding of solidarity rooted in sameness and relative proximity. This may be the dominant traditional interpretation of solidarity, as in notions of working-class solidarity (although even there differences within the working class were elided). Nevertheless, in a globalizing world it is also possible to identify alternative, more inclusive, conceptualizations of solidarity such as a 'cosmopolitan solidarity', which values diversity and 'multiplicity' over 'sameness and unity' (Beck 2005: 141), or 'reflective solidarity', appeals to which rest on 'our awareness of and regard for those multiple interconnections in which differences emerge' (Dean 1996: 16). Writing in the wake of the British public's response to the Indian Ocean tsunami, Ray Pahl has argued that: 'there are now forms of compassion and social solidarity that stretch across the world', for 'globalisation has increased our solidarities of compassion' (2005: 35).

It might be argued in response that, nevertheless, in practice, many people in affluent welfare states may be more likely to feel such solidarity towards people perceived as different to themselves when the latter remain at a distance on the other side of the world than when they migrate to their own backdoor, laying a claim to the 'global redistribution of citizenship status' (Yeatman 1994: 80). It is this dynamic and the growing diversity to which it gives rise that have prompted fears that 'the more different we become from one another and the less we share a moral consensus or a sense of mutual obligation and belonging, the less happy we may be to support a generous welfare state' (Goodhart 2005: 156).

The conclusion reached by commentators such as David Goodhart, editor of the influential *Prospect* journal, is that 'when solidarity and diversity pull against each other', public policy should favour solidarity (2004: 35). Others, while acknowledging the potential tension between the two, dispute that it is inevitable (Banting and Kymlicka 2004; Pearce 2004). A number of social scientists have used empirical analysis of welfare states and the example of Canada to argue that the evidence does not support the view that increasing diversity resulting from immigration necessarily erodes support for the welfare state (Banting 2004, 2006; Taylor-Gooby 2005). Moreover, as John Clarke has argued:

> solidarities are not naturally occurring phenomena: they are the result of political-cultural work that builds connections and identifications. Social democracy in its many European forms has had to build solidarities across social divisions – notably those of class and gender – to sustain the construction and enlargement of welfare states.
>
> (Clarke 2004: 156)

To question the pessimism of those who pose an ineluctable conflict between solidarity and diversity in welfare state politics is not, however, to deny the importance of the issue, particularly in the context of the vitriolic politics of asylum and immigration in Europe at the turn of the twenty-first century. The significance of the asylum issue, in particular, for Fraser's own project of reframing justice in a globalizing world, is brought out in an essay by Stephen Castles on the sociology of forced migration. Asylum and other forms of forced migration are, he argues: 'a central aspect of social transformation in the contemporary world' and are 'amongst the most important social expressions of global connections and processes' (2003: 30, 24), including processes of exclusion and inclusion which exacerbate inequalities.

The hysterical demonization of asylum-seekers by sections of the media and some politicians has fed hostility towards them in the UK and many other European countries. A study of media reporting of refugees and asylum seekers in the UK found that it is 'characterized by the inaccurate and provocative use of language' and of negative, threatening, imagery. As a result of 'the overwhelmingly negative media coverage', 'asylum seekers and refugees feel alienated, ashamed and sometimes threatened'. Many of those interviewed 'reported direct experience of prejudice, abuse or aggression from neighbours and service providers which they attributed to the way in which the media informs public opinion' (Buchanan *et al.* 2003: 9). In other words, they are, to quote Fraser's definition of disrespect: 'being routinely maligned or disparaged in stereotypic public cultural representations and/or in everyday life interactions' (1997: 14).

The roots of this disrespect are both cultural and socio-economic. Culturally asylum-seekers are perceived as the 'Other'. They also all too often appear 'as the physical embodiment of the external threat to jobs, living standards and welfare' in a globalizing world (Castles 2003: 20). As such, it is easy to blame them for the deficiencies of the welfare state, as suggested by a couple of opinion polls. The first found that nearly three-fifths of those questioned thought that asylum seeking was now a major reason why health and education were overburdened (*Guardian*, 13 February 2003). In the second, among those questioned who believed that other people 'seem to get unfair priority over you when it comes to public services and benefits', a fifth, unprompted, mentioned - asylum-seekers and a fifth mentioned new immigrants as those getting unfair priority (Duffy 2004). Yet the recent history of European welfare states' response to forced migration has primarily been one of 'differential exclusion' (Bloch and Schuster 2002: 408) and of the erosion of social rights (Dwyer 2005; Schuster 2005).

Here we have a politics of anti-recognition and anti-redistribution, which are all too integrated. The counter politics must likewise integrate the two. The challenge is how progressives can articulate a convincing politics of solidarity in difference that will extend solidarity to in-comers from beyond a nation's borders.

Conclusion

This chapter has engaged with the work of Nancy Fraser from the perspective of critical social policy. Such a perspective confirms the relevance of her writings to both social policy and social politics. In her most recent work she highlights the importance of the question of the 'who' of justice (Fraser 2005). It has been suggested here that there are a number of groups suffering economic and cultural injustice *who* are to a greater or lesser extent invisible in Fraser's own writings but who exemplify much of her own analysis and who are important to any project of social justice: disabled people, people living in poverty and asylum-seekers. They too should be recognized within the frame of social justice.

Notes

1 Esping-Andersen is a leading welfare-state analyst whose earlier work was widely criticized by feminist scholars for its neglect of gender.
2 The reference to adult members of society is indicative of the silence around children in Fraser's work. Yet some children too are involved in a politics of recognition and are trying to make a reality of the participatory right contained in the UN Convention on the Rights of the Child.
3 In its ten year child care strategy, the Government notes that high quality child care will require 'a step-change ... in the quality and stability of the workforce' (HM Treasury 2004: 45). It has established a Children's Workforce Development Council and has asked it to report on the impact of reward packages on recruitment and retention (*0–19*, March 2006).

References

Adair, V.C. (2005) 'US working-class/poverty-class divides', *Sociology*, 39, 5: 817–834.
APPGP (1999) *Policy, Poverty and Participation*, London: All-Party Parliamentary Group on Poverty.
Banting, K. (2004) *Diversity, Solidarity and the Welfare State: International Experience and British Debates*, London: Canada House.
Banting, K. (2006) 'Ethnic diversity and the welfare state: a North American perspective', in S. Delorenzi (ed.) *Going Places: Neighbourhood, Ethnicity and Social Mobility*, London: Institute for Public Policy Research.
Banting, K. and Kymlicka, W. and others (2004) 'Too diverse? Replies to David Goodhart's essay, which posed the notion that values of diversity and solidarity can conflict', *Prospect*, March: 1–10.

Barry, C. and Pogge, T.W. (eds) (2005) *Global Institutions and Responsibilities*, Oxford: Blackwell Publishing.

Beck, U. (2005) 'Inequality and recognition: pan-European social conflicts and their political dynamic', in A. Giddens and P. Diamond (eds) *The New Egalitarianism*, Cambridge: Polity Press.

Bennett, F. (2005) *Gender and Benefits*, Manchester: Equal Opportunities Commission.

Bloch, A. and Schuster, L. (2002) 'Asylum and welfare: contemporary debates', *Critical Social Policy*, 22, 3: 393–414.

Buchanan, S., Grillo, B., Threadgold, T. and Mosdell, N. (2003) *What's the Story? Results from Research into Media Coverage of Refugees and Asylum-seekers in the UK*, London: Article 19.

Cameron, C., Mooney, A. and Moss, P. (2002) 'The childcare workforce: current conditions and future directions', *Critical Social Policy*, 22, 4: 572–595.

Castles, S. (2003) 'Towards a sociology of forced migration and social transformation', *Sociology*, 37, 1: 13–34.

Clarke, J. (2004) *Changing Welfare Changing States: New Directions in Social Policy*, London: Sage.

Commission on Poverty, Participation and Power (2000) *Listen Hear! The Right to be Heard*, Bristol: The Policy Press.

Coole, D. (1996) 'Is class a difference that makes a difference?', *Radical Philosophy*, 77: 17–25.

Dean, J. (1996) *Solidarity of Strangers: Feminism after Identity Politics*, Berkeley: University of California Press.

Duffy, B. (2004) 'Free rider phobia', *Prospect*, February: 16.

Duncan, S. and Edwards, R. (1999) *Lone Mothers, Paid Work and Gendered Moral Rationalities*, Basingstoke: Macmillan.

Dwyer, P. (2005) 'Governance, forced migration and welfare', *Social Policy and Administration*, 39, 6: 622–639.

Edwards, C. and Imrie, R. (2003) 'Disability and bodies as bearers of value', *Sociology*, 37, 2: 239–256.

Esping-Andersen, G. (2002) *Why we Need a New Welfare State*, Oxford: Oxford University Press.

Fraser, N. (1987) 'Women, welfare and the politics of needs interpretation', *Hypatia*, 2, 1: 103–119.

Fraser, N. (1995) 'Pragmatism, feminism, and the linguistic turn', in S. Benhabib, J. Butler, D. Cornell and N. Fraser *Feminist Contentions: a philosophical exchange*, New York and London: Routledge.

Fraser, N. (1997) *Justice Interruptus*, New York and London: Routledge.

Fraser, N. (1999) 'Social justice in the age of identity politics: redistribution, recognition and participation', in L. Ray and A. Sayer (eds) *Culture and Economy after the Cultural Turn*, London: Sage.

Fraser, N. (2001) 'Recognition without ethics', *Theory, Culture and Society*, 18, 2–3: 21–42.

Fraser, N. (2003) 'Social justice in the age of identity politics: redistribution, recognition and participation', in N. Fraser and A. Honneth *Redistribution or Recognition? A Political-Philosophical Exchange*, London and New York: Verso.

Fraser, N. (2005) 'Reframing justice in a globalizing world', *New Left Review*, 36: 69–88.

Fraser, N. and Gordon, L. (1994) '"Dependency" demystified: inscriptions of power in a keyword of the welfare state', *Social Politics*, 1, 1: 4–31.

Fraser, N. and Naples, N. (2004) 'To interpret the world and to change it: an interview with Nancy Fraser', *Signs*, 29, 4: 1103–1124.

Goodhart, D. (2004) 'Too diverse?', *Prospect*, February: 30–37.

Goodhart, D. (2005) 'Britain's glue: the case for liberal nationalism', in A. Giddens and P. Diamond (eds) *The New Egalitarianism*, Cambridge: Polity Press.

Goodlad, R. and Riddell, S. (2005) 'Social justice and disabled people: principles and challenges', *Social Policy and Society*, 4, 1: 45–54.

Hewitt, P., McRobbie, A., Campbell, B. *et al.* (2004) 'Debating feminism: roundtable discussion', *Renewal*, 12, 3: 15–29.

HM Treasury (2004) *Choice for Parents, The Best Start for Children: a Ten Year Strategy for Childcare*, London: HM Treasury/The Stationery Office.

Hutchings, K. and Dannreuther, R. (eds) (1999) *Cosmopolitan Citizenship*, Basingstoke: Macmillan.

Jones, C. (1999) *Global Justice: Defending Cosmopolitanism*, Oxford: Oxford University Press.

Knijn, T. and van Wel, F. (2001) 'Careful or lenient: welfare reform for lone mothers in the Netherlands', *Journal of European Social Policy*, 11, 3: 235–251.

Lewis, J. (2000) 'Work and care', in H. Dean, R. Sykes and R. Woods (eds) *Social Policy Review 12*, Newcastle: Social Policy Association.

Lewis, J. (2001) 'The decline of the male breadwinner model: implications for work and care', *Social Politics*, 8, 2: 152–169.

Lister, R. (1997; 2nd edn 2003) *Citizenship: Feminist Perspectives*, Basingstoke: Macmillan.

Lister, R. (2002) 'The dilemmas of pendulum politics: balancing paid work, care and citizenship', *Economy, Theory and Society*, 31, 4: 520–532.

Lister, R. (2004) *Poverty*, Cambridge: Polity Press.

Lister, R. (2005) 'Being feminist', *Government and Opposition*, 40, 3: 442–463.

Meekosha, H. (1998) 'Body battles: bodies, gender and disability', in T. Shakespeare (ed.) *The Disability Reader*, London and New York: Continuum.

Mepham, D. (2005) 'Social justice in a shrinking world', in N. Pearce and W. Paxton (eds) *Social Justice: Building a Fairer Britain*, London: Politico's.

Morris, J. (1993) *Independent Lives*, Basingstoke: Macmillan.

Morris, J. (1996) 'Introduction', in J. Morris (ed.) *Encounters with Strangers: Feminism and Disability*, London: Women's Press.

Morris, J. (2005) *Citizenship and Disabled People*, London: Disability Rights Commission.

Oliver, M. (1996) *Understanding Disability: from Theory to Practice*, Basingstoke: Macmillan.

Olson, K. (2002) 'Recognizing gender, redistributing labor', *Social Politics*, 9, 3: 380–410.

O'Neill, O. (2000) *Bounds of Justice*, Cambridge: Cambridge University Press.

Orloff, A. (2002) 'Explaining US welfare reform: power, gender, race and the US policy legacy', *Critical Social Policy*, 22, 1: 96–118.

Owen, S. (2003) 'The pay's the thing', *0–19*, June: 8–9.

Pahl, R. (2005) 'Hidden solidarities that span the globe', *New Statesman*, 17 January: 34–35.

Pearce, N. (2004) 'Diversity versus solidarity: a new progressive dilemma?', *Renewal*, 12, 3: 79–87.

Peel, M. (2003) *The Lowest Rung*, Cambridge: Cambridge University Press.

Phillips, A. (2003) 'Recognition and the struggle for political voice', in B. Hobson (ed.) *Recognition Struggles and Social Movements*, Cambridge: Cambridge University Press.

Ridge, T. (2002) *Childhood Poverty and Social Exclusion*, Bristol: The Policy Press.

Russell, H. (ed.) (1996) *Speaking from Experience*, Manchester: Church Action on Poverty.

Schuster, L. (2005) 'A sledgehammer to crack a nut: deportation, detention and dispersal in Europe', *Social Policy and Administration*, 39, 6: 606–621.

Scott, G., Brown, U. and Campbell, J. (2003) *Visible Childcare: invisible workers*, Glasgow: Scottish Poverty Information Unit.

Sennett, R. (2003) *Respect*, London: Allen Lane.

Shakespeare, T. (2000) 'The social relations of care', in G. Lewis, S. Gewirtz and J. Clarke (eds) *Rethinking Social Policy*, London: Sage.

Shakespeare, T. (2005) 'Disabling politics? Beyond identity', *Soundings*, 30: 156–165.

Silvers, A. (1997) 'Reconciling equality to difference: caring (f)or justice for people with disabilities', in P. DiQuinzio and I.M. Young (eds) *Feminist Ethics and Social Policy*, Bloomington and Indianapolis: Indiana University Press.

Taylor, C. (1992) 'The politics of recognition', in A. Gutmann (ed.) *Multiculturalism and the Politics of Recognition*, Princeton: Princeton University Press.

Taylor-Gooby, P. (2005) 'Is the future American? Or, can Left politics preserve European welfare states from erosion through growing "racial" diversity?', *Journal of Social Policy*, 34, 4: 661–672 (updated in S. Delorenzi (ed.) (2006) *Going Places: Neighbourhood, Ethnicity and Social Mobility*, London: Institute for Public Policy Research).

Toynbee, P. (2002a) *Hard Work: A Challenge to Low Pay*, London: Smith Institute.

Toynbee, P. (2002b) 'It will be a tragedy if the firefighters are crushed', *Guardian*, 27 November.

UKCAP (1997) *Poverty and Participation*, London: UK Coalition against Poverty.

Veit-Wilson, J. (1998) *Setting Adequacy Standards*, Bristol: The Policy Press.

Watson, N., McKie, L., Hughes, B., Hopkins, D. and Gregory, S. (2004) '(Inter)dependence, needs and care: the potential for disability and feminist theorists to develop an emancipatory model', *Sociology*, 38, 2: 331–350.

White, S. (2003) 'Republicanism, patriotism, and global justice', in D.A. Bell and A. de-Shalit (eds) *Forms of Justice*, Lanham, Boulder, New York and Oxford: Rowman & Littlefield Publishers.

Wilkinson, R. (2005) *The Impact of Inequality*, London and New York: Routledge.

Witcher, S. (2005) 'Mainstreaming equality: the implications for disabled people', *Social Policy and Society*, 4, 1: 55–64.

Wolfe, A. and Klausen, J. (2000) 'Other people', *Prospect*, December: 28–33.

Wootton, B. (1955) *The Social Foundations of Wage Policy*, London: Allen & Unwin.

Yar, M. (1999) 'Beyond Nancy Fraser's perspectival dualism', *Economy and Society*, 30, 3: 288–303.

Yeatman, A. (1994) *Post-modern Revisionings of the Political*, London and New York: Routledge.

10 Needs, rights and transformation

The adjudication of social rights in South Africa

Sandra Liebenberg

Introduction

The South African Constitution is well known for the inclusion of a range of social rights in its Bill of Rights.[1] These rights, along with the civil and political rights in the Bill of Rights, are enforceable by the courts (section 38 of the Constitution). However, this development has not been uncontroversial. Groups associated with business interests in South Africa have argued that it is inappropriate to give the courts powers to dictate issues of social policy to the executive and legislature as this violates the doctrine of separation of powers.[2] Progressives have also argued that justiciable social rights vest too much power in an unaccountable judiciary and erode the power of both the democratically elected parliament as well as civil society.[3]

Debate has also focused on precisely how the courts should enforce the duties imposed by these rights, particularly the extent to which the courts should affirm an enforceable right to the provision of basic needs by those who lack access to these needs. In the South African context, this is a plight affecting a substantial portion of our population, and must also be contextualized in relation to the high degree of inequality existing in our society. The Constitutional Court has handed down eight major judgments in which it has established the foundations of its jurisprudence on the social rights in the Constitution.[4]

This chapter explores the relationship between a jurisprudence of basic needs and the transformative goals of the South African Constitution. The question that interests me is whether a jurisprudence relating to the fulfilment of social needs can have transformative potential, and if so, under what conditions? I draw extensively on Nancy Fraser's integrated theory of justice to develop a theoretical understanding of the relationship between social rights and transformation.

Social justice, transformation and 'non-reformist reform'

Social justice under a transformative Constitution

The South African Constitution is widely described as a transformative Constitution (Klare 1998; Albertyn and Goldblatt 1998; Van der Walt 2001; Moseneke

2002; Botha 2003).[5] Unlike many classic liberal constitutions, its primary concern is not to restrain State power, but to facilitate a fundamental change in unjust political, economic and social relations in South Africa.[6] Thus, the preamble of the Constitution proclaims that it was adopted 'so as to – [h]eal the divisions of the past and establish a society based on democratic values, social justice and fundamental human rights'. The founding values of the Constitution refer to 'the achievement of equality', 'non-racism and non-sexism' and 'a system of democratic governance that is accountable, responsive and open' (section 1).

The commitment to social justice is central to the transformative goals and processes of our Constitution, and must infuse the interpretation of the Bill of Rights. In the Fourth Bram Fischer Memorial Lecture, the Deputy Chief Justice, Dikgang Moseneke, describes the important role of social justice in constitutional adjudication:

> [I]t is argued here that a creative jurisprudence of equality coupled with substantive interpretation of the content of 'socio-economic' rights should restore social justice as a premier foundational value of our constitutional democracy side by side, if not interactively with, human dignity, equality, freedom, accountability, responsiveness and openness.
>
> (Moseneke 2002: 314)

By arguing that a conception of social justice should inform our interpretation of rights claims, I am aligning myself with critical legal theorists who argue that it is necessary 'to step outside of' rights discourse in order to fill rights with legal and institutional meaning.[7]

Social justice as 'participatory parity'

Notions of social justice are of course highly contested in a pluralist society. Any theory of social justice that is to do real work in interpreting and adjudicating constitutional claims must be compatible with a diversity of opinions regarding the good life. This is a pre-requisite in a constitutional dispensation such as our own that takes seriously the equal autonomy and moral worth of human beings.[8] At the same time, it must supply sufficiently determinative criteria for adjudicating concrete cases. Finally, it must be consonant with the values and ethos of the Constitution.

Nancy Fraser's theory of social justice based on the principle of participatory parity meets these criteria (Fraser 1997, 2000, 2005; Fraser and Honneth 2003). This principle recognizes the right of all to participate and interact with each other as peers in social life. As such it is compatible with a plurality of different views of the good and ethical disagreements. At the same time, she develops specific criteria for assessing whether institutional arrangements accord people 'the status of full partners in social interaction' (Fraser and Honneth 2003: 229). Formal notions of equality are rejected as insufficient. Instead, her theory focuses on the substan-

tive requirements to ensure that everyone has access to 'the institutional prerequisites of participatory parity' (ibid.: 229), particularly the economic resources and
the social standing needed to participate on a par with others.[9]

Fraser identifies two major obstacles to social justice conceived in terms of promoting greater parity of participation in social life and overcoming institutional
patterns of subordination of different classes and groups. The first, misrecognition,
entails a form of status subordination 'in which institutionalized patterns of cultural value impede parity of participation for some' (ibid.: 87). This involves systemic forms of discrimination and disadvantaging of certain groups on grounds
such as race, gender and sexual orientation. Examples are marriage laws that
exclude same-sex partnerships, social-welfare policies that stigmatize single
mothers as sexually irresponsible scroungers and policing practices that associate
black persons with criminality (Fraser 2000: 114). A second major obstacle to participatory parity arises when some actors lack the necessary resources to interact
with others as peers (ibid.: 116). This distributive dimension 'corresponds to the
economic structure of society, hence to the constitution, by property regimes and
labour markets of economically defined categories of actors, or classes, distinguished by their differential endowments of resources' (ibid.: 117). Thus, according to Fraser, social injustice has (at least) two analytically distinct dimensions:
misrecognition and maldistribution (ibid.: 116). These forms of injustice, while
analytically distinct,[10] overlap and interact causally with each other. Fraser
describes the nature of this intertwinement as follows:

> Economic issues such as income distribution have recognition subtexts:
> value patterns institutionalized in labour markets may privilege activities
> coded 'masculine', 'white' and so on over those coded 'feminine' and
> 'black.' Conversely, recognition issues – judgements of aesthetic value, for
> instance – have distribution subtexts: diminished access to economic
> resources may impede equal participation in the making of art. The result
> can be a vicious circle of subordination, as the status order and the eco-
> nomic structure interpenetrate and reinforce each other.
>
> (Ibid.: 118)

By theorizing a two-dimensional concept of social justice, Fraser also aims at
countering the recent tendency of recognition struggles (particularly in the form
of 'identity politics') to displace the distributive dimension of social justice and
to reify rigid group identities (ibid.: 110–113). A project aimed at advancing
social justice must seek to address both dimensions *and* consider the impact of
their interrelationship. Such a project aims at overcoming systemic patterns of
racial, gender, class and other forms of subordination.

Affirmation, transformation and 'non-reformist reform'

Fraser goes on to consider institutional reforms and strategies that can serve to
promote greater participatory parity along both the axes of recognition and

redistribution, 'while also mitigating the mutual interferences that can arise when those two aims are pursued in tandem' (Fraser and Honneth 2003: 72–73). She clarifies, however, that she is not aiming to devise 'institutional blueprints', but to delimit the range of possible policies and programmes that are compatible with the requirements of justice while leaving the weighing of the choices within the range to citizen deliberation (ibid.: 72).

Fraser distinguishes two broad strategies for remedying injustice that cut across the redistribution–recognition divide: *'affirmation'* and *'transformation'* (ibid.: 74). The distinction between these remedies relates to the level at which distributional and recognition injustices are addressed. As Fraser explains:

> Affirmative strategies for redressing injustice aim to correct inequitable outcomes of social arrangements without disturbing the underlying social structures that generate them. Transformative strategies, in contrast, aim to correct unjust outcomes precisely by restructuring the underlying generative framework.[11]
>
> (Ibid.: 74)

In the context of distributive justice the 'paradigmatic example' of an affirmative strategy is the liberal welfare state which aims to redress maldistribution through income transfers. In contrast, a transformative strategy would address the underlying causes of an unjust distribution, for example, changing the division of labour, the forms of ownership and other deep structures of the economic system (ibid.: 74). In the context of recognition injustices, affirmative and transformative strategies can also be distinguished (ibid.: 75–76).

One of the key disadvantages of affirmative strategies to remedy maldistribution such as social assistance programmes is that they tend to provoke 'a recognition backlash'. They can mark out the beneficiaries as 'inherently deficient and insatiable, as always needing more and more' (ibid.: 77). Their net effect can be 'to add the insult of disrespect to the injury of deprivation' (ibid.: 77). This is illustrated by the many gender stereotypes surrounding welfare programmes aimed at mothers and children. In the South African context this is exemplified by popular perceptions that the child support grant encourages young women to become pregnant and encourages 'dependency' on the State (Goldblatt 2005; Fraser 1989: 144–160). In contrast, transformative strategies by tending to cast entitlements in universalist terms promote solidarity and reduce inequality 'without creating stigmatized classes of vulnerable people perceived as beneficiaries of special largesse' (Fraser and Honneth 2003: 77). Transformative strategies also have their difficulties. Strategies aimed at transforming the underlying conditions of economic injustice may seem remote for those faced with the struggle to meet immediate daily needs. They stand to benefit much more directly from income transfers that help meet subsistence needs. It can thus be much more difficult to mobilize communities in pursuance of transformative goals (ibid.: 78).

However, according to Fraser, the dilemma of substantively problematic affirmative strategies and politically impractical transformative strategies is not intractable. Affirmative programmes can have transformative effects if they are consistently pursued. They can both meet people's needs within existing institutional frameworks and set in motion 'a trajectory of change' in which deeper reforms become practical over time (ibid.: 78). She elaborates:

> By changing incentive and political opportunity structures, they expand the set of feasible options for future reform. Over time their cumulative effect could be to transform the underlying structures that generate injustice.
>
> (Ibid.: 79–80)

Fraser calls these interventions 'non-reformist reforms' (ibid.: 79).[12] An example of such a 'non-reformist reform' in the South African context might be a universal basic income grant. Such a grant together with other social programmes assists people in their struggle to meet basic survival needs. At the same time, it creates the security and space needed both for greater participation in economic activities as well as popular mobilization around deeper reforms. By providing women in poor communities with an independent source of income, it also expands the set of choices available to them and assists in challenging women's subordination within the family and community.[13] In this way an affirmative remedy such as a basic income grant can set in motion a series of changes which can have a transformative impact over time.

An illustration of the interaction of affirmative and transformatory remedies in the context of legal strategies to advance entitlements to social benefits is provided by Lucy Williams in her account of welfare labour rights advocacy in the US. She documents how civil and welfare rights movements in the late 1960s and early 1970s were able to effectively mobilize around the legal breakthroughs in cases such as *King* v. *Smith*[14] in which the Supreme Court interpreted social security legislation as creating by statute a categorical entitlement to the receipt of cash assistance for families.[15] The right to a hearing prior to the termination of benefits under the AFDC programme won in *Goldberg* v. *Kelly*[16] was seen as 'a vehicle to empower recipients – to make them less afraid of losing subsistence benefits in retaliation for taking collective action' (Williams 1998: 575).

Furthermore, Williams demonstrates how winning recognition for the right to welfare assistance introduced 'a radically destabilizing concept into US legal discourse in two distinct but related ways' (ibid.: 578). First, by creating an entitlement that redistributed income, it exposed 'the socially created nature of all background rules of entitlement and exposed their distributive significance – that is their role in maintaining inequality'. In other words, if rights are constructed it implies that they can be reconstructed so as to promote greater social equity (ibid.: 578). If poverty is not natural but a result of political, legal and social choices, it can also be redressed through political will combined with appropriate social and legal reforms. Second, the concept of a welfare entitlement illustrated the notion that entitlements could accrue to people outside of individual effort and exchange in traditional labour markets. In doing so, it 'challenged the idea of a neutral and natural definition of effort and exchange' (ibid.: 578). The privileging of the 'public' space of labour markets in traditional social insurance programmes renders other forms of valuable social contributions, such as the care-giving functions traditionally performed by women, invisible. Welfare entitlements have the potential to validate such unrecognized social roles. It also exposes the false dichotomy between traditional notions of independence associated with wage work and dependency associated with the receipt of government benefits (ibid.: 579). The concept of a welfare benefit ('not the meagre amount of actual benefits') theoretically gives some workers an alternative to wage work. In this way it helps surface the reality of dependency in wage work relationships created by the employer's superior market power (ibid.: 579).

Ultimately, however, Williams argues that the progressive movement failed to exploit the transformative potential of the welfare entitlement concept (ibid.: 580–581). She argues that welfare and labour rights advocates unwittingly played into a discourse that reinforced the economic *status quo* and thus failed to advance a more fundamental redistribution. Welfare lawyers did this by fixating on government transfer policy and failing to adequately expose the contingency and distributional implications of the background rules of property and contract.[17] Labour lawyers failed to challenge the privileging of waged work over family, care giving in the organization and distribution of social benefits. In so doing, they alienated many potential allies and perpetuated a male discourse of citizenship in the public sphere (Williams 2002: 114). Thus, Williams illustrates how an affirmative strategy (the winning of entitlement to a welfare benefit) had substantial transformative potential. However, this potential was not realized as the underlying structures and choices generating deep inequalities in the US have not been effectively challenged.[18]

Social justice, democracy and adjudication

Adjudication and participatory parity

Fraser's project is to articulate a philosophical theory of social justice under contemporary conditions (Fraser and Honneth 2003: 70–72). She also examines the institutional arrangements, the broad types of policies and reforms that can advance participatory parity under contemporary social conditions. In this context, she explores the interplay between affirmative and transformative remedies as outlined above. It is no simple task to consider the implications of her theory in the context of the adjudication of social rights claims. Karl Klare observes: the fact 'that South Africa opted to accomplish some significant portion of their law-making through adjudication is a decision fraught with institutional consequences' (Klare 1998: 147).[19]

Fraser's conception of social justice is inextricably linked to the notion of participatory parity in which patterns of institutionalized value or lack of access to resources deny to certain groups the possibility of participating on a par in social processes. It rejects formal equality as insufficient:

On this view, anything short of participatory parity constitutes a failure of equal respect. And denial of access to parity's social prerequisites makes a mockery of a society's professed commitment to equal autonomy. Participatory parity constitutes *a radical democratic interpretation of equal autonomy.*

(Fraser and Honneth 2003: 229)

She observes that, although participatory parity supplies a powerful justificatory standard: 'it cannot be applied monologically, in the manner of a decision procedure' (ibid.: 42). There is 'no wholly transparent perspicuous sign that accompanies participatory parity, announcing its arrival for all to see' (ibid.: 43). Instead, 'the norm of participatory parity must be applied dialogically and discursively, through democratic processes of public debate' (ibid.: 43). Yet, adjudication is supposed to represent precisely 'a decision-making procedure' in which judges are given the power to pronounce authoritatively on what justice requires in the case under consideration.[20]

The impact of judicial review on democratic processes has been a major subject of academic debate in political theory and constitutional law (Botha 2000; Lenta 2004). In the context of highly contested social rights claims, the democratic objection to adjudication acquires a particular intensity.[21] Libertarians traditionally object to social rights on the substantive basis that they entrench an unacceptable role for the State and the courts in resource redistribution.[22] However, there is also an objection to the judicial review of social rights from the perspective of democracy. It is argued that social rights guarantees allow for a vast array of institutional and policy measures in contrast to the relatively clear and uncontested normative obligations imposed by civil and political rights.[23] According to critics, both representative and participatory democracy are undermined by giving judges the power to decide highly contested issues of public policy. Thus, Davis articulated his opposition to the inclusion of socio-economic demands as fully justiciable constitutional rights in the South African Constitution in the following terms: 'It elevates judges to the role of social engineers, concentrates power at the centre of the state and consequently erodes the influence of civil society' (Davis 1992: 489).[24]

Many academic contributions that seek to justify the role of the courts in the adjudication of social rights focus on questions of institutional politics, that is, the impact of judicial review on the functioning of the legislative and executive branches of government. This is raised most frequently in discussions of the 'counter-majoritarian' dilemma created by the institution of judicial review. For example, it is pointed out that in recent times the legislature has declined in political influence in comparison to the executive which 'has burgeoned in size, influence over the legislature and power over the citizenry' (Pieterse 2004: 388). As executives and bureaucracies are usually only indirectly accountable to the people, and given their extensive power to affect people's socio-economic well-being, there is an evident need for mechanisms to hold them accountable for their decisions. In many constitutional democracies, citizens have increasingly turned to the courts to protect their rights, including in the realm of socio-economic interests (ibid.: 388). However, it is the implications of the adjudication of basic needs claims for participatory politics that I am interested in exploring further. If the adjudication of basic needs claims operates to obstruct radical participatory democracy and depoliticizes questions concerning the definition and meeting of needs, it will ultimately undermine the project of advancing fundamental transformation in South Africa.[25] If we are to maximize our prospects of developing a transformative jurisprudence on social rights, we should at least be conscious of the potential impact of adjudication on participatory politics.

Adjudication and the 'politics of need interpretation'

In order to understand the potential effects of adjudication on transformative strategies, it is necessary to examine more closely what Fraser refers to as 'the politics of needs interpretation' (Fraser 1989: 163). She describes needs claims as 'nested' in that they are 'connected to one another in ramified chains of "in order to" relations' (ibid.: 163). Thus it is relatively uncontroversial to argue that homeless people, who live in non-tropical climates, need shelter 'in order to' survive (what Fraser calls 'thin needs'). However, as soon as we descend to lesser levels of generality – to questions such as 'precisely what form of shelter do people need?' and 'what else do they need in order to sustain their homes?' – controversy proliferates. As the chains of 'in order to' relations are progressively unravelled, the deeper becomes the level of political contestation and disagreement. As Fraser observes:

> Precisely how such chains are unravelled depends on what the interlocutors share in the way of background assumptions. Does it go without saying that policy designed to deal with homelessness must not challenge the basic ownership and investment structure of urban real estate. Or is that the point at which people's assumptions and commitments diverge?
>
> (Ibid.: 163)

Thin theories of need assume that the issue is only whether various predefined needs 'will or will not be provided for' (ibid.: 164). In so doing they ignore the underlying relational chains and 'deflect attention' from a number of important political questions (ibid.: 163–164).

Fraser identifies the politics of needs to comprise 'three moments that are analytically distinct but interrelated in practice' (ibid.: 164). The first is the struggle to validate the need in question as a legitimate political concern. The second constitutes the struggle over the definition or interpretation of the need. The third moment is the struggle over the implementation of the need (ibid.: 164). She identifies two major institutions which serve to depoliticize needs discourses in the course of these struggles. One strategy is to define the needs as questions of personal as opposed to public responsibility. Here the family is seen as a major institution for meeting the needs in question.[26] A second prevalent strategy is to cast the needs in questions 'as impersonal market imperatives, or as "private" ownership prerogatives, or as technical problems for managers and planners, all in contradistinction to political matters' (ibid.: 168). In this case, the depoliticization of needs occurs through the institutions of the market economy in the capitalist system. The effect of such depoliticizing discourses is to perpetuate class, gender and race relations of domination and subordination.

Adjudication in a constitutional democracy such as South Africa is a significant socio-cultural forum in all three moments of the politics of needs.

The first moment: recognizing needs as entitlements

The inclusion of a range of socio-economic rights as justiciable rights in the 1996 South African Constitution can be seen as a successful struggle by various political actors and civil society organizations to establish the meeting of these needs as objects of constitutionally mandated State responsibility (Liebenberg and Pillay 2000).[27] By placing a constitutional obligation on the State to ensure that everyone has access to a variety of socio-economic rights, the meeting of the needs in question are clearly recognized as a public matter, and not simply to be relegated to the 'private' domestic or market sphere.[28]

The very distinction between 'justiciable' civil and political rights versus non-justiciable socio-economic rights is in itself deeply political. It privileges negative liberty and the existing economic *status quo*, and obscures the costs and policy dimensions of civil and political rights (Liebenberg 1995: 84; Pieterse 2004: 397, 398). In constitutional democracies where adjudication is an important component of a country's fundamental governance structures, the exclusion or weak enforcement of socio-economic rights can have the effect of marginalizing the interests of the poor and masking the socio-economic barriers to more egalitarian social relations.[29] By contrast, the inclusion of social rights transforms the issue of unmet needs into a question of entitlement.[30]

The constitutional status of these rights clearly does not avoid on-going contestation and the emergence of 'reprivatization' discourses aimed at re-establishing the needs in question as matters for the family or the market to deal with. The institutional implications of such discourses involved the cutting back of social security programmes, the privatization of national assets and the deregulation of private enterprises. As Fraser observes: 'discursively, it means depoliticization' (Fraser 1989: 172). In the current era of neo-liberalism, social assistance and social insurance programmes in many countries are being privatized or cut back. This presents a new set of challenges for asserting the State's role in the public provision of social benefits to mitigate current inequalities in access resources. The constitutional recognition of justiciable social rights provides oppositional social movements with a potentially powerful tool to assert the state responsibility for meeting basic needs.

The second and third moments: interpreting and implementing needs as rights

How does adjudication relate to the two further dimensions of needs struggles in late capitalist societies? The second moment is the struggle around 'the interpreted *content* of contested needs once their political status has been successfully secured' (Fraser 1989: 173). The third moment corresponds to the processes and institutions through which the need in question is implemented and administered. These moments frequently result in the proliferation of expert needs discourses and the creation of agencies for the satisfaction of the need in question. These discourses are aimed at translating 'politicized needs into administrable needs' (ibid.: 174). Expert needs discourses tend to be depoliticizing by repositioning the people whose needs are in question as individual 'cases'. As Fraser explains: 'they are rendered passive, positioned as potential recipients of predefined services rather than as agents involved in interpreting their needs and shaping their life conditions' (ibid.: 174).

Judicial interpretations of social rights can powerfully shape political discourse and administrative practice in both these dimensions. Daniel Brand describes the powerful political and symbolic role of the courts around needs discourses:

> First, courts' adjudication of socio-economic rights claims becomes part of the political discourse, even a medium through which this discourse partly plays out …. Second, courts also occupy a symbolic, or perhaps more accurately, an exemplary role with respect to poverty and need discourses – their vocabulary, the conceptual structures they rely on, the rhetorical strategies they employ infiltrate and so influence and shape the political discourses around poverty and need.
>
> (Brand 2005a: 24)[31]

The adjudication of social rights in the South African courts has the potential both to reinforce and counter reprivatization discourses around needs, and to deepen or erode participatory democracy. Thus, the jurisprudence can assert the role of the political community in meeting basic needs, or it can explicitly or implicitly endorse the primary role of the market or family in meeting these needs. For example, the Court held in the *Grootboom* judgment that the duty to meet the unqualified right of children to shelter protected in section 28 of the Constitution rested primarily on their parents or family. Only when family care was lacking (for example, when children were abandoned or removed from family care) did the state become responsible for the provision of shelter (*supra*, note 4, paras 76–77; for a critique of this reasoning, see Sloth-Nielsen 2001).

Moreover, the adjudication of social rights can divert attention from the underlying conditions that give rise to economic deprivations by taking existing resource distributions for granted and failing to engage questions concerning the allocation and prioritization of state resources. While judicial restraint may be understandable from the perspective of institutional relations with the other branches of government, it nonetheless serves to 'naturalize' systemic socio-economic inequalities. Brand's main critique of the Constitutional Court's jurisprudence is that it tends to endorse an institutional concept of politics in which communities and civil society are viewed as passive recipients of needs predefined by the political branches of government. He identifies as problematic, not so much the fact that the court defers, 'but what it is that it defers to'; deference is to the formally constituted official branches of government and downplays the role of participatory democracy in the interpretation and satisfaction of needs (Brand 2005a: 31–33).

In interpreting socio-economic rights, courts authoritatively declare that a certain standard of provisioning fulfils or fails to fulfil the constitutional obligation. In so doing, judicial discourse can serve to artificially curtail democratic debate on the underlying changes needed to transform social relations so as to eliminate conditions of deprivation and inequality. To borrow Fraser's terminology, adjudication can serve to 'occlude the interpretative dimension of needs politics, the fact that not just satisfactions but *need interpretations* are politically contested' (Fraser 1989: 164). To return to our earlier distinction, while the adjudication of social rights claims may sometimes achieve affirmative remedies, they may simultaneously deflect attention from more transformative strategies to remedy social injustice.

Once the court has interpreted and upheld a social rights claim, the focus shifts to the implementation of the court's judgment. In this process, judicial discourse can tend to position poor litigants and the class they represent as passive beneficiaries of the court's order instead of active participants in defining their needs and the methods of their implementation. An illustration of a more empowering approach is the Constitutional Court's judgment in the *PE Municipality* case in which the Court held that, in the absence of special circumstances, it would not ordinarily be just and equitable for a court to order the eviction of a community from land 'if proper discussions, and where appropriate, mediation, have not been attempted' (*supra* note 4, paras 43, 39–47).

As Fraser observes, these are highly complex struggles as social movements aim at establishing State provision of various needs in question, but 'oppose the administrative and therapeutic need interpretations' (Fraser 1989: 175). Even when needs become depoliticized through the administration of need satisfaction, Fraser records 'a countertendency that runs from administration to client resistance and potentially back to politics' (ibid.: 177).[32]

Enhancing participatory parity

Despite its depoliticizing tendencies, the adjudication of social rights can also serve to enhance participatory politics. In his contribution to the early social rights debates, Haysom articulated a justification from the perspective of participatory democracy for including a basic floor of justiciable social rights in the Constitution:

> By constitutionalising selected socio-economic rights, society is elevating certain rights to a necessary condition for the exercise of a *minimum* civic equality. This in turn, establishes the conditions for democracy for the effective use of civil and political rights …. This article goes no further than arguing that a minimum floor of rights should be constitutionalised to enrich political contest and democratic participation – not by limiting political choice but by facilitating real participation in social and political rights.
>
> (Haysom 1992: 461; see also Michelman 1979)

Fraser argues in favour of translating justified needs claims into social rights, despite left criticisms that they obstruct radical social transformation, on the basis that they 'begin to overcome some of the obstacles to the effective exercise of existing rights' (Fraser 1989: 183). Thus, they can help to transform a formalist conception of classic liberal rights into substantive rights (ibid.: 183). In other words, the inclusion of social rights in a Bill of Rights can help infuse a substantive dimension into the Bill of Rights as a whole.

The South African Constitutional Court's explicit endorsement of the concept of the interrelationship and interdependence of all the rights in the Bill of Rights underscores this point (*Grootboom, supra* note 4, paras 23, 44; *TAC, supra* note 4, para. 78; *Khosa, supra* note 4, paras 49, 52). Social rights have an important role to play in securing civil and political participation while civil and political rights in turn can help facilitate greater civic mobilization around issues of resource distribution. By emphasizing the interdependence and interrelatedness of the Bill of Rights as a whole, the courts help to counter some of the recognition problems associated with social rights and the social benefit programmes they facilitate. This in turn helps establish the conditions for a more inclusive, equitable public debate regarding the measures needed to transform unjust social and economic relations.

Fraser insists that the norm of participatory parity must be applied dialogically and discursively through democratic processes of public debate. At the same time, she emphasizes that fair democratic deliberation concerning the merits of redistribution and recognition claims 'requires parity of participation for all actual and possible deliberators' which in turn requires just distribution and reciprocal recognition. She argues that eliminating this circularity in democratic justice requires that we 'work to abolish it in practice by changing social reality …. By arguing publicly that the conditions for genuine democratic public argument are currently lacking, one expresses the reflexivity of democratic justice in the process of struggling to realize it practically' (Fraser and Honneth 2003: 43–44). In this context, the courts can serve as a forum for highlighting the needs of those marginalized in official political processes and thereby enhance democratic participation in the meeting of socio-economic needs. But if social rights are to make a meaningful contribution to transformation, it is vital that they are substantively interpreted by the courts. If individuals and groups are unable to reliably enforce their claims to the provision of subsistence needs, the role of socio-economic rights in enhancing participatory parity becomes largely illusory.

In the following section, I outline some of the main challenges facing the Constitutional Court in developing a jurisprudence on social rights that can enhance participatory parity and transformation in South Africa.

Developing the transformative potential of social rights jurisprudence

South Africa has had a long history of colonialism and apartheid with strong patriarchal underpinnings (Terreblanche 2002; Gouws 2005). Given these accumulated historical injustices, the full realization of social rights will require deep-seated structural changes over time. Can the courts play a meaningful role in facilitating these fundamental changes? I outline five challenges that must be met if South Africa's social rights jurisprudence is to fulfil its transformative potential.

Giving substance to reasonableness review

The Court has been generally reluctant to interpret the social rights provisions in the Constitution as creating individual entitlements to the provision of basic needs by the state (Liebenberg 2002; Bilchitz 2003). Instead it has held that the positive duty imposed by these rights on the state is primarily a duty to act reasonably. The Court has developed a number of substantive criteria for assessing the reasonableness of government's conduct or omissions, including the requirement that programmes must be designed and implemented in a way that is capable of facilitating the realization of the relevant rights, they must cater for groups in urgent need, and must be transparent and participatory (*Grootboom*, *supra* note 4, paras 39–46; *TAC*, *supra* note 4, paras 67–79, 123). The model of reasonableness review has been applied by the Court to require the state to adopt a housing programme catering for those in urgent need and living in intolerable conditions (*Grootboom*, *supra* note 4), to provide anti-retroviral treatment throughout the public health sector so as to reduce the risk of mother-to-child transmission of HIV during childbirth (*TAC*, *supra* note 4), and to extend social assistance grants to permanent residents as a category of non-citizens (*Khosa* case, *supra* note 4). The judgment in favour of the applicants in Khosa was based on an interdependent reading of the right of access to social assistance (s 27) and the right to equality (s 9) in the Bill of Rights. The Court has also held that the state will be placed under a heavy burden to justify the reasonableness of depriving people of their existing access to social rights. In these situations, justification must occur in terms of the stringent criteria of the general limitations clause in the Bill of Rights (s 36). In the latter context, it has declared unconstitutional legislation that allowed sales-in-execution of poor people's homes for trifling debts without judicial oversight (*Jaftha*, *supra*, note 4).

Reasonableness review has the advantage of being a flexible, context-sensitive model of review for socio-economic rights claims (Liebenberg 2005). Thus, the Court held in the *Grootboom* case that the reasonableness of a set of measures in giving effect to particular socio-economic rights has to be assessed in the light of their social, economic and historical context as well as the context of the Bill of Rights as a whole (*supra* note 4, para. 43). In this sense, 'reasonableness review' avoids closure and creates the on-going possibility of challenging socio-economic deprivations in the light of changing contexts. Thus, 'reasonableness review' can facilitate the creation of a participatory, dialogical space for considering social rights claims. This is exemplified by the way in which a dynamic social movement in South Africa, the Treatment Action Campaign (TAC), has been able to use reasonableness review to win a major victory in the provision of appropriate medical treatment to reduce the risk of the transmission of HIV from mother to child (Heywood 2003). This victory was a significant breakthrough in the broader transformative strategy of the TAC to achieve a general anti-retroviral programme announced by government in August 2003 for people living with HIV/AIDS. The TAC and other civil society organizations were able to use the criteria for a reasonable programme established in the *Grootboom* case and the mother-to-child transmission case in broad-based advocacy for a general anti-retroviral roll-out programme (Heywood 2005).

Despite these positive features, it is important to recognize that reasonableness review can easily come to represent a very deferential standard of review. Davis argues that the concept of reasonableness can be moulded by the courts 'so that, on occasion, it resembles a test for rationality and ensures that the court can give a wide berth to any possible engagement with direct issues of socio-economic policy' (Davis 2004: 5). The danger is that reasonableness review becomes a proxy for the courts endorsing the State's own views about the justifiability of its policies.[33]

The challenge is thus to continue advocating for a substantive interpretation of reasonableness. In evaluating the reasonableness of the State's acts or omissions, the central consideration should be the position of the claimant in society, the history and nature of the deprivation experienced and its impact on her and others in a similar situation.[34] A particular focus of this inquiry should be the impact of the deprivations in question on the ability of the affected groups to participate as peers in society. Close attention should be paid to the interaction of the obstacles to participatory parity identified by Fraser, namely the lack of access to economic and social resources, the social stigma and stereotypes associated with poverty, and their interaction with other forms of recognition of injustices such as race, gender, sexual orientation and disability. In explicitly considering these factors, the courts are well positioned to highlight the impact of macro-injustices on particular claimants in concrete situations. Justice Albie Sachs describes the responsibility of the courts to strive to achieve justice for the litigants before them against a backdrop of systemic social inequality:

> The inherited injustices at the macro level will inevitably make it difficult for the courts to ensure immediate present-day equity at the micro level. The judiciary cannot of itself correct all the systematic unfairness to be found in our society. Yet it can at least soften and minimise the degree of

injustice and inequity which the eviction of the weaker parties in conditions of inequality of necessity entails.

(*PE Municipality* case, *supra* note 4, para. 38)

The real challenge for social rights litigation is situations where large groups are currently excluded from social provisioning. This is illustrated by South Africa's current social security system. Provision is made for those formally employed through social insurance schemes, and for the payment, from public funds, of social grants to certain targeted vulnerable groups (children, the aged and those living with disabilities). However, no social assistance is provided for children of 14 years and older and adults under 60 years (for women) and 65 years (for men) who live in poverty and are affected by long-term structural unemployment. For this group (approximately 8.4 million people) the right of access to social security, including social assistance, protected in section 27(1)(c) of the Constitution, is largely illusory. It remains to be seen whether the courts will, when confronted by a relevant case, require the State to adopt positive measures to close this gap in social security provisioning. Of relevance in this context is the obligation recognized by the UN Committee on Economic, Social and Cultural Rights of the State to formulate and implement a national strategy and plan of action to address access to socio-economic rights by the whole population. This strategy and plan of action must be formulated, and periodically reviewed, on the basis of a participatory and transparent process, and must include indicators and benchmarks by which progress can be closely monitored.[35] Even if the courts cannot order the entire gap in social security provisioning to be immediately closed, they can at least require participatory planning and the taking of concrete steps towards the full realization of this important social right.

Placing the claimants and the nature and history of the deprivation experienced at the centre of the reasonableness inquiry will help keep the focus on the systemic social and economic barriers to a more egalitarian society.

Robust remedies

Second, the courts can use their wide remedial powers to grant more effective remedies in social rights cases. Thus, for example, the courts can require the State to put in place a plan or programme that facilitates the changes needed, and to take concrete and targeted steps in terms of that plan (Trengove 1999). In this context, the Constitutional Court should overcome its reluctance to grant supervisory remedies in order to facilitate the long-term structural reforms required to realize socio-economic rights (Pillay 2002). Supervisory orders have a rich potential not only for the courts to monitor the implementation of such orders, but also to enhance the participation of both civil society and the State institutions supporting constitutional democracy in socio-economic rights litigation. Courts can also give forms of tangible relief to those experiencing immediate deprivations to avoid irreparable threats to life, health and future development. The nature and extent of this relief will depend on the context, but must reflect the conviction expressed in the *Grootboom* case that a society 'must seek to ensure that the basic necessities of life are provided to all if it is to be a society based on human dignity, freedom and equality' (*supra* note 4, para. 44). Transformation is thus promoted by calling into question existing unjust resource distributions and affirming rights to social and economic benefits where previously no such rights were recognized (see van der Walt's discussion of Frank Michelman's needs-based theories, 2004).

A transformative discourse

The courts can also contribute to transformation by the nature of their discourse in socio-economic rights judgments. This rhetorical role is important even where the courts feel constrained by institutional politics from making orders that will have an extensive impact on existing budgetary allocations. Thus, the courts can resist the temptation to focus only on 'thin' needs, and instead strive to expose the underlying patterns of social injustice that generate the deprivations in question. The judgment of the Court in the *PE Municipality* case is an excellent illustration of how courts can engage with the historical, socio-economic, political and legal factors behind the eviction of poor people from their homes in South Africa (*supra* note 4, paras 8–23). Judicial discourse of this nature helps to counter the depoliticizing tendencies of adjudication by locating the needs in question within a broader historical and social context of systemic injustice.

Furthermore, the courts can assist in destabilizing existing stereotypes and perceptions about the role of publicly provided benefits in society. This is illustrated by the manner in which Justice Yvonne Mokgoro in the *Khosa* case subverts the normal discourse around social assistance creating dependency on the State by highlighting its role in relieving the burden on poor communities and fostering the dignity of permanent residents (*supra* note 4, para. 76). Finally, the court's discourse can serve as a constant reminder that the redress of poverty and inequality are questions of political morality and a collective social responsibility. This is illustrated again in the *Khosa* case by the following observation of Mokgoro J:

> Sharing responsibility for the problems and consequences of poverty equally as a community represents the extent to which wealthier members of the community view the minimal well-being of the poor as connected with their personal well-being and the well-being of the community as a whole. In other words, decisions about the allocation of public benefits present the extent to which poor people are treated as equal members of society.
>
> (*supra* note 4, para. 74)

Through discourse of this nature, the courts contribute to countering the 'recognition backlash' associated with the provision of social benefits to the poor.

It is the responsibility of the courts to keep at the forefront of public consciousness the vast chasm between the vision of a just society reflected in the Constitution and social reality. As the Acting Chief Justice Pius Langa (as he then was) noted in the *Modderklip* case:

> The fact that poverty and homelessness still plague many South Africans is a painful reminder of the chasm that still needs to be bridged before the constitutional ideal to establish a society based on social justice and improved quality of life for all citizens is fully achieved.
>
> (*supra*, note 4, para. 36)

Transforming background common law rules

In a market economy, common law background rules structure access to and distribution to resources. Thus, Brand (2005b: 39) argues:

> Although the development of constitutional socio-economic rights to establish new and unique constitutionally based remedies is an important endeavour on its own, to explore the full transformative potential of socio-economic rights, sustained critical engagement also with these common law background rules is crucial.[36]

Social rights also impacts on the common law through the adoption of legislation to give effect to these rights, for example, legislation providing substantive and procedural protection against arbitrary evictions. The constitutional cases relating to evictions and homelessness in South Africa have contributed to deconstructing hierarchical and absolute notions of property rights. The interest of poor people in the protection of their homes and in avoiding homelessness is now a highly relevant factor in eviction cases, and property is no longer the ultimate trump card. In other areas, the courts have been less willing to transform common law rules in the light of socio-economic rights commitments.[37]

Although it is beyond the scope of this chapter, the transformatory potential of the courts' social rights jurisprudence will not be realized without broader forms of the processes and practices of adjudication to make them more accessible and participatory. As Fraser (1989: 182) notes, procedural considerations are an essential element of assessing competing need interpretations: 'In general, procedural considerations dictate that, all other things being equal, the best need interpretations are those reached by means of communicative processes that most closely approximate ideals of democracy, equality and fairness'. Institutional reforms in the South African context should encompass achieving equitable access to quality legal services, improving mechanisms for the implementation of social rights judgments and transforming judicial ideology and culture.[38]

The challenges of globalization

The constitutional adjudication of human rights is premised on the responsibility of the national state. Section 7(2) of the South African Bill of Rights places the responsibility on the state to 'respect, protect, promote and fulfil the rights in the Bill of Rights'. However, like all nation states South Africa faces the challenges of globalization which have profound and multi-faceted implications for the state's capacity to enact far-reaching social programmes. This is exemplified by a court challenge brought by a group of pharmaceutical multinational companies to legislation enacted by the State to promote access to affordable medicines, including measures providing for generic substitution, parallel importation of patented medicines and a transparent medicine pricing system.[39] The Treatment Action Campaign intervened as *amicus curiae* ('friend of the court') in the case, and after intense national and international public pressure, the companies abandoned their challenge (Heywood 2001).

As in many other countries, service delivery in South Africa is affected by tendencies towards privatization and commodification (on privatization of water services in South Africa, see Kok 2005).

Globalization thus creates unprecedented challenges for the normative foundations of social rights litigation premised on the primary responsibility of the national state. In this context, Fraser's invitation to reconsider the frame of distributional, recognition and representation struggles is timely (Chapter 2). It invites critical reflection on creative strategies of integrating national, regional and global struggles around social rights (Greenstein 2004).

Conclusion

There will probably be an enduring tension between the depoliticizing tendencies of social rights adjudication and its transformative potential. Those engaged in social rights litigation need to be conscious of both tendencies and seek to minimize the former while maximizing the prospects to realizing the latter. The winning of affirmative social benefits through litigation can create a favourable terrain for broader mobilization around deeper reforms. A substantive jurisprudence on social rights can facilitate 'non-reformist reforms' and advance transformation in South Africa. In particular, it can serve to enhance the participatory capabilities of those living in poverty and expose the socially constructed nature of poverty and inequality. At its best it should constantly remind us of our constitutional commitment to establishing a society based on social justice, and facilitate the inclusion of marginalized voices in the debate on what is required to achieve such a society. However, we cannot take for granted that this transformative trajectory will be found. Exploring the theoretical underpinnings of important concepts to our constitutional democracy such as social justice and transformation can help us in finding our way.

Notes

1 This chapter is a revised and updated version of the article published in the *Stellenbosch Law Review* 1 2006 1. I would like to thank Lourens du Plessis, André van der Walt and Jan Theron for comments and inspiration.

These rights include equitable access to land (s 25(5)); housing (s 26); health care, food, water and social security (s 27); and education (s 29). Sections 26(2) and 27(2) require the state to 'take reasonable legislative and other measures, within its available resources, to achieve the progressive realisation' of the rights in these sections.

2 These arguments were made by a group of civil society organizations led by the Free Market Foundation in opposing the inclusion of social rights in the Constitution during the certification process: *Ex parte Chairperson of the Constitutional Assembly: In re Certification of the Constitution of the Republic of South Africa 1996* 1996 (10) BCLR 1253 (CC).

3 This argument is discussed in greater detail in 'Adjudication and participatory parity', below.

4 *Soobramoney* v. *Minister of Health, KwaZulu* 1997 (12) BCLR 1969 (CC); *Government of the Republic of South Africa and Others* v. *Grootboom and Others* 2000 (11) BCLR 1169 (CC) [hereafter '*Grootboom*']; *Minister of Health* v. *Treatment Action Campaign and Others* 2002 (10) BCLR 1033 (CC) [hereafter '*TAC*']; *Minister of Public Works and Others* v. *Kyalami Ridge Environmental Association and Others* 2001 (7) BCLR 652 (CC); *Khosa* v. *Minister of Social Development; Mahlaule* v. *Minister of Social Development* 2004 (6) BCLR 569 (CC) [hereafter '*Khosa*']; *Port-Elizabeth Municipality* v. *Various Occupiers* 2004 (12) BCLR 1268 (CC) [hereafter '*PE Municipality*']; *Jaftha* v. *Schoeman and Others; Van Rooyen* v. *Stoltz and Others* 2005 (1) BCLR 78 (CC) [hereafter '*Jaftha*']; *President of RSA and Another* v. *Modderklip Boerdery (Pty) Ltd and Others* 2005 (8) BCLR 786 (CC) [hereafter '*Modderklip*']. For a comprehensive analysis of South Africa's jurisprudence on socio-economic rights, see Liebenberg (2007, forthcoming).

5 Klare (1998: 150) describes transformative constitutionalism as:

> a long-term project of constitutional enactment, interpretation, and enforcement committed (not in isolation, of course, but in a historical context of conducive political developments) to transforming a country's political and social institutions and power relationships in a democratic, participatory, and egalitarian direction.

6 *S* v. *Makwanyane* 1995 (6) BCLR 665 (CC) para. 262; *Bato Star Fishing (Pty) Ltd* v. *Minister of Environmental Affairs and Tourism* 2004 (7) BCLR 687 (CC para. 74); *Minister of Finance* v. *Van Heerden* 2004 (11) BCLR 1125 (CC para. 74); *Rates Action Group* v. *City of Cape Town* 2004 (12) BCLR 1328 (C) para. 100.

7 Thus Klare (1998: 101) argues:

> One must appeal to more concrete and therefore more controversial analyses of the relevant social and institutional contexts than rights discourse offers; and one must develop and elaborate conceptions of and intuitions about human freedom and self-determination by reference to which one seeks to assess rights claims and resolve rights conflicts.

8 The South African Constitutional Court has held that the recognition of the equal moral worth of people requires respect for difference and a diversity of views and lifestyles: See, e.g., *Prince* v. *President, Cape Law Society* 2002 (2) SA 794 (CC), para. 49.

9 Participatory parity is described as constituting '*a radical democratic interpretation of equal autonomy*. Far more demanding than standard liberal interpretations, this principle is not only deontological but also substantive' (Fraser and Honneth 2003: 229).

10 She argues that under 'capitalist conditions, neither is wholly reducible to the other' (Fraser 2000: 118).

11 She clarifies that the distinction 'is *not* equivalent to reform versus revolution, nor to gradual versus apocalyptic change. Rather, the nub of the contrast is the level at which injustice is addressed: whereas affirmation targets end-state outcomes, transformation addresses root causes' (Fraser and Honneth 2003: 74).

12 She credits the idea of non-reformist reform to Gortz (1967).

13 The phased introduction of a basic income grant was one of the key proposals to close the large gap in social security provisioning made by the government-appointed Committee of Inquiry into a Comprehensive Social Security System in South Africa (2002). There is also a coalition of civil society organizations, the Basic Income Grant Coalition, mobilizing in support of this proposal (see www.big.org.za). For a discussion of the transformative potential of an unconditional basic income grant, see Fraser in Fraser and Honneth (2003: 78–79).

14 392 US 309 (1968).

15 The relevant programme, Aid to Families with Dependent Children (AFDC), provided means-tested cash benefits from tax revenues to indigent families with children.

16 397 US 254 (1970).

17 The consequences, according to Williams, are that welfare law 'becomes a market corrective technique, an adjunct to private law, rather than a redistributional hub' (Williams 2002: 113–114).

18 For a comparative review of US and South African developments in the use of rights-based strategies to address poverty, see Williams (2005).

19 He cites Duncan Kennedy's critique of adjudication (1997: 2):

> The diffusion of law-making power reduces the power of ideologically organized majorities, whether liberal or conservative, to bring about significant change in any subject-matter heavily governed by law. It empowers the legal fractions of intelligentsias to decide the outcomes of ideological conflict among themselves, outside the legislative processes. And it increases the appearances of naturalness, necessity; and relative justice of the status quo, whatever it may be, over what would prevail under a more transparent regime.

20 In this role the judge is cast in the role of the 'platonic philosopher-kings of yore' (Davis 1992: 483). See also the discussion by Fraser in Fraser and Honneth (2003: 70–71) on the 'appropriate division of labour between theorist and citizenry'. The metaphor of dialogue has gained currency in describing the process of judicial review under a supreme Constitution, particularly in describing the interaction between the judiciary and legislature. This represents a less authoritarian and more democracy-enriching model of judicial review than the monological model (see, e.g., Roach 2005: 537). But while certain reforms to litigation processes can enhance the diversity of voices able to participate in litigation, at the end of the day the court ultimately has the power 'to privilege some interpretations over others' (Botha 2000: 573). Patrick Lenta (2004: 29) observes: 'Judges most often write in a monological voice that effaces the appearance of freedom of choice, and presents the verdict as forced by the logic of the situation itself ...'

21 It is naturally possible to constitutionalize social rights without necessarily vesting significant power in the judiciary to enforce them directly (Michelman 2003). This could entail, e.g., including them in the Constitution as directive principles of State policy following the examples of India, Namibia and Ireland. However, in the case of India, the judiciary has utilized the directive principles to infuse substantive content into traditional civil rights, such as the right to life (Shah 1999: 435). In the South African context, other constitutional institutions, particularly the SA Human Rights Commission, have significant functions in relation to socio-economic rights, including an information-gathering and monitoring role in terms of s 183 (3) of the Consti-

tution. In this article, I focus specifically on the implications of vesting power in the courts to directly adjudicate socio-economic rights claims.

22 See, for example, the discussion by Davis (1992: 477) of the views of Nozick developed in *Anarchy, State and Utopia* (1974).

23 See the discussion by Davis (1992: 478–479) of Ronald Dworkin's distinction between 'choice insensitive issues' which are equated with basic civil and political rights which are enforceable by the judiciary, and 'choice sensitive issues' which are equated with socio-economic policy choices which are best resolved through democratic processes. Thus, Davis argues that whilst judicial interpretation is inevitably indeterminate, in the case of 'first generation rights', 'judicial interpretation is often predictable because background norms are uncontested' (ibid.: 484). In contrast, judicial interpretation of 'second generation' rights inevitably involves contested policy choices, and is hence far less predictable.

24 Davis (1992: 489). Lenta highlights the democratic erosion that occurs through judicial decision-making in the following terms:

> The fact that constitutional courts are regarded as the forum for deciding fundamental questions facing the political community in the areas of employment, education, housing, freedom of association among many others, decreases the number of decisions left for the political arena and contributes to the erosion of politics.
>
> (Lenta 2004: 29)

25 Fraser distinguishes between the following concepts: Institutional politics in terms of which 'a matter is deemed "political" if it is handled directly in the institutions of the official governmental system, including parliaments, administrative apparatuses, and the like'. This 'official political' contrasts with what is handled by institutions that are defined as being outside the official political system like 'the family' and 'the economy' ('even though in reality they are underpinned and regulated by the official political system'). The second concept is 'discursive political' or 'politic*ized*'. In this sense 'something is "political" if it is contested across a range of different discursive areas and among a range of different publics'. This contrasts with 'what is not contested in public at all and with what is contested only in relatively specialized, enclaved, and/or segmented publics' (Fraser 1989: 166).

26 I would also add that the amorphous 'community' also falls into this category of 'privatizing' the needs in question, e.g., by cutting back on state care for mental health patients on the supposition that they will be cared for by 'the community' or that 'the community' can take care of AIDS-orphans.

27 This struggle has not been comprehensively documented. For an abbreviated account, see Liebenberg and Pillay (2000: 19–20).

28 In the Constitutional Court's landmark judgment in the *Grootboom* case, *supra*: para. 40, it is emphasized that 'the national sphere of government must assume responsibility for ensuring that laws, policies, programmes and strategies are adequate to meet the State's section 26 obligations'.

29 As Scott and Maklem (1992: 29) argued:

> Perhaps the strongest reason for including a certain number of economic and social rights is that by constitutionalizing half of the human rights equation, South Africans would be constitutionalizing only part of what it is to be a full person. A constitution containing only civil and political rights projects an image of truncated humanity. Symbolically, but still brutally it excludes those segments of society for whom autonomy means little without the necessities of life.

30 As Fraser (1989: 182) observes: 'After all, conservatives traditionally prefer to distribute aid as a matter of need *instead* of right precisely in order to avoid assumptions of entitlement that could carry egalitarian implications'. Van der Walt (2004: 196) makes the similar point that the power of Michelman's translation of a moral

obligation arising from extreme need into a Constitution duty 'is that social theory and practice do not remain locked into needs talk, but take place within the traditionally powerful discourse of rights'.

31 On the use of rights-based discourses in social rights advocacy in South Africa, see Wilson (2004) and Heywood (2005).

32 She cites the example of clients of social-welfare programmes in the US joining together '*as clients*' to challenge administrative interpretations of their needs: 'They may take hold of the passive, normalized, and individualized or familialized identities fashioned for them in expert discourses and transform them into a basis for collective political action' (ibid.: 180–181).

33 See Fredman's (2005) critique of the Supreme Court of Canada's approach in *Gosselin* v. *Quebec (Attorney General)* 2002 SCC 84 to the review of social security regulations in Quebec which discriminated in the provision of welfare benefits against persons under 30 years of age.

34 In this respect, socio-economic rights jurisprudence converges with substantive equality jurisprudence, particularly in relation to the test for unfair discrimination and the Court's approach to restitutionary equality: *Harksen* v. *Lane No* 1998 (1) SA 300 (CC) para. 53; *Minister of Finance* v. *Van Heerden* 2004 (11) BCLR 1125 (CC) paras 25–32. For a discussion of this convergence, see De Vos (2001).

35 General Comment No 14 (Twenty-second session, 2000) *The right to the highest attainable standard of health (art. 12 of the International Covenant on Economic, Social and Cultural Rights)*, UN doc. E/C.12/2000/4, para. 43(f); General Comment No 15 (Twenty-ninth session) *The right to water (arts 11 and 12 of the International Covenant on Economic, Social and Cultural Rights)* UN doc E/C. 12/2002/11, para. 37(f).

36 *Introduction to Socio-economic Rights in the South African Constitution* (2005) 39. The impact of social rights on the common law may also take place through the adoption of legislation to give effect to these rights, e.g., legislation providing substantive and procedural protection against arbitrary evictions.

37 *Afrox Healthcare (Pty) Ltd* v. *Strydom* 2002 (6) SA 21 (SCA); see the discussion in Brand (2005b: 41–42).

38 For a discussion of the problems of judicial ideology and culture in the context of socio-economic rights adjudication, see Pieterse (2004: 396–399). On the broader institutional reforms needed in relation to social rights litigation, see Gloppen (2005).

39 *Pharmaceutical Manufacturers' Association and Others* v. *President of the Republic of South Africa and Others* Case No. 4183/98, High Court (Transvaal Provincial Division), March 2001.

References

Albertyn, C. and Goldblatt, B. (1998) 'Facing the challenges of transformation: difficulties in the development of an indigenous jurisprudence of equality', *SAJHR*, 14: 248–276.

Bilchitz, D. (2003) 'Towards a reasonable approach to the minimum core: laying the foundations for future socio-economic rights jurisprudence', *SAJHR*, 19: 1–26.

Botha, H. (2000) 'Democracy and rights: constitutional interpretation in a postrealist world', *THRHR*, 63: 561–581.

—— (2002) 'Metaphoric reasoning and transformative constitutionalism (part 1)', *Journal of South African Law (TSAR)*, 4: 612–627.

—— (2003) 'Metaphoric reasoning and transformative constitutionalism (part 2)', *Journal of South African Law (TSAR)*, 1: 20–36.

Brand, D. (2005a) 'The "politics of need interpretation" and the adjudication of socio-economic rights claims in South Africa' in A.J. van der Walt (ed.) *Theories of Social and Economic Justice*, Stellenbosch: Sun Press, 17–36.

—— (2005b) 'Introduction to socio-economic rights in the South African Constitution' in D. Brand and C. Heyns (eds) *Socio-Economic Rights in South Africa*, Pretoria: Pretoria University Press, 1–56.

Committee of Inquiry into a Comprehensive Social Security System in South Africa (2002) *Transforming the Present – Protecting the Future: Report of the Committee of Inquiry into a Comprehensive System of Social Security in South Africa*, National Department of Social Development, Pretoria: Government Printers.

Davis, D. (1992) 'The case against the inclusion of socio-economic demands in a Bill of Rights except as Directive Principles', *SAJHR*, 8: 475–490.

—— (2004) 'Socio-economic rights in South Africa: the record of the Constitutional Court after ten years', *ESR Review*, 5: 3–7.

De Vos, P. (2001) '*Grootboom*, the right of access to housing and substantive equality as contextual fairness', *SAJHR*, 17: 258–276.

Fraser, N. (1989) *Unruly Practices: Power, Discourse and Gender in Contemporary Social Theory*, Minneapolis: University of Minnesota Press and Polity Press.

—— (1997) *Justice Interruptus: Critical Reflections on the "Postsocialist" Condition*, New York: Routledge.

—— (2000) 'Rethinking Recognition', *New Left Review*, 3: 107–120.

—— (2005) 'Reframing justice in a globalizing world', *New Left Review*, 36: 1–19.

Fraser, N. and Honneth, A. (2003) *Redistribution or Recognition? A Political–Philosophical Exchange*, London: Verso.

Fredman, S. (2005) 'Providing equality: substantive equality and the positive duty to provide', *SAJHR*, 21:163–315.

Gloppen, S. (2005) 'Social rights litigation as transformation: South African perspectives' in P. Jones and K. Stokke (eds) *Democratising Development: the Politics of Socio-Economic Rights in South Africa*, Leiden: Martinus Nijhoff Publishers, 153–180.

Goldblatt, B. (2005) 'Gender and social assistance in the first decade of democracy', *Politikon*, 32: 329–257.

Gortz, A. (1967) *Strategy for Labour: a radical proposal*, trans. Nicolaus and Ortiz, Barton: Beacon Press.

Gouws, A. (ed.) (2005) *(Un)thinking Citizenship: Feminist Debates in Contemporary South Africa*, Aldershot, Hants: Ashgate.

Greenstein, R. (2004) 'Socioeconomic rights, radical democracy and power: South Africa as a case study' in N. Gordon (ed.) *From the Margins of Globalization: Critical Perspectives on Human Rights*, Lexington, MD: Lexington Books, 87–126.

Haysom, N. (1992) 'Constitutionalism, majoritarian democracy and socio-economic rights', *SAJHR*, 8: 451–463.

Heywood, M. (2001) 'Debunking "conglomo-talk": a case study of the amicus curiae as an instrument for advocacy, investigation and mobilisation', *Law, Democracy and Development*, 5: 133.

—— (2003) 'Preventing mother-to-child HIV transmission in South Africa: background, strategies and outcomes of the Treatment Action Campaign Case against the Minister of Health', *SAJHR*, 19: 278–315.

—— (2005) 'Shaping, making and breaking the law in the campaign for a national HIV/AIDS treatment plan' in P. Jones and K. Stokke (eds) *Democratising Development: The Politics of Socio-Economic Rights in South Africa*, Leiden: Martinus Nijhoff Publishers, 181–243.

Kennedy, D. (1997) *A Critique of Adjudication (fin de siècle)*, Cambridge: Harvard University Press.

Klare, K. (1991) 'Legal theory and democratic reconstruction: reflections on 1989', *UBC Law Review*, 25: 69–103.

—— (1998) 'Legal culture and transformative constitutionalism', *SAJHR*, 14: 146–188.

Kok, A. (2005) 'Privatisation and the right to access to water' in K. De Keyter and F.G. Isa (eds) *Privatisation and Human Rights in the Age of Globalisation*, Antwerp: Intersentia, 259–287.

Lenta, P. (2004) 'Democracy, rights disagreements and judicial review', *SAJHR*, 20: 1–31.

Liebenberg, S. (1995) 'Social and economic rights: a critical challenge' in S. Liebenberg (ed.) *The Constitution of South Africa from a Gender Perspective*, Cape Town: The Community Law Centre at the University of the Western Cape in association with David Philip, 79–96.

—— (2002) 'South Africa's evolving jurisprudence on socio-economic rights: an effective tool in challenging poverty?', *Law, Democracy and Development*, 6: 159–191.

—— (2005) 'Enforcing positive socio-economic rights claims: the South African model of reasonableness review' in J. Squires, M. Langford and B. Thiele (eds) *The Road to a Remedy: Current Issues in the Litigation of Economic, Social and Cultural Rights*, Australian Human Rights Centre, The University of New South Wales with Centre on Housing Rights and Evictions, 73–88.

—— (2006) 'Needs, rights and transformation: adjudicating social rights', *Stellenbosch Law Review*, 17: 1–36.

—— (2007, forthcoming) 'South Africa', in M. Langford (ed.) *Socio-Economic Rights Jurisprudence: Emerging Trends in Comparative and International Law*, Cambridge: Cambridge University Press.

Liebenberg, S. and Pillay, K. (2000) *Socio-Economic Rights in South Africa: a Resource Book*, The Socio-Economic Rights Project, Community Law Centre, University of the Western Cape.

Michelman, F. (1979) 'Welfare rights in a constitutional democracy', *Wash Univ. LQ*, 3: 659–701.

—— (2003) 'The constitution, social rights, and liberal political justification', *1 Con*: 13–34.

Moseneke, D. (2002) 'The fourth Bram Fischer Memorial Lecture: transformative adjudication', *SAJHR*, 18: 309–317.

Nozick, R. (1974) *Anarchy, State and Utopia*, Oxford: Basil Blackwell.

Pieterse, M. (2004) 'Coming to terms with judicial enforcement of socio-economic rights', *SAJHR*, 20: 383–417.

Pillay, K. (2002) 'Implementation of *Grootboom*: implications for the enforcement of socio-economic rights', *Law, Democracy and Development*, 6: 255–277.

Roach, K. (2005) 'Constitutional, remedial and international dialogues about rights: the Canadian experience', *Texas International Law Journal*, 40: 537–576.

Scott, C. and Maklem, P. (1992) 'Constitutional ropes of sand or justiciable guarantees? Social rights in a new South African constitution', *Univ of Penn LR*, 142: 1–148.

Shah, S. (1999) 'Illuminating the possible in the developing world: guaranteeing the human right to health in India', *Vand J Transnat'l L*, 32: 435–485.

Sloth-Nielsen, J. (2001) 'The child's right to social services, the right to social security, and primary prevention of child abuse: some conclusions in the aftermath of *Grootboom*', *SAJHR*, 17: 210–231.

Terreblanche, S. (2002) *A History of Inequality in South Africa: 1652–2002*, Pietermaritzburg: University of Natal Press/KMM Review Publishing.

Trengove, W. (1999) 'Judicial remedies for violations of socio-economic rights', *ESR Review*, 1: 8–10.

Van der Walt, A. (2001) 'Tentative urgency: sensitivity for the paradoxes of stability and change in the social transformation decisions of the Constitutional Court', *SA Public Law*, 16: 1–27.

—— (2004) 'A South African reading of Frank Michelman's Theory of Social Justice' in H. Botha, A. Van der Walt and J. Van der Walt (eds) *Rights and Democracy in a Transformative Constitution*, Stellenbosch: Sun Press, 163–211.

Williams, L. (1998) 'Welfare and legal entitlements: the social roots of poverty' in D. Kairys (ed.) *The Politics of Law: a Progressive Critique*, New York: Basic Books, Inc., 569–590.

—— (2002) 'Beyond labour law's parochialism: a re-envisioning of the discourse of redistribution', in J. Conaghan, R.M. Fischl and K. Klare (eds) *Labour Law in an Era of Globalization: Transformative Practices and Possibilities*, Oxford: Oxford University Press, 93–114.

—— (2005) 'Issues and challenges in addressing poverty and legal rights: a comparative United States/South African analysis', *SAJHR*, 21: 436–472.

Wilson, S. (2004) 'Taming the Constitution: rights and reform in the South African constitution education system', *SAJHR*, 20: 418–447.

Index